MW00582658

Violence in Scripture

INTERPRETATION
Resources for the Use of Scripture in the Church

INTERPRETATION

RESOURCES FOR THE USE OF SCRIPTURE IN THE CHURCH

Patrick D. Miller, *Series Editor*
Ellen F. Davis, *Associate Editor*
Richard B. Hays, *Associate Editor*
James L. Mays, *Consulting Editor*

OTHER AVAILABLE BOOKS IN THE SERIES

Ronald P. Byars, *The Sacraments in Biblical Perspective*
Robert W. Jenson, *Canon and Creed*
Patrick D. Miller, *The Ten Commandments*

JEROME F. D. CREACH

Violence in Scripture

INTERPRETATION *Resources for the Use of Scripture in the Church*

WESTMINSTER
JOHN KNOX PRESS
LOUISVILLE · KENTUCKY

First edition
Published by Westminster John Knox Press
Louisville, Kentucky

13 14 15 16 17 18 19 20 21 22—10 9 8 7 6 5 4 3 2 1

Book design by Drew Stevens
Cover design by designpointinc.com

Library of Congress Cataloging-in-Publication Data

Creach, Jerome F. D. (Jerome Frederick Davis), 1962–
    Violence in scripture / Jerome F. D. Creach.—First edition.
        pages cm.—(Interpretation: resources for the use of scripture in the church)
    Includes bibliographical references.
    ISBN 978-0-664-23145-3 (hardback)
    1. Violence in the Bible. I. Title.
    BS1199.V56C74 2013
    220.8'3036—dc23

                                                                            2013019670

♾ The paper used in this publication meets the minimum requirements of the American National Standard for Information Sciences—Permanence of Paper for Printed Library Materials, ANSI Z39.48-1992.

Westminster John Knox Press advocates the responsible use of our natural resources. The text paper of this book is made from 30% postconsumer waste.

To Page

hinnāk yāpâ raʿyātî

CONTENTS

ACKNOWLEDGMENTS

A book on a topic as controversial and currently relevant as violence in the Bible is a challenging project. My work has been made immensely easier and more enjoyable, however, by the help of many friends, colleagues, and family members. I wish to express my deepest thanks to Pat Miller, who invited me to contribute this volume to the series and for his interest in the shape and content of the book along the way. Ellen Davis has been a patient and incredibly helpful editor. Her own work as a scholar has long been an inspiration to me, and the influence of that work is evident in this book. Numerous other colleagues shared insights that improved the work. Among them are Clint McCann, Steve Tuell, and Ron Tappy. I must also give special thanks to Dale Allison, who co-taught a course on violence in the Bible with me at Pittsburgh Theological Seminary. He provided more insight on New Testament issues than this volume's guidelines allow me to show.

I must also express my thanks to two organizations that provided funding for work on this project. In 2005 I received a generous grant from the Louisville Institute for a consultation of pastors on the problem of violence in the Bible. The Institute also gave as part of the grant program money for a period of research and writing. In 2007 I received a Theological Research Grant from the Association of Theological Schools. That grant provided me with a summer of work unencumbered by any other professional duties.

As always I must thank my wife, Page, for her encouragement and support. But mostly, the time spent writing this book was simply mixed with other dimensions of life together. She and our children, Adair and Davis, constantly reminded me of how blessed I am.

SERIES FOREWORD

This series of volumes supplements Interpretation: A Bible Commentary for Teaching and Preaching. The commentary series offers an exposition of the books of the Bible written for those who teach, preach, and study the Bible in the community of faith. This new series is addressed to the same audience and serves a similar purpose, providing additional resources for the interpretation of Scripture, but now dealing with features, themes, and issues significant for the whole rather than with individual books.

The Bible is composed of separate books. Its composition naturally has led its interpreters to address particular books. But there are other ways to approach the interpretation of the Bible that respond to other characteristics and features of the Scriptures. These other entries to the task of interpretation provide contexts, overviews, and perspectives that complement the book-by-book approach and discern dimensions of the Scriptures that the commentary design may not adequately explore.

The Bible as used in the Christian community is not only a collection of books but also itself a book that has a unity and coherence important to its meaning. Some volumes in this new series will deal with this canonical wholeness and seek to provide a wider context for the interpretation of individual books as well as a comprehensive theological perspective that reading single books does not provide.

Other volumes in the series will examine particular texts, like the Ten Commandments, the Lord's Prayer, and the Sermon on the Mount, texts that have played such an important role in the faith and life of the Christian community that they constitute orienting foci for the understanding and use of Scripture.

A further concern of the series will be to consider important and often difficult topics, addressed at many different places in the books of the canon, that are of recurrent interest and concern to the church in its dependence on Scripture for faith and life. So the series will include volumes dealing with such topics as eschatology, women, wealth, and violence.

The books of the Bible are constituted from a variety of kinds of literature such as narrative, laws, hymns and prayers, letters, parables, miracle stories. To recognize and discern the contribution and importance of all these different kinds of material enriches and enlightens the use of Scripture. Volumes in the series will provide help in the interpretation of Scripture's literary forms and genres.

The liturgy and practices of the gathered church are anchored in Scripture, as with the sacraments observed and the creeds recited. So another entry to the task of discerning the meaning and significance of biblical texts explored in this series is the relation between the liturgy of the church and the Scriptures.

Finally, there is certain ancient literature, such as the Apocrypha and the noncanonical gospels, that constitutes an important context to the interpretation of Scripture itself. Consequently, this series will provide volumes that offer guidance in understanding such writings and explore their significance for the interpretation of the Protestant canon.

The volumes in this second series of Interpretation deal with these important entries into the interpretation of the Bible. Together with the commentaries, they compose a library of resources for those who interpret Scripture as members of the community of faith. Each of them can be used independently for its own significant addition to the resources for the study of Scripture. But all of them intersect the commentaries in various ways and provide an important context for their use. The authors of these volumes are biblical scholars and theologians who are committed to the service of interpreting the Scriptures in and for the church. The editors and authors hope that the addition of this series to the commentaries will provide a major contribution to the vitality and richness of biblical interpretation in the church.

The Editors

Introduction

The Nature and Scope of the Problem

One of the greatest challenges the church faces today is to interpret and explain passages in the Bible that seem to promote or encourage violence. It is perhaps not an exaggeration to say that the Bible in this regard is a major problem for Christians, both for the church's own theology (what it says it believes) and for the church's presentation of itself to the world (who the church says it is). Since the terrorist attacks of September 11, 2001, there has been intense interest in the way religious faith sometimes encourages violence. Although much initial discussion focused on the Qur'an and the faith of the 9/11 hijackers, it was not long before the connection between faith and violence turned to Christian Scripture. About one year after the attacks of 9/11, in his presidential address to the Society of Biblical Literature, John Collins rightly declared that "any reader of the Bible should have had a flash of recognition" ("Zeal of Phinehas," 3). Historian Philip Jenkins goes even further in his assessment of the Bible's violent content. In a 2010 interview with National Public Radio, Jenkins declared that the Bible has more bloody passages than the Qur'an and may pose more difficult ethical problems than the Muslim holy book (npr.org; March 18, 2010).

Jenkins holds up 1 Samuel 15 as particularly egregious. In this chapter the prophet Samuel addresses King Saul with divine directions for how to treat an old enemy called the Amalekites: "Thus says the LORD of hosts, 'I will punish the Amalekites for what they did in opposing the Israelites when they came up out of Egypt. Now go and attack Amalek, and utterly destroy all that they have; do not spare them, but kill both man and woman, child and infant, ox and sheep, camel and donkey'" (vv. 2–3).

This passage reveals at least three crucial dimensions of the problem of violence in the Bible. First, there is a problem of how God is described and portrayed. The Bible seems to present God as vengeful and destructive against those who oppose God's will. Second, the passage raises questions about the behavior and moral identity of the people of God. Do those who identify with the God of the Bible have license to kill in God's name? Do they see themselves as having a special privilege in the human community, to the point of justifying genocide to promote their own security? Finally, this story highlights a key issue about the unity and authority of the Bible. While 1 Samuel 15 is quite troubling, many parts of the Bible seem to present a message that refutes Samuel's words to Saul. The most obvious example is Jesus' command to his disciples to love their enemies (Matt. 5:44). The question arises, therefore, how can the church read passages like 1 Samuel 15 as part of its Scripture? Surely the order to slaughter the Amalekites should not inform Christian behavior toward enemies. But how is such a passage to be read in the midst of a Bible that includes Jesus' injunctions to nonviolence?

These questions are not new and did not originate in the modern era. Indeed, they represent one of the earliest conflicts the church faced. In the second century a Christian leader in Rome named Marcion (d. ca. 160 CE) rejected large portions of the Bible on grounds that the God portrayed was different from the God of Jesus Christ. Although his objections are often characterized as a rejection of the Old Testament, Marcion also eschewed portions of the New Testament that shared this view of God (e.g., Rev. 19:11–16). He declared that the God portrayed in much of the Bible was "judicial, harsh, mighty in war," as compared to Jesus' Father, who is "mild, placid, and simply good and excellent" (Tertullian, *Against Marcion* 1.6; for a discussion of other implications of Marcion's ideas see Head, "Foreign God"). The church rejected Marcion's views as heretical and kept Scripture intact. Nevertheless, the questions Marcion raised have never disappeared, and many in the church continue to struggle to answer them.

Despite the ancient origins of the controversy over violence in the Bible, it nevertheless has taken on unique dimensions in our time. Although Marcion represented a movement within the faith, the increasing secularization of society in Europe and North America has seen the rise of critics of the Bible from outside the church as well (see especially Schwartz, *Curse of Cain*). Modernity itself presents challenges to the Bible's authority in this regard. It raises the prospect of making human reason the primary guide to morality and making Enlightenment ideals the judge over the content of biblical texts (see E. Davies, "Morally Dubious Passages").

In the midst of all this mistrust of the Bible and the general sense of dis-ease that persists in our culture over the violent content of portions of Scripture, many Christians are at a loss as to how to think about the matter. As a result, many people who grew up reading and loving the stories of the Bible now feel alienated from their Scripture. They assume they must either repress certain biblical texts by assigning them a secondary, nonauthoritative status, or they must reject them altogether.

The Purpose of This Book

This book is written for those who wish to read the Bible as Scripture and who seek ways to interpret the Bible's violent passages as integral parts of the Bible's authoritative word to the church. Hence readers will find in the book empathy for the biblical text, even with passages that seem to advocate violence. Such empathy is born of at least two convictions about how to read the Bible as a whole and how to treat individual passages that seem to promote violence. First, although there is no one right way to read the Bible, it is useful to read it as a testimony to Jesus Christ, as Christians have for centuries. Whatever method of reading one chooses, it is probably necessary to read the Bible with some organizing center as a guide to understanding the whole. That is, one must decide what the Bible is in order to make sense of it. Reading the whole Bible with Christ as its center is one way that may aid in understanding passages that seem to promote violence.

3

It is important to recognize that this type of reading does not impose meaning on the Bible that it does not already have. Rather, it directs attention to and highlights particular aspects of the Bible as central or normative. This recognition is particularly important for understanding the effect of such choices on the Old Testament. For example, some have read Jesus' parable of the Good Samaritan (Luke 10:25–37) as a repudiation of a narrow Old Testament idea of who is one's neighbor that allows one to ignore or even attack a "nonneighbor." But instead, reading the Bible as a work that points to Christ highlights a lesson firmly grounded in the Old Testament's identity of the neighbor that included foreigners living in Israel's midst. Indeed, Leviticus 19:18 expresses the particular law addressed in the story of the Good Samaritan when it says, "you shall love your neighbor as yourself." Later in the same chapter, the same language of love and inclusion is extended to foreigners: "The alien who resides with you shall be to you as the citizen among you; *you shall love the alien as yourself,* for you were aliens in the land of Egypt" (v. 34; cf. Exod. 23:9). In other words, Jesus did not offer a corrective to Old Testament ideas of hating those outside one's kinship group. Rather, Jesus identified those more inclusive portions of the Old Testament understanding of who the neighbor is as normative. Therefore, it is most accurate to say that Jesus presents for Christians an authoritative *interpretation* of the Old Testament, not a repudiation of it. To be sure, this type of reading does not remove all the difficulties with passages that seem to promote violence. It does, however, suggest we not give up on such passages too easily.

This perspective resonates with Augustine's view of charity, the notion that every portion of the Bible directs the reader's attention either to how one loves God or to how one loves the neighbor. With such an understanding, the interpreter's task is to discern how a particular passage should be understood to discern its revelatory character (*Christian Doctrine* 3.10.14).

A second conviction that guides this book is that the Bible itself conceives violence as action that is opposed to God and God's desires for the world. Many modern people have an abstract notion of violence, as seen in the definition of violence as "physical force intended to hurt, damage, or kill something or someone" (*Oxford American College Dictionary,* 1575). The Bible, however, seems to present violence as destruction that has a particular motivation.

4

Violence is action that arises from motivations of greed, selfishness, and a desire for power and control over others. Thus violence is action that defies the authority of God and threatens the just order God intends (von Rad, *Theology*, 1:157). It is probably this understanding of the term that led to its use in the cry for help— "Violence!"—that appears in passages like Jeremiah 20:8; Habakkuk 1:2; and Job 19:7.

It may be helpful to observe that the first occurrence of the primary Hebrew term translated "violence" (*ḥāmās*) is in Genesis 6:11 in an explanation for why God brings the flood to destroy the creation: "the earth was corrupt in God's sight, and the earth was filled with violence" (on the theological use of *ḥāmās* see Stoebe, "חָמָס *ḥāmās* violence"). Hence although the Bible frequently portrays God destroying and killing, it presents these actions as the divine response to and correction of the violence of humans. Indeed, the Bible seems to distinguish God's destructive actions for corrective and redemptive purposes from violence that is performed by humans. Read this way, therefore, the whole of Scripture may be understood rightly as a grand testimony *against* violence.

Approaching Texts That Seem to Promote Violence

Given the perspective toward violence in the Bible just described, how is it possible to construe the whole Bible as a book that advocates nonviolence? How shall we interpret texts that seem to promote violence? In the pages that follow I will attempt to answer these questions, and the following assumptions will guide the discussion:

1. *The understanding of violence as human action that opposes the reign of God is communicated in part by the order and shape of the canon.* In this regard the set of creation stories in Genesis 1 and 2 are crucial. As I discuss in chapter 1, Genesis 1:1–2:4a presents a remarkable picture of God creating the world without conflict or combat. This portrait of God is striking because it contrasts sharply with the Babylonian creation epic called *Enuma Elish* that would have been well known at the time Genesis 1:1–2:4a was written. The Babylonian epic presents the Babylonian god Marduk creating the world by engaging in violent combat with other deities who

5

represent chaos. Since the two creation stories depict the creation with an identical order of things created, it seems likely that the Genesis account was meant as a response to and refutation of the Babylonian story. In any case, the notion that God creates through speaking and not through violent conflict is quite unique in the ancient Near East.

Though Genesis 2:4b–25 does not address the issue directly, this passage does present God's intentions to shape a world without violence. Thus the opening of the canon gives an important cast to the violence that appears later. Violence clearly appears as a human intrusion into the order of creation. Furthermore, God's destructive activity is God's attempt to correct what humans have damaged and upset for the sake of the future of the creation. Thus God's involvement in destructive activity is understood as corrective and redemptive in nature.

2. *In addition to the broad structures of the canon that help frame difficult passages, many passages that may seem to promote violence have within them self-correcting features that actually counter the violence they seem at first to allow.* Passages that seem to promote violence or encourage violent action often contain features that require us to question such a reading. Indeed, one problem in some efforts to argue against texts that seem to promote violence is that such efforts are based on too simple a reading of those texts. It is often as Ellen Davis says, "When we think we have reached the point of zero-edification, then that perception indicates that we are not reading deeply enough; we have not probed the layers of the text with sufficient care" ("Critical Traditioning," 741). Davis illustrates this conviction by showing how certain troubling passages contain dimensions that indicate the author is wrestling with the difficulty in our presence. A good example of this phenomenon is the conquest story in the book of Joshua. This story includes the idea that the Israelites are to destroy all the residents of the land. But within the story Rahab the harlot is not only not destroyed, she becomes a model of faith by which the Israelites seem to be measured (Josh. 2). Davis calls this kind of shaping "critical traditioning." An author or editor has passed on a story (a tradition), but with it he or she has also passed on a critical reflection that now presents a more complex and nuanced reality.

3. *The historical circumstances in which portions of the Bible were written speak against any easy justification of violence.* One

might assume the opposite, that this type of reading requires an admission that the Bible at many points allows and even advocates violence. For example, it would require the informed reader to admit that placing enemies under the ban was a practice in the ancient Near East known from documents outside the Bible. Therefore, Moses' order to "utterly destroy" all the people of the land the Israelites occupied in the conquest of Canaan would have to be read against this backdrop of sanctified slaughter (Deut. 7:2).

This kind of historically informed reading, however, informs the reader only about the world in which Moses' order would have been understandable. The actual time of composition might suggest a significantly different meaning. Indeed, most of the accounts of wars and bloody conflicts in the Old Testament were composed long after the times depicted in the text. Moreover, some periods of composition were marked by Israel's utter powerlessness. In such a setting a story about Israel going to battle and slaughtering all its enemies would have a very different meaning than if written when Israel had the ability to attack and conquer the enemy. A brief consideration of two important times of composition of some of the biblical material helps illustrate the point.

One period in which much of the Old Testament seems to have been written is the seventh century BCE, during the reign of Josiah (d. 609 BCE). Josiah ruled the kingdom of Judah when the mighty Assyrian Empire was waning in power. The Assyrians had destroyed Israel (the northern kingdom) a century earlier (722 BCE), but now their decline left a vacuum of power that allowed Josiah to revive memories of the golden age of David and Solomon. Part of Josiah's program was a set of religious reforms associated with the values expressed in Deuteronomy: the people of God would live in a land promised to Israel's ancestors; they would worship this God alone (Deut. 6:5), in one place God would choose (Deut. 12), and the king would serve as the primary example of religious faithfulness for the people (Deut. 17:14–20). The book of Deuteronomy and the so-called Deuteronomistic History (Joshua through Kings) were largely compiled during Josiah's reign. This literary complex recalled the times of Moses and David in order to inspire religious purity in the time of the writing.

The implications of this understanding of the time Deuteronomy through Kings were composed are very significant for our understanding of violence in the Bible. That is, the authors of the

7

story of the wars of David and the conquest of Canaan composed the stories to inspire people of Josiah's day to religious devotion to God alone. The narratives would not have served as a mandate to put enemies under the ban. In fact, the enemies in the stories themselves—Canaanites and Philistines, for example—no longer existed in any form recognizable from the narratives. The accounts of battle therefore provided a dramatic narrative portrait of what it meant to be devoted exclusively to the Lord, not as a mandate to kill people.

The second crucial time period for the composition of much of the Old Testament came just after Josiah's lifetime when Babylonians conquered the kingdom of Judah and took its leading citizens into exile (587–539 BCE). Most Old Testament books were completed during this time, and the canon as we know it today began to take shape. The impetus for the present arrangement of Old Testament books and the final judgments about their content was this experience of defeat and humiliation. In the period after the exile and into the New Testament era, circumstances did not change significantly. Those who put the Old Testament into its present form and those who composed the New Testament lived as a colonial people, controlled by one of the great empires. Hence their perspective was not that of a people who could consider violent response to their aggressors.

4. *The early church promoted spiritual interpretations of passages that seem to promote violence, and those interpretations have more validity than many modern readers have recognized.* Interpreters like Origen and Augustine insisted that passages like 1 Samuel 15 were not meant to be read literally as if to prescribe behavior toward one's enemies. Rather, the injunction to kill, they said, was a figurative way of urging a purer faith. In that way of thinking the Amalekites are emblematic of vices and sinfulness that the believer must reject in order to serve God fully.

This way of reading the Bible has fallen out of favor with many modern readers. Indeed, in the modern world the figurative interpretations of the early church do not seem adequate. Modern scholars have regularly denounced symbolic interpretations on grounds that such interpretations of texts that present violence simply deny what those texts clearly say. But a close reading of passages that seem to promote violence often indicates that those early interpreters were more insightful than sometimes thought. Two points in

8

support of allegorical interpretation are important. First, as suggested in the previous section, a careful consideration of the historical context of writing often presses the reader toward figurative interpretation. That is, if the text recalls a violent event or practice that occurred long before the time of writing, one must ask why the recollection is made. For any story to have meaning for a later audience it must have had some degree of symbolical or emblematic significance.

Paul Ricoeur has laid a philosophical foundation for this type of interpretation in his discussion of the function of language. He notes that written texts stand between language and lived experience and are therefore by nature open to the life of the reader. That is, written texts by nature are not limited to the events they narrate or by the historical circumstances that produced them (*Conflict of Interpretations*, 66). As Ricoeur says, such a narrative creates its own world and invites readers into it that they may be transformed or shaped by that world. Written for this purpose, the story does not simply report an event or occurrence; rather, it *redescribes* reality (Ricoeur, "Narrative Function," 194–95). It tells about something in the past but for the benefit of those hearing in the present. Although such stories may have historical events behind them, they are attempts not primarily to reconstruct the past but to give meaning to the present.

The symbolic importance of texts that seem to promote violence is evident also in the biblical worldview in which creation and order are constantly set over against chaos and evil. Therefore, the reader must always consider the possibility that descriptions of enemies and portrayals of warfare are not to be read literally. Instead, they represent forces that oppose God and God's intention for the creation, not merely historical foes of God's people. A good example of this symbolical character, to be explored in chapter 2, is the portrait of Pharaoh and the Egyptians in the book of Exodus. When a new pharaoh arises "who did not know Joseph" (Exod. 1:8), he immediately sets out to undo the creational work accomplished among the Israelites. Indeed, the note that "the Israelites were fruitful and prolific" and "they multiplied" (Exod. 1:7) is a clear indication that God was accomplishing through the Israelites what God intended for humankind (Gen. 1:28). Pharaoh's acts against the Israelites, however, identify him essentially as the anticreator.

9

5. *The Bible sometimes presents and approves destructive action for the sake of liberation from oppression, but judgment and justice are presented as God's prerogative, not the right or responsibility of humans.* This point has two important implications. First, the Bible—and its apparent promotion of violence—emerges from the life of a people who are surely closer in character to those in the third world than to those in North America or Western Europe. It is important to recognize that many biblical texts that include so-called violent imagery are directed against the great empires of the ancient world (Egypt, Assyria, Babylon, Rome). Hence those in North America who read such texts should perhaps not ask first if the text incites *them* to violence, but if the text might incite someone else to violence *against them.* Or, more true to the character of most such texts, the question is whether a text with violent imagery calls on or pictures God in opposition to the North American reader. Second, although the Bible often speaks strongly about judgment on those who oppress the poor and powerless, the poor and powerless are not called to take up arms against their oppressors. Rather, they are called to rely on God, the ultimate judge and arbiter of justice.

A Summary of the Book

Before we delve into the larger discussion of violence in the Bible, it may be helpful to summarize the content of the book in order to give the reader a guide to what will be found in the pages that follow. The first three chapters deal primarily with the portrait of God acting destructively, and the theological problems that portrait poses for the church. The discussion begins in chapter 1, however, on a positive note by exploring ways the beginning of the canon presents God as distinctly not violent. The chapter focuses particularly on the creation stories in Genesis 1–2 and the significance of their place at the beginning of the canon. These accounts give a rather remarkable perspective on God's relationship to violence that sets the tone for the rest of the Bible. Genesis 1:1–2:4a portrays God as one who creates without doing battle or engaging in conflict. This picture of God strikingly contrasts with the depiction of most ancient Near Eastern deities involved in creation, who were said to create by means of violent warfare. In light of the typical description of creation in other creation stories, the first picture of God in the Bible is noteworthy for its emphasis on God's nonviolent creative work. After the initial creation story many other passages present God doing battle with cosmic enemies, much like the typical depiction of ancient gods did. But the presence of Genesis 1:1–2:4a at the beginning of the canon relativizes such accounts. Genesis 1:1–2:4a appears as normative by virtue of its canonical position. The picture of God as nonviolent, in turn, suggests a normative picture of human beings who are created in the image of God. They should act nonviolently in imitation of God whom they represent on earth (1:26–30). A similar understanding of God's intentions for humankind appears in 2:4b–25. There humans are created to care for and protect the earth and to act in partnership with one another.

When humans begin to harm each other in Genesis 4 it is clearly an affront to God's intentions for the world. By 6:11 violence has spread over the entire creation, and God must act to restore the creation to the order God intended. Hence it becomes apparent that much of the Bible's description of violence and destruction is related directly to God's desire to maintain the proper order in creation. Furthermore, what is often understood as God's violence is actually God acting to protect the creation itself or the creation, following the will of God, rising up in rebellion against those who would ruin it.

An important part of this portrait of God as creator and of humans made in the image of God is the role of Abraham and his descendants as God's representatives on earth. When God calls Abraham (Gen. 12:1–3) God narrows the focus of human blessing and responsibility to this one man and his family. Thus Abraham and his descendants will be the primary conduit of blessing for humankind and the ones primarily responsible for maintaining "justice and righteousness," which counteract violence (Gen. 18–19).

In chapter 2 I explore the meaning and significance of the description of God as a warrior, which appears for the first time in Exodus 15:3. If Genesis portrays God as nonviolent, working for the well-being of the whole creation, Exodus may seem to present a very different understanding of God. In this chapter I will point out, however, that the notion of God as warrior is intimately connected to the portrait of God as creator in at least two ways. First, God's actions against Pharaoh and the Egyptians in Exodus 1–15 are actually extensions of God's role as creator. Pharaoh appears as

11

the anticreator, as one opposed to the order of the creation as it is being worked out in the descendants of Abraham. Thus the nonhuman elements rise up against Pharaoh and act as God's agents to protect Israel. Second, God's actions as warrior are linked directly to God's concern for justice. God's battle against the Egyptians represents a trial, and the Egyptians fall because they are guilty of violating God's order and intentions. It is also noteworthy that God acts as a warrior without the assistance of humans. God fights for Israel, but Israel does not fight. In chapter 2 I will also explore how this paradigm of God's sole action as warrior plays out in Psalms 24 and 46 and in Isaiah 63:1–6, passages that suggest further that God's actions as warrior are aimed at establishing, or reestablishing, peace and stability in the creation.

In chapter 3 I treat the other side of the idea of God as warrior, namely, the notion that some people are enemies of God. I explore three such enemies: the people of Sodom (Gen. 18–19), the pharaoh of the exodus (Exod. 1–15), and Amalek (Exod. 17). I will suggest, however, that these three enemies are not presented as historical figures in the narrow sense, but as symbols of evil, emblems of total depravity like those humans in Genesis 6 who ruined the creation with violence. I will linger over 1 Samuel 15, one of the most difficult passages in the Bible to incorporate into a Christian understanding of violence. I will attempt to show that Amalek indeed represents the forces opposed to God's purpose for creation. Primary evidence of this view of Amalek is seen in the identity of Haman in Esther as a descendant of Agag, the Amalekite king Saul was commanded to destroy.

In chapters 4 through 7 I turn to the biblical picture of the people of God. One initial problem is simply that a group of people are identified as *the people of God*. I also treat this problem at points in chapters 1 through 3. A natural complement to the choice of one group of people is the rejection or subordination of the needs of other groups. As difficult as that problem is, I do not try to remove the tension completely, for to do so would deny the personal nature of God. It would also miss a fundamental theological idea that begins with the choice of Abraham and Sarah (Gen. 12:1–3; see above)—that God chooses to bless humankind through the agency of this one family. I will note, however, that the identity of Israel as God's beloved is not simple or crass favoritism. Through Israel God works for justice in the world, and sometimes those outside Israel are identified as models of faithfulness.

In chapter 4 I address perhaps the most difficult problem, the ban and the conquest of Canaan as prescribed in Deuteronomy and narrated in Joshua 1–12. These subjects are for many people the primary stumbling blocks for reading the Old Testament as Scripture. I will suggest, however, that both the ban and the conquest have important emblematic dimensions that may reflect the intention of the authors who originally presented them. The ban is prescribed as action the Israelites are to take against the Canaanites as they enter the promised land (Deut. 7:2). But the nature of the language about the ban in Deuteronomy along with the likely date of the writing about the ban in this case suggest that the command to annihilate all Canaanites is a symbolic injunction to purify the faith, not a literal command to kill people. The presentation of the conquest in Joshua 1–12 is also complex and must be interpreted with two points in mind. (1) The story presents the conquest as the action of God; therefore, any attempt to claim the account as justification for war or conquest is misguided. (2) Some of the Canaanites who are defeated are actually portrayed in the narrative as models of faith; therefore, anyone who would identify with the Israelites in the story must do so with humility, recognizing that those outside the main group are sometimes models of faith.

In chapter 5 I treat the book of Judges, which has violence as part of its plot as much as or more than any other biblical book. Furthermore, many identify it as a book that approves or at least tolerates violence, particularly violence against women. I will attempt to show, however, that Judges does not condone violence. To the contrary, violence in Judges appears as a primary sign that Israel lost its way in relationship to God, and the violence against women in the book is a primary sign of how Israel failed to acknowledge and be guided by God's reign.

In chapters 6 and 7 I discuss several forms of "seeking vengeance." In chapter 6 I deal with prophetic action, mainly by Elijah and Elisha, and prophetic speech, mainly the oracles against foreign nations and predictions of final judgment (including the New Testament description of hell). A concern for justice underlies each subject here. I recognize a tension between the necessity of judgment for the sake of justice and the promise of forgiveness

13

and renewal. The accent in every case—the last word—is not on retributive justice but on restoration.

In chapter 7 I examine the violent language and imagery in the imprecatory psalms. These psalms that call on God to bring destruction on the enemy are problems precisely because they are prayers. As such they seem to contradict Jesus' instructions to pray for enemies (Matt. 5:44). I will point out, however, that these prayers express essentially the same petition as in the Lord's Prayer for God's kingdom to come "on earth as it is in heaven" (Matt. 6:10). Hence the imprecatory psalms are a crucial part of the Bible's witness against injustice and a call for justice. The chapter explores this conviction by treating the most difficult psalms of vengeance: Psalms 109, 137, and 139.

In the final chapter (chap. 8) I conclude the discussion by addressing a subject that is anticipated by and touches on every other chapter in some way: the relationship of the life and teachings of Jesus to the Old Testament. As already noted, this has been a key issue in the church's struggle over violence since at least the time of Marcion. In this chapter I have two primary goals. First, I attempt to show that Jesus' teachings do not reject the Old Testament but rely on it. Nevertheless, Jesus gives ways of reading the Bible in relation to violence that necessarily shifts the focus for Christians. The issue is not so much that the Old Testament contains instructions and stories that have values Jesus then rejected. The issue rather is that Jesus' special focus on the concern for violence calls for similar attention to the matter throughout the canon.

The second goal of the final chapter is to show that the Old Testament has dominant themes that make it quite compatible with the teachings of Jesus on violence. For example, the Old Testament emphasizes that God is sovereign, and hence God has exclusive prerogative over war and other forms of destruction. The Old Testament presents the ideal stance before God as one of dependence, recognizing that only God can provide true security. Ideas like this are so pervasive they may be seen as providing a framework that encourages nonviolence—and reliance on God to bring justice—in ways quite similar to Jesus' teachings.

It will be apparent that in these eight chapters I do not address 14 the problem of violence comprehensively. A few notes about the limits of the discussion may be helpful. Here I do not address the issue of sacrifice, a foundational theme that permeates much of the Bible. Those interested in the subject may wish to pursue it through the perspective of René Girard, whose work in relation to the Bible is summarized well in James Williams's book, *The Bible, Violence, and the Sacred*. Likewise, I do not address the topic of atonement, which would go well beyond the purview of a study of violence in the Bible. Those interested may consult the book by Williams just mentioned as well Mark Heim's work, *Saved from Sacrifice*. Finally, I do not attempt to deal extensively with the legal material in the Old Testament. For an entrée into that material, one should read Patrick Miller's book *The Ten Commandments* in this series.

CHAPTER 1

Setting the Stage

Violence, Creation, and Calling

The creation story in Genesis 1:1–2:4a presents two remarkable claims that set the stage for an understanding of violence in the rest of the Bible: first, this account declares that God created the world without conflict or combat and God called the creation at every stage "good" (1:4, 12, 18, 21, 25, 31). This claim is noteworthy because it runs counter to other ancient Near Eastern creation stories in which creation results from the creator god doing battle with chaotic forces, forces presented as implicitly *not* good. Hence the Bible opens with a powerful alternative story about the nature of God who creates, about the nature of the creation itself, and about the way God exercises power over the creation. Second, the story says this same God made humankind in God's image and likeness, thus appointing humans as divine representatives on earth (1:26–28). Although the notion of humans made in God's image should not be reduced to the function of ruling over the earth, that aspect of humanity's role is quite significant if the depiction of God in Genesis 1 is taken seriously. It would seem to suggest that human beings are to exercise authority as God does, namely, in order to establish and maintain the well-being or *shalom* of the whole creation (see Middleton, "Created in the Image," 341). Genesis 2:4b–25 continues this portrait of God and humankind. Here God makes the human and places the human on earth to care for it as a gardener, not to rule over it as a tyrant.

Thus Genesis 1–2 presents a view of God and an expectation for humankind that suggest violence will represent a major disruption of the order God intended. The violence that eventually enters creation and threatens to undo it is an intrusion that results from human rebellion. God's subsequent involvement in violence is therefore an effort to deal with the violence instead of giving creation up to it (see Fretheim, "I Was Only," 374).

The notion that God did not give creation up to violence is interesting in light of the argument of Paul in Romans 8:18–25. There Paul says the creation "was subjected to futility." Paul seems to refer to the curse of the ground that Genesis 3:17–19 says came because of human rebellion. Paul seems to suggest that the curse remains in effect. But Paul argues nevertheless that God in Christ is working to restore creation and bring it to fruition. The point is that this redemptive work may be observed in the Old Testament as well. The creation's "groaning in labor pains" (Rom. 8:22) is seen throughout the Old Testament. Indeed, the fulfillment of creation in Christ is anticipated in the Old Testament's insistence that God has been working to redeem and restore the intended order (Isa. 11:6–9).

Genesis 1:1–2:4a and the Idea of Creation by Combat

As already noted, the vision of God and creation in Genesis 1:1–2:4a is quite distinctive when viewed in the ancient Near Eastern context. For much of the past century, however, this distinctiveness was obscured as scholars focused more attention on how creation accounts from the ancient Near East shared certain features. In 1895 Hermann Gunkel published a groundbreaking work that inadvertently pushed the literary and theological distinctiveness of Genesis 1:1–2:4a out of sight. Gunkel's work, which focused on creation and chaos, made the point that ancient Near Eastern peoples, including the ancient Israelites, conceived creation largely as a battle between the creator god and forces of disorder (*Creation and Chaos*, 21–114). The main extrabiblical text Gunkel used to argue this point was the (then) newly discovered Babylonian creation account called *Enuma Elish*. The Babylonian story reports how Marduk (the chief god) defeated and slew Tiamat

18

(who represented the chaotic ocean) and created the world from her body. The same general scenario appears in the cycle of stories about Baal from the ancient city of Ugarit. Baal also battles enemies represented by bodies of water, Prince Sea and Judge River. His defeat of the enemy then marks the founding or restoring of the world (Middleton, "Created in the Image," 342–44). Such battles seemed to represent a pattern in ancient Near Eastern creation stories; "creation" was the result of a deity establishing mastery over the elements, and the elements themselves were understood as recalcitrant, represented by rival deities who were distinctly evil.

Gunkel and others thought ancient Israelites shared this conception of creation because the theme of creation by conflict appears in biblical texts as well. Three Old Testament passages clearly include the thematic elements of chaos battle that characterize other ancient Near Eastern creation stories: Job 26:7–14; Psalms 74:12–17; and 89:5–14 (6–15 Heb.). Each of these passages describes God doing battle with an enemy that represents the forces of chaos. For example, Psalm 89:9 (10 Heb.) declares, "You rule the raging of the sea; when its waves rise, you still them." The passage then describes God crushing the sea monster Rahab (v. 10 [11 Heb.]) to provide evidence that God rules over all (vv. 11–13 [12–14 Heb.]). Job 26 also depicts God conquering "the Sea," striking down Rahab (v. 12), and piercing the "fleeing dragon" (v. 13). In Psalm 74 the enemies God defeats are listed as "the sea," "the dragons" (*tannînîm*; v. 13) and Leviathan (v. 14).

Based on texts like these Jon Levenson makes a strong case that the Old Testament's notion of creation is really about God pushing back unruly (watery) forces. Evil, in turn, is symbolized by the continuing threat of chaos, represented by elements of the natural world (*Creation and Persistence of Evil*). Later Old Testament apocalyptic material (as in Dan. 7–12) and some New Testament texts of the same kind (Revelation) present a kind of cosmic warfare in which God battles forces of evil. Some of these texts describe the force of evil like the chaotic forces God tamed in Genesis 1:1–2:4a. With these connections in mind, it may seem desirable to think first and foremost of God as one "at war" with evil (see Boyd, *God at War*; note that this theological portrait intends to encourage human *nonviolence* by recognizing that the battle is with cosmic, not human, forces; see Eph. 6:12).

Genesis 1:1–2:4a certainly has important parallels of a general sort with the Babylonian creation story. For example, the two accounts report the events of creation in nearly identical order. Both stories report the taming of waters, the establishment of a vault in the heavens, the appearance of dry land, the emergence of plants and finally animals. In both accounts the deity creates humans after placing boundaries on the waters and bringing forth other forms of life. Some more specific parallels are present also. The name Tiamat in the Babylonian epic is quite similar to the word for "the deep" (tĕhôm) in Genesis 1:2. Although the words may not be from the same root, the sound of the term tĕhôm calls to mind the Babylonian goddess.

But significantly Genesis 1:1–2:4a does not present any conflict between God and the elements that are ordered. Whereas *Enuma Elish* depicts the chaotic elements as rival deities, Genesis 1:1–2:4a completely demythologizes them. Water is just water. Sun, moon, and stars are just lights. God has no rival and thus has no need to conquer the elements in order to establish divine kingship (as Marduk does in *Enuma Elish*).

The picture of God's creative work does not involve God fighting the natural world; moreover, it seems the elements of the world are willing participants in the act of shaping and ordering the creation. The particular verb forms used to express God's wishes for creation in Genesis 1:1–2:4a are a clear sign of this distinctive feature. The verbs are not imperatives and thus are not commands as such. They are jussives, third-person forms that suggest a more collaborative relationship. Although jussives may serve as weak commands, similar to imperatives, they are nevertheless distinctive in that they express wishes and invite participation: "Let there be light" (1:3); "Let there be a dome in the midst of the waters" (1:6); "Let the waters under the sky be gathered together into one place, and let the dry land appear" (1:9). These statements are not the demands of a despot. They are rather the invitations of one who invites the elements as partners in the creative process.

The invitational character of the verbs is then matched by statements to the effect that certain parts of the creation also participated directly in the creation. Genesis 1:12 says, for example, "*The earth* brought forth green plants." The word 'ereṣ, "earth," is the subject of the verb. Hence the sentence seems to say that God turns over some of the creative work to parts of the creation itself.

20

The same is true in Genesis 1:20–21 when God invites the waters to teem with living creatures. God does not have to create the water creatures directly; the sea simply begins to swarm with them. To be sure, the account says that after God invited the waters to "bring forth" (v. 20), "God created" the creatures in the sea (v. 21). This seems to indicate, however, that God "creates" by including and partnering with the elements rather than dominating them (see also "God made" in 1:25). It is also noteworthy that the sea creatures are named *tannînîm,* the same label given to the monsters of the sea in Psalm 74:13. In Genesis 1:21 these creatures are merely part of what came forth, fully within God's intention. A similar picture appears in Psalm 104:26, which mentions Leviathan as a creature of the sea that presents no threat. Indeed, one viable translation of the verse suggests that Leviathan is God's playmate: "There go the ships, and Leviathan that You formed to sport with" (see Levenson, *Creation and Persistence of Evil,* 17; Levenson suggests that Leviathan in this passage is God's "rubber duckey"!).

Perhaps the most profound example of the creation participating in further creation is Genesis 1:26. God uses first-person plural speech when declaring the plan to create humankind: "*Let us* make humankind in *our* image." "Let us" seems to suggest that members of the divine council worked with God to create humans. Although the idea of a divine council is not very well developed in the Old Testament, a number of texts portray God with heavenly attendants who go out to do God's bidding (Job 1:6–12; Ps. 82). Genesis 1:26 seems to draw on this idea to present the notion that God involves others in making the world.

A final sign of God inviting participation is that God gives humans the task of continuing the work of creation. Here God does speak in imperatives, but the commands essentially give humans a share in the continuation of God's work: "Fill the earth and subdue it." The implication is that creation was not "complete" in an absolute or abstract sense even though God "finished" (2:1–2). God did not create and then step back and allow the creation to run on its own. Rather, God made the world for continual shaping and reshaping. That ongoing creative work would include the participation of the created elements themselves, especially human beings (1:28; see Fretheim, "Book of Genesis," 346).

The uniqueness of God's invitation to the creation in Genesis 1:1–2:4a becomes especially clear when we compare this passage

21

with the creation account in *Jubilees* 2, a Jewish text from the first century BCE that relies on the Genesis account and indeed presents itself as an alternative version of it. The *Jubilees* version is careful to say that God alone made everything. For example, *Jubilees* 2:11 declares, "And on the fifth day he created great sea monsters in the depths of the waters, for these were the first things of flesh that were created by his hands, the fish and everything that moves in the waters, and everything that flies, the birds and all their kind" (R.H. Charles, *The Apocrypha and Pseudepigrapha of the Old Testament* [Oxford: Clarendon Press, 1913]). The water does not produce the creatures that live in it; the earth does not bring anything forth; indeed, *Jubilees* says only that God created and everything was made "by his hands." Likewise, God does not consult members of the heavenly court when creating humankind (VanderKam, "Genesis 1 in Jubilees 2," 313–14, 318–19).

Jubilees is careful to trace everything the Jewish people practiced unequivocally to the creative work of God in the beginning (VanderKam, "Genesis 1 in Jubilees," 319–21). But the narrative that opens the canon simply does not make such a claim. Moreover, in presenting God's openness to the creation itself, Genesis 1:1–2:4a suggests that the God of the Bible will be significantly different from the other deities of the ancient Near East. Although sovereign and powerful, this God does not operate by sheer force. Indeed, the portrait of God's creation in Genesis 1:1–2:4a perhaps suggests that in creating the world God risked imperfection and rebellion for the sake of participation. But at the very least this passage does not portray God as a warlike creator like Marduk. Here God does not combat a single chaotic force. Instead, God invites the elements of the world to participate in the making of order. And when this was accomplished, God declared it "very good" (Gen. 1:31).

This understanding of creation has important ethical implications. As William Brown states, these stories of how the world began "presume a seamless connection between cosmos and society" (*Ethos of the Cosmos*, 2). They were told to highlight and enhance certain political and military realities in the real world. In the case of *Enuma Elish*, the story supported the imperial conquests of the Babylonian monarchy. The Babylonian kings, bearing the "image" of Marduk, went out to battle to create order out of the peoples they conquered. Thus the Babylonian story of creation provided theological justification for Babylon's world domination. Or, as Paul Ricoeur puts it, this story legitimates a "theology of power" (*Symbolism of Evil*, 195–98). If the Bible's accounts of creation were simply another version of the "creation-by-conflict" stories, they too would seem to encourage violence and conquest, albeit by Israel and those who identify with Israel. But this does not seem the appropriate reading of such stories. Rather, the biblical creation accounts seem to be repudiations of coercive force.

Perhaps the most obvious reason for reading the biblical creation accounts as counters to the Babylonian notion of imperial power is the placement of Genesis 1:1–2:4a at the beginning of the Bible. To be sure, Genesis 1:1–2:4a seems to be an anomaly among the creation stories of the ancient Near East and in comparison to other creation texts in the Bible. As already noted, Job 26 and Psalms 74 and 89 describe God creating and shaping the world through combative action. But Genesis 1:1–2:4a is a significant anomaly since it appears in such a special place in the canon.

This text was likely composed by a Priestly author during the Babylonian captivity (587–539 BCE). The writer almost certainly knew the Babylonian creation epic and perhaps even composed the work as a response to it. That this account was then placed at the opening of the primeval history perhaps indicates that the portrait of God in Genesis 1:1–2:4a was normative for those who gave the Old Testament canon its present shape. Indeed, this first creation account is appropriately read as a "Divine Protocol" that "epitomizes divine procedure and purpose" (McBride, "Divine Protocol," 7). As the Bible unfolds, violence enters the created order and threatens to overtake it (Gen. 6:11 speaks of the creation being "ruined" or "corrupt" because it was filled with violence), and God will eventually engage the violent forces of the world (Gen. 6–9). But the account of God creating without violence in Genesis 1:1–2:4a "now serves as the overture to the entire Bible, dramatically relativizing the other cosmologies" (Levenson, *Creation and Persistence of Evil*, 100). Hence from the very beginning the Bible suggests that violence is not part of God's intention for the world. Anyone who acts coercively and violently goes directly against the example of the God who created.

The three biblical texts that do present a clear creation-by-combat motif also give clues that suggest we read them as other than imperialistic claims by ancient Israel. Job 26 is not connected to any political agenda. It seems to present God's conflict with the

23

elements only to highlight Job's powerlessness vis-à-vis the all-powerful Creator. Psalms 74 and 89 do connect God's creation combat with the political agenda of David. Psalm 89 is a particularly good example because it lists the conquests of David in direct parallel to the actions of God in creation. Psalm 89:9–10 (10–11 Heb.) describes God's rule over the sea and recalls God's crushing of Rahab the chaos monster. Then in a parallel section expressing God's favor for David, God says, "I will set his hand on the sea and his right hand on the rivers" (89:25 [26 Heb.]). When the larger context of Psalm 89 is considered, however, this glorious image of David appears much less than supportive of an imperialistic agenda. Indeed, in verse 38 (39 Heb.) the psalm turns to a lament over the downfall of the monarchy: "But now you have spurned and rejected him; you are full of wrath against your anointed." Although the exact occasion of the psalm is debated, it is clear that the final form of the work is a complaint about the failure of the king (see Clifford, "Psalm 89"). The grand creation-combat language that seems to support the political aspirations of the Israelite monarchy is merely a foil for the complaint about royal failure. Psalm 74 similarly speaks of God's victory over Leviathan and the rebellious waters (vv. 12–15) as part of a complaint that the Jerusalem temple has been overrun by Israel's enemies.

That the language of combat emerges from a situation of abject defeat and helplessness in both Psalms 74 and 89 is crucial for understanding the significance of that language. The violent actions of Mesopotamian gods like Marduk is linked directly to the association of those gods with power-grabbing political figures and the territories in which they ruled. As Thorkild Jacobsen says, "this cruelty goes hand in hand with the growing politization of the gods who come to embody more and more the political interests of their cities and countries" (*Treasures of Darkness*, 231). In Psalms 74 and 89, however, the language of divine combat does not support political domination. Rather, it promises that the cruelty of those supported by the likes of Marduk will not reign forever, that the Creator God will one day set things right in the world (in this regard see also Isa. 51:9–11). But this message does not encourage revenge seeking—the recipients are powerless to attempt that. Rather it provides hope that the world is not ultimately at the mercy of whichever nation, with its god, happens to come out on top in the most recent struggle, hope that the strongest force in the world is in fact fair and just and ultimately will defend the powerless.

In the Image of God: A Call to Nonviolence

In light of this distinctive picture of God in Genesis 1:1–2:4a, the notion that humankind is created in the image of God would seem to have quite significant implications for how humans act as God's agents on earth. As J. Richard Middleton aptly says, "This opening canonical disclosure of God and humanity constitutes, not only a normative framework for interpreting the rest of Scripture, but also a paradigm or model for exercising of human power in the midst of a world filled with violence" ("Created in the Image?" 355). Ellen Davis makes a similar connection between reading Genesis 1 and acting rightly, but she emphasizes the liturgical character of the passage: "As a liturgical poem, Genesis 1 is giving form to a certain way of seeing the world, and accurate perception provides an entrée to active participation in the order of creation" (*Scripture, Culture, and Agriculture*, 43).

If we take seriously that the divine image placed upon humans is delineated in concert with the portrait of God's nonviolent creation, the call to peacemaking and cooperative living would seem essential. A closer consideration of the meaning of the divine image enhances this idea.

Biblical scholars and theologians have pondered the meaning of "the image of God" for centuries, but without much agreement on its meaning and significance. One common assumption about the image of God, however, is that it has a functional dimension. Humans represent God's sovereignty on earth and thus occupy a royal "office" in God's cosmic administration (on the expression of this idea in Ps. 8 see Mays, *Psalms*, 66–67). Just as kings in Egypt and Mesopotamia were identified as bearing the image of God, so all humans represent God's royal sovereignty in the first creation account.

A broader understanding of the significance of the divine image may be available, however, from records created by certain ancient Near Eastern kings themselves. It was common for warrior kings to set up victory stelae in the lands they conquered so

25

their "images" might be always present to those vanquished. For example, after one of his victories the Assyrian king Ashurnasirpal (883–859 BCE) said, "At that time I fashioned an image of my own likeness, the glory of my power and my glory I inscribed thereon, and in the midst of the mountain of Enki, in the city of Assur-nâsir-pal, at the (river) source, I set it up" (Luckenbill, *Ancient Records,* 1:143, §441). Kings like Ashurnasirpal set up monuments not just for the purpose of memorializing their victories, but also to declare their sovereignty and to warn their defeated foes against rebellion (see the discussion of Strong, "Shattering the Image of God," 630).

The idea that God created humans in God's image in Genesis 1:26–27 takes on an important cast against this backdrop. Those who first read or heard Genesis 1:26–27 perhaps understood the image of God as a grand testimony to God's "victory" over the disordered elements of the cosmos. The image of God placed upon humans seems to be God's testimony concerning his mastery over the natural world. As John Strong puts it, "Humankind was to be a testimony to Chaos that YHWH defeated it and that it was YHWH who brought order to the world" ("Israel as a Testimony," 96). If this is the meaning of "the image of God," however, the testimony humans are intended to demonstrate would seem to have a radically different character than is sometimes recognized. The image of God seems first to be a repudiation of the declarations of violence and domination made by ancient Near Eastern kings. Indeed, if the analogy of God's image to the image of Assyrian kings is accurate, then God's image is intended to convey the notion that God has exercised authority that is shaped by divine openness, seen in that God creates by inviting, collaborating, and empowering. God includes the elements of the disorganized, chaotic world to participate in the creative process. By doing so, God sets the stage for proper human behavior on God's behalf, behavior of those who represent the divine image.

The context of the divine image in Genesis 1:26–27 suggests at the very least that to act on God's behalf—to bear God's image—means *not* to act imperialistically and coercively. Put more positively, those who bear the image of God are called to practice patience and to exercise authority through an invitational stance toward others. When God decides to "make humankind in our image" (Gen. 1:26), God truly sets the stage for a kind of life that guards against violence.

26

It is worth noting also that 1:1–2:4a may have something more specific to say about how Israel conducted itself in possessing the land of Canaan. Walter Brueggemann sees an important connection between God's command for humans to "subdue" (*kbš*) the earth and Israel's occupation of the promised land ("Kerygma of the Priestly Writers," 109). Specifically, Brueggemann makes an interesting link between the creation account and the fact that Israel was landless at the time of the passage's composition. He suggests the creation account therefore is meant to encourage Israel that it will once again have a place in the land. If that is so, two emphases in the Priestly tradition are important: first, God is the owner of the land and Israel is allowed to occupy it only as an obedient tenant (Lev. 25:23); second, the fruitfulness of the land will depend on Israel's obedience to God, not on Israel's domination or manipulation of it (Lev. 26:3–5, 9, 18–20). This call to obedience and humility is particularly important for the exilic audience. For them the mandate to subdue the earth was both an encouragement to possess the land and a warning that they would fail, as they had before, if they did not live according to the justice, compassion, and faithfulness that God's law demanded (see Davis, *Scripture, Culture, and Agriculture,* 60).

Sabbath: Beneficial Use of Time

Genesis 1:1–2:4a ends not with humans crowned as the image of God, but with God resting (2:2) and God blessing the seventh day (2:3). This conclusion implies that God carefully and sympathetically shaped time for beneficent purposes just as God shaped the elements of the universe for such purposes. And, like the rest of God's creative work in 1:1–2:4a, God's rest acts as a deterrent to violence.

According to Genesis 2:2–3, God's rest was not just God ceasing from activity after God completed the world. In fact, the world was not "completed"; humans were charged with continuing the creative work. Verse 2a says, "*On the seventh day* God *finished* the work he had done." Then verse 2b: "*he rested on the seventh day* from all the work he had done." In other words, God's rest on the seventh day was also God's work. The seventh day involved a work of completing and ceasing. This, in turn, provided the model for the observance of Sabbath. According to Exodus 20:11 the notion

27

of keeping Sabbath is grounded precisely in God's resting at the end of creation.

Sabbath is directly related to the prevention of violence in that it calls the human to recognize God's reign. As already observed, the failure to recognize God's sovereignty is the beginning of and motivation for violence. It should not be a surprise that Karl Barth begins his discussion of ethics with a discussion of Sabbath. He notes appropriately that the purpose of Sabbath is to bring humankind into "a deliberate non-continuation, a temporal pause, to reflect on God and His work and to participate consciously in the salvation provided by Him and to be awaited from Him" (*Church Dogmatics* III/4:50). The Jewish philosopher and theologian Abraham Heschel took this idea of Sabbath further; it was for him a day to prevent violence in its many forms:

> To set apart one day a week for freedom, a day on which we would not use the instruments which have been so easily turned into weapons of destruction, a day for being with ourselves, a day of detachment from the vulgar, of independence of external obligations, a day on which we stop worshipping the idols of technical civilization, a day on which we use no money, a day of armistice in the economic struggle with our fellow men and the forces of nature—is there any institution that holds out a greater hope for man's progress than the Sabbath?
>
> (*Sabbath*, 28)

In other words, Sabbath is a time to remember that the world belongs to God. For Heschel, "being with ourselves" means not trying to control everything around us, recognizing that the world does not revolve around us, that we are part of the larger creation. That recognition, in turn, fosters a more open and humble approach to the world.

The laws that derive from the concept of Sabbath make clear that the main implications of Sabbath observance are ethical in nature and are intended to prevent violence through the economic system (see Miller, *Ten Commandments*, 135–49). They have the protection of the poor particularly in view. For example, Exodus 23:11 states: "but the seventh year you shall let it rest and let it lie fallow, so that the poor of your people may eat; and what they leave the wild animals may eat. You shall do the same with your vineyard, and with your olive orchard." Thus the end of God's creative work

(God's ordering of time) is like the beginning (the ordering of the material world); it provides a world order intended to prevent violence and abuse.

Genesis 2:4b–25

The second creation story in Genesis 2:4b–25 complements the first. Biblical scholars have often sharply divided 2:4b–25 from 1:1–2:4a on grounds that the two accounts belong to different sources and were written in different times and circumstances. Regardless of the original independence of the two stories, however, 2:4b–25 now continues the message of 1:1–2:4a with an expanded view of God's six days of creating and shaping the world and human beings. The second creation story is like the first in that it presents the purpose of human beings to be God's caregivers of the earth, to reflect the goodness of God.

The role of human beings in 2:4b–25 is defined first by the human's relationship to the earth. When 2:7 says God made the first human from the dust of the ground, it refers to that one as *'ādām*, a word that derives from the same root as "ground" or "soil" (*'ădāmâ*). Thus the human comes from and is dependent on the earth. All the other living things, both plants (2:9) and animals (2:19), came from the ground as well. The human, however, was given the special task of caring for the ground out of which he had been taken. This calling is described by two words: *'ābad* and *šāmar* (2:15). Most modern translations render the first term "till" and the second term "keep." As Ellen Davis points out, however, the Hebrew words used here are not terms that typically describe horticultural activity (*Getting Involved with God*, 192). Rather, these terms most often denote worship and religious service. The term *'ābad* has the sense of "serve" or give deference (Exod. 9:1, 13). Therefore, the implication of the man being put in the garden "to serve" seems to be that human needs are secondary to the needs of the earth. The man is literally meant to be a servant of the creation and of the ground. The second term, *šāmar*, is often connected to keeping Torah (Exod. 13:10). Thus as Terence Fretheim says, "what it means to 'keep' the soil is akin to what it means to keep the commandments" (*God and World*, 53). In some texts this word also refers to care for the poor and vulnerable (Pss. 16:1; 17:8).

29

Although this language can be used to communicate other types of service and caregiving, it is striking in this context of agriculture. It seems clear the human is appointed as one responsible for preventing abuse and misuse, for keeping God's creation intact.

Just as the image of God in Genesis 1:26–28 relates to and subverts the abusive actions of ancient Near Eastern kings, so also the picture of the human as the divinely appointed gardener in Genesis 2 draws from the realm of royal power and presents an alternative to it. It was common for conquering kings to confiscate plants on their conquests and then to plant gardens signifying their victories (see W. Brown, *Seeing the Psalms*, 67–71). The gardening activity of these kings thus symbolized their dominance. But God's horticultural work seems to derive from a completely different motivation. God plants a garden and places the human, God's representative, in it to serve it rather than dominate it. This subtle portrayal of the role of humans on earth is important for what it says about the human's relationship to violence. The role of the man in the garden is essentially to keep the land from violence by serving the interests of the land and its creatures. This becomes even more apparent in the story of Cain and his punishment for murdering his brother. Abel's blood cries out "from the ground," the ground the humans were to protect from violence. Cain is therefore cursed "from the ground" (4:11) and "driven from the soil" (4:14).

Genesis 2:4b–25 also makes a profound statement about the intended relationship between man and woman. The second creation account appears almost like a commentary on 1:26–28, the story of God creating humankind in God's image. Genesis 1:28 is careful to say that both male and female were made in the image of God and that the two sexes together make humankind complete. Although some interpreters have tried to find in this statement a hierarchical relationship between men and women, there is little evidence in the text for such a view (see the discussion of Barth, *Church Dogmatics* III/4:116–240). Furthermore, if 2:4b–25 is understood as an expansion of 1:1–2:4a, the intended mutuality between the sexes at the beginning of the Bible is rather remarkable. Genesis 3:16 does include among the curses on humankind man's dominance of woman, but this is clearly presented as the result of human sin, not as God's intention. Hence just as violence in general

30

appears in Genesis as a human intrusion into God's design, so the subtle forms of violence that arise from male/female hierarchy are also against the Creator's intent.

The first hint at the woman's role is in the statement that God initiated a search for a "helper" for the man (*'ēzer*; 2:18, 20). This term does not seem to imply subordination nor does it identify the woman's role with childbirth, as some have thought. Indeed, God is identified as a "helper" in some texts (e.g., Exod. 18:4; Deut. 33:7; Ps. 20:3). The woman's role as helper reflects the fact that humans were meant to live in community, to enjoy mutual support, and the basis of such communal support is the relationship between man and woman (Westermann, *Genesis 1–11*, 227).

It also says nothing negative about the woman's status that she is taken from the "side" (traditionally "rib") of the man. As the man's response to the woman indicates, the point is that the woman is of the same kind as the man ("This at last is bone of my bones and flesh of my flesh," v. 23a). It would be anachronistic to interpret such statements as indications of gender-blindness. They do, however, express an ideal of male-female relationships that is rather unique in the ancient Near East (see Frymer-Kensky, *Studies in Bible*, 185–93). This concern for right relationships between men and women, in turn, had potential to prevent the kind of violence against women that would plague Israel later, particularly in the book of Judges (see chap. 5 below).

As already noted, the rest of the Bible will testify to many acts of violence against women that arise from a depreciation of the role of women highlighted here. The "fall" described in Genesis 3 leads to a curse on humankind, a curse marked in part by constant forgetting of the intended role of the two sexes. This testimony to the ideals of mutual sharing and appreciation between women and men should be particularly apparent to Christian readers in light of the New Testament's understanding of creation's renewal in Christ. When Paul declares that in Christ "there is no male and female" (Gal. 3:28), he harks back to God's creative intentions now lost. Likewise, when Ephesians says "clothe yourselves with the new self" (4:24), it refers in part to men and women being "subject to one another out of reverence for Christ" (5:21). This notion of a new humanity seems to acknowledge that in Christ something has been regained in the relationship between women and men.

31

Genesis 4:1–16: The First Violent Act

If Genesis 1:1–2:4a and 2:4b–25 lay out the nature of God and God's intentions for humankind, the chapters that follow largely narrate human failure and divine efforts to repair the damage that results. This has long been considered the purpose of the story in Genesis 3. The story of the garden has traditionally been read as *the* explanation for the disruptions in God's world that appear in the rest of the primeval history, and for the rest of history (Rom. 5:12–21). But Genesis 3 is only part of the story of the fall. Genesis 4 should perhaps be read as a continuation and completion of the account in Genesis 3 (see Hauser, "Linguistic and Thematic Links"). Indeed, the story of Cain and Abel may be even more important in this regard. At the very least, Genesis 4 explains the beginnings of violence.

This story portrays the first murder, the first death by violent means. But more than that, the account associates this violent act with *sin*. The word "sin" (Heb. *haṭṭā't*) appears for the first time in the story of Cain and Abel. Although the story in Genesis 3 reports the first human rebellion against God's commands, and thus the essential character of sin, the word itself occurs in Genesis 4 in relation to Cain's violent action against his brother (see Barr, *Garden of Eden*, 1–20).

Genesis 4 raises numerous difficult questions, for example, why does God accept Abel's offering but reject Cain's (4:4–5)? Does the story reflect rivalry between farmers and ranchers? But Genesis 4 shows little interest in such questions. Verses 3–5 simply set the stage: Abel has what Cain desires. The story seems to reflect the basic notion that human conflict arises from one person's desire to have what another person possesses. René Girard proposes that such desire is the root of all violence (see *Things Hidden*, 7). This part of the story seems to vindicate Girard's thesis, at least from the perspective of the Genesis narrative. Genesis 4:3–5 explicates the first incidence of mimetic desire, the desire to have what belongs to another. Verse 7 seems to indicate that Cain's real problem is not that he lacks an acceptable offering, but rather his reaction to the fact that his brother's offering is accepted. God says, "If you do well, will you not be accepted?" "Being accepted" is linked with the right response to the favor shown to another.

In verse 7 sin is introduced, and it is inextricably linked to violence. But sin here is not so much an action one does as a predator waiting for one vulnerable enough to be devoured: "Sin is lurking at the door; its desire is for you." The word "desire" here is the same word 3:16 uses to describe the desire of a woman for her husband; that desire is presented as negative because it comes in the context of a lack of mutuality that resulted from alienation from God. It is an unhealthy aspect of human life, a sign that one has been taken over by alien forces and now lives enslaved to them. Hence the story seems to suggest that sin is the all-consuming desire to have what belongs to another (Exod. 20:17). But Cain is not powerless. God declares, "You must master it." Sin is at once an outside force and something that evokes an internal struggle. The Syriac and Aramaic versions will later add to the account to the effect that Cain was born of the devil and that the evil one controlled him (Levine, "Syriac Version," 73–74). But Genesis 4 says nothing of the sort. The heart of that struggle and the central issue in the understanding of sin in Genesis 4 is Cain's desire for the approval Abel enjoys.

After the report of Cain's murder and God's attempt to prevent such violence from spreading on the earth, a significant event occurs. Cain builds a city and names it for his firstborn son, Enoch (4:17). In the context of Genesis 1–11 this is significant because it identifies the first human civilization, founded by the first murderer (Williams, *Bible, Violence, and the Sacred*, 27). As Girard says, the story of Cain and Abel serves to "lay bare the beginnings of culture" (Girard, *Things Hidden*, 146–48; cf. Williams, *Bible, Violence, and the Sacred*, 35). That is, the very organization of human life is traced to the exiled murderer, Cain, who now lives east of Eden (4:16). Such stories are common in the ancient world. But unlike the myth of the founding of Rome, for example, in which Romulus killed Remus and his death is justified, in Genesis 4 Abel's murder is roundly condemned (4:9; Girard, *Things Hidden*, 146, 148–49). The Genesis story also casts suspicion over all "independent" or self-serving human efforts to organize, build, and develop, all of which becomes clearer in the stories of the flood (Gen. 6–9) and the tower of Babel (11:1–9). Augustine later identifies the earthly human community, the "city," as that which comes from Cain; all those who live there have hope only in God, who redeems them and makes them citizens of the city of God (Augustine, *City of God* 15.1).

33

The Flood Story: Is God Destructive After All?

Although the Bible opens with a portrait of God creating with the cooperation of the creation itself, in Genesis 6–9 God is so heartsick that he destroys the whole human race, along with every other creature, except Noah, his family, and pairs "of every kind" of creature. Therefore, the story may seem to reveal that God gave in to the violence that had become so prominent in the world. God may appear to some readers like a parent who spirals out of control when the children become unruly.

But a close reading of the flood story shows that God neither gave in to violence nor acted rashly. Rather, the flood story is really about God's struggle to maintain creation in the face of humanity's spread of violence. As William Brown puts it, "As creation's integrity or ethos is violated through unchecked violence, creation is (re)saturated by the flood" (*Ethos of the Cosmos*, 58). Indeed, divine judgment amounts to the return of the precreation state in an attempt to correct creation and reestablish the order necessary for life. As Brown goes on to say, "chaos, properly speaking, lies not in the deluge per se but in the flood's cause: violence and corruption, which have accompanied blessing's growth through the ten generations like a hidden parasite that in the end has overtaken its host" (*Ethos of the Cosmos*, 58–59).

It may be helpful to note that the flood story does not speak of God's wrath. Instead of anger the predominant emotion attributed to God is sadness. The story begins with God grieving over the creation gone awry (6:6). Furthermore, the last portion of the story begins with the note, "but God remembered Noah and all the beasts and all the cattle that were with him in the ark" (8:1a), and then God begins to create again (8:1b, "And God made a wind blow over the earth"; see 1:2, "But a wind from God was hovering over the waters"). Hence God should not be understood as one who reacts rashly to human sinfulness. Instead, much of what appears to be God's destructive activity grows out of divine suffering and mourning over the creation. The destruction that is portrayed is not God's angry response to sinfulness; it is God's action of last resort to correct the creation.

34 In this way the flood story follows logically the story of creation in 1:1–2:4a in which God showed himself as Creator to be nonviolent. God as Creator invited the creation to participate in

the creative work and formed humans particularly to represent this work among the other creatures. In so doing, God appeared open and vulnerable to the creation. It was human beings who introduced violence into God's world, contrary to God's intentions (4:1–16). To begin to address these issues we will look more closely at the story itself. The first consideration is the genre, or literary type, that Genesis 6–9 represents.

The Question of Genre

There is no denying that the flood story portrays God destroying what God had previously created. God declares to Noah, "For my part, I am going to bring a flood of waters on the earth, to destroy from under heaven all flesh in which is the breath of life; everything that is on the earth shall die" (Gen. 6:17). The following chapter then presents God doing just as God promised. But we must take into account the nature of the story—its genre and purpose—in order to evaluate what the story says about God. In the following discussion I suggest that the purpose of the story is to present the reason creation continues, not why God destroyed it in the flood.

Like most of Genesis 1–11, Genesis 6–9 is a richly symbolic narrative that tells of events in primeval time in order to explain the origins of certain aspects of the world today. For example, at the end of the account God places his bow in the clouds as a sign that God will never again flood the whole earth (9:13–17). The rainbow is a reminder that rain comes and goes in cycles, that God only gives what is necessary to water the earth.

Such "myths" are different from stories that are cast as historical narratives. To be sure, myth in the Old Testament has been woven together with such texts; myth has been "historicized" (and history, in turn, has been mythicized). But mythic texts are most concerned to link typical experiences to an original or paradigmatic experience. They are symbolically rich stories that use images and narratives to enable us to look more deeply into our "ordinary" experience. Thus Genesis 6–9 operates on a different set of assumptions than narratives that have a historicized chronology. It differs, for example, from the story of Hezekiah in 2 Kings 18–20, which displays a strong interest in dating and parallel historical circumstances ("In the third year of King Hoshea son of Elah of Israel, Hezekiah son of Ahaz of Judah began to reign"; 2 Kgs. 18:1).

35

Genesis 6–9 gives no dates or historical circumstances that tag the flood in relation to other events. Rather it begins with a story of divine beings having sex with women and creating a race of giants (6:1–4)! This is hardly something that can be verified. The point is this: the flood story belongs to a genre intended to explain why things are the way they are or why humans experience the world as they do. It was not meant to be read as an historical account, unlike 2 Kings 18–20.

Understanding the nature and purpose of the flood story should alter the way the story is read in relation to God's destructive activity. Indeed, although the story portrays God making "an end to all flesh" (Gen. 6:13), it does not intend to say that God actually made an end to all flesh, at least not in the same way other stories report historical events. If then Genesis 6–9 is not really a record of God destroying the whole earth, what is its purpose and message?

The Message of the Story

Genesis 6:1–4

Genesis 6:1–4 seems to present the initial reasons for the flood that God brings on the earth. The brief account notes first that when people began to multiply on earth "daughters were born to them" (v. 1). Then the "sons of God *saw*" the human daughters and "*took* wives for themselves of all that they chose" (v. 2). Here the "sons of God" seem to be heavenly beings like those who attend God's throne (Pss. 29:1; 82:1) and whom God appoints to oversee various territories and peoples on earth (Deut. 32:8). The book of 1 *Enoch* (dating to the Hellenistic period, ca. 200 BCE) explains the matter much this way. It identifies the "sons of God" as angels who fell from the purpose God gave them (1 *Enoch* 6–7). The main point Genesis 6:2 makes is that these heavenly beings were in a position of power over humans, and they overstepped the bounds of that power (see the account of David, who "*saw*" that Bathsheba was beautiful and "*took*" her for his wife; 2 Sam. 11:2–4). The result of their union, however, is an unnatural elevation of humans to semi-divine status. Hence God determines to limit the presence of the divine spirit, the breath of life, to one hundred twenty years (Gen. 6:3; cf. 2:7).

36

The story concludes with a summary statement about the result of the union of divine and human beings: the children born to them are great heroes (Gen. 6:4b). This may be intended, however, as an ironic statement. The great heroes are not named and are no longer known at all. The implication seems to be that they were not as important as they thought. The final expression, "warriors of renown," reinforces this message. The expression in Hebrew is literally "men of the name" (*'anšê haššēm*), and yet the names of these heroes are completely forgotten. It is also worth noting that later, in 11:1–9, the people of the earth again try to make themselves more than they are when they attempt to "make a name for themselves" (v. 4). In that story the problem is precisely that humans do not know their place before their creator. So also in 6:1–4 humans (after procreating with the "sons of God") are identified by their "name" that they make for themselves, not by the name of God or by a name God gives them. Although the passage does not say that these humans are violent, this self-importance is the root of violence.

Genesis 6:5–8, 11–13

After the account of the sons of God taking women as wives, the flood story proper begins with two explanations of why God brought the devastation on the earth. The two explanations are typically assigned to different authors or sources (6:5–8 to the Priestly writer; 6:11–13 to the Yahwist writer). What is important here is that both introductions to the flood narrative relate to violence, albeit the violence of humans, not God.

Genesis 6:5–8 does not mention violence specifically, but it does seem to point to the root causes that are evident in the humans God made. God saw "that the wickedness of humankind was great on the earth" (v. 5a). The word translated "wickedness" (*rā'â*) is closely related to the word rendered "evil" (*ra'*) in the next part of the verse (v. 5b) (both are from the same root). When this term refers to human activity it typically signifies evil against humans as well as against God (see Isa. 11:9). It is the opposite of "good" (*ṭôb*), the word that characterizes the world God made (Gen. 1:31). Therefore, what God saw in the humans God had created was a level of rebellion that threatened to reverse the intentions God had in the beginning (see Stoebe, "רעע *r'* to be bad," 1252–53). Verse 5b

37

characterizes the level of activity against God by saying, "the inclination of the thoughts of their hearts was only evil continually." The word for "inclination" (*yēṣer*) has the sense of "shape" or "form." In other words, the verse is saying that humans had all developed hearts and minds that were "evil-shaped," inclined toward destruction. As we have already observed, this orientation away from God and God's intentions is the catalyst for *ḥāmās*, "violence." That is the picture 6:5–8 gives of the human race.

The evil intention of humankind is matched by the sorrow of God over the state of the world God had created. As 6:7 says, "So the LORD said, 'I will blot out from the earth the human beings I have created—people together with animals and creeping things and birds of the air, for I am sorry that I have made them.'" God's response to human evil in this case is not anger or wrath but sorrow. The description of God's "condition" is one of divine pathos. God mourns or grieves (as in 38:12; Jer. 31:15). Another description of God occurs at the end of Genesis 6:6 with a word that means to be distressed, indignant, or saddened (*yit'aṣṣēb*; note this same verb appears in 34:7 to describe the feelings of Dinah's brothers after she is raped). Hence God's decision to "blot out from the earth the human beings" (v. 7) comes in relation to divine sorrow. Walter Brueggemann appropriately puts 6:5–8 in the context of the larger picture of God in Genesis:

> In our discussion of 1:1–2:4a, we have seen that God's creative power was not coercive and authoritarian. Rather, it is invitational and permit-granting. While God wills creation to be turned toward him, he does not commandeer it. So in this narrative, bringing the world to trust and obedience is not done by God's fiat. Rather, it is done by the anguish and grief of God, who enters into the pain and fracture of the world.
>
> (*Genesis*, 79)

As the story proceeds we learn that the world does not come to trust and obedience. God's *attempt* to so bring the world, however, is through God's own suffering and vulnerability.

Genesis 6:11–13 describes human corruption explicitly in terms of violence. Verse 11 says the "earth was filled with violence," and in verse 13 God restates the point in his speech to Noah. The term that accompanies *ḥāmās*, "violence," is *šḥt*, "to ruin" or "to be ruined." Violence seems like a disease that breaks out and spoils everything. It is not only human hearts that are affected (as in vv. 5–8), but the whole earth or land. Because all is spoiled, the only remedy is to start over, which is the intention of God's action to "make an end to all flesh." "All flesh" seems to include animals as well as human beings, and indeed all life forms are killed in the flood. But the expression "all flesh" refers only to humans in other judgment texts (see, e.g., Deut. 5:26). Therefore, the judgment that "all flesh corrupted its way upon the earth" seems to pin the blame solely on human beings. Hence Genesis 6:11–13 seems to say that God found it necessary to end all life on earth because human beings had made life untenable. On this point Calvin notes that the animals died because "the earth was like a wealthy house" and animals were part of that household. Further, Calvin says, "neither asses, nor oxen, nor any other animals had done evil; yet being in subjection to man when he fell, they were drawn with him into the same destruction" (*Genesis*, 1:250).

God's method of destroying the earth is popularly conceived as a flood. But Genesis describes the event as more—it was a reversal of creation. This is expressed in 7:11, which notes that "the fountains of the great deep burst forth" and "the windows of the heavens were opened." The picture here is of the primeval ocean that God pushed back in creation (1:2–6) now gushing forth past the limits God once set. Likewise, the heavenly vault God established to hold back the waters above the earth loses its effectiveness. In Genesis 1 creation was characterized first and foremost by the control of the waters—waters above and waters below given set limits. But the creation God once protected from these waters is ruined, so the waters bring it to an end. This reversal of the order of creation is thus God's reaction to humankind's overstepping its bounds and spreading violence over the earth. Now the waters are allowed to go beyond their boundaries in order to address the problem. The entire event is said to result from God's suffering. God had risked the divine self in creating the world. Now God decides with grief and regret to start over.

Genesis 8:20–22

The elements of the flood story that follow immediately upon God's decision to destroy the earth are well known: the animals entered the ark (though rather less familiar is the note that of the clean

39

animals Noah took seven pairs of those animals that could be sacrificed; 7:2–3); the flood came (7:11–24); the ark came to rest on the mountains of Ararat (8:1–5); Noah sent out raven and dove to discover dry ground (8:6–12); finally Noah, his family, and the animals came off the ark (8:13–19).

The details of the conclusion to the story may be less familiar, but they are perhaps the greatest clue to the central intention of the account. Genesis 8:20–22 reports that Noah made sacrifices. God then declared he would never again destroy the earth by covering it with water. Most importantly, verse 21 states that God made this decision despite the fact that humankind had not changed. This is perhaps the most important theological statement in the story. On this matter several points need further attention.

First, there are questions about the nature and purpose of Noah's acts of sacrifice. The reason for the sacrifices is not given. They seem to be purely expressions of thanks (Westermann, *Genesis 1–11*, 454). Verse 21a reports God's reaction to the sacrifices with striking anthropomorphic imagery: "the LORD smelled the pleasing odor." In other Old Testament texts this description communicates God's acceptance (Exod. 29:18; Lev. 1:9; Ezek. 6:13). There is no hint that Noah's sacrifices appease God's anger or make atonement for sins (see von Rad, *Genesis*, 122–23). Hence God's decision to allow humans to continue seems purely God's own. It is not motivated by any sacrificial mechanism.

Verse 21aβ-b gives God's decision about the future of the creation and God's relationship to it. The NRSV translation illustrates the difficulty: "I will never again curse the ground because of humankind, *for* the inclination of the human heart is evil from youth; nor will I ever again destroy every living creature as I have done." In this translation, the passage seems to make two contradictory statements. It seems to say that God decided to preserve the creation *because* humans continued their bent toward evil. The key here is the meaning of the Hebrew particle (*kî*) that NRSV translates "for." This word often does have a causative meaning. In this case, however, it makes more sense to take it as concessive, "even though" (see similar use of the term in Jer. 49:16). Indeed, what God's statement indicates is that God decided not to destroy the earth again, *despite* the fact that humankind had not become any more obedient. God simply chose to become more patient. Again, Brueggemann says it well: "The flood has effected no change in

40

humankind. But it has effected an irreversible change in God, who now will approach his creation with an unlimited patience and forbearance" (*Genesis*, 81). Calvin addresses the point of God's grace here by saying that if God gave humankind what it deserved, "there would be a necessity for a daily deluge" (*Genesis*, 1:284). But God does not give the world what it deserves.

Another issue in this verse is that the reference to the land being cursed seems out of place. The judgment just described was the destruction of all living things in the flood. Yet the passage here refers to God's curse of the ground, which seems to reach back to 3:17 and 4:11–12. Some scholars explain the reference as a mistake of some sort. But as it stands the reference to the curse of the ground coupled with the reference to the flood is quite appropriate. It draws together the consequences of all human rebellion, rebellion that was punished in the deluge, and indicates that God reversed the penal measures earlier prescribed. The reference to the curse of the ground refers to the curse given to Adam (3:17) and to Cain (4:11–12). On account of their disobedience ("because of humankind"; 8:21aα) God earlier declared that the ground would rebel against them. The ground was cursed so it became difficult for Adam to till it; Cain was "cursed from the ground" so that he could not gain any produce from it and thus had to wander about unable to be "rooted" himself (4:12). Genesis 8:21 makes the remarkable claim that this curse is no longer valid, even though humans have apparently learned nothing from these experiences. God will "never again curse the ground" just as God will never "again destroy every living creature."

This remarkable ending to the flood story reveals the real point of the account as a whole. It shows that the story is not so much about why God destroyed all living things in the flood—the rottenness of humankind is clear enough; rather it answers the question of why God allows the creation now to exist. Genesis 8:20–22 indeed makes the point that humankind did not change as a result of the ordeal. The judgment on humans in 6:5–8 and 11–13, including the violence that humans perpetrated and spread throughout the created order, is still as bad as ever. God has simply decided to be more gracious since humans have not become more obedient. This point gives a very important cast to the issue of God's destructive activity in the flood. Genesis 6–8 portrays great destruction at the hands of God. That cannot be denied. But it seems the story is

41

not told to make that point. Rather, the devastation of the flood is a foil for a more important point, namely, that the Lord is "a God merciful and gracious, slow to anger and abounding in steadfast love and faithfulness" (Exod. 34:6).

Genesis 9:1–17: God's Concessions to Violence

As the flood story concludes, God blesses Noah and his sons, just as God blessed the first humans in 1:30: "Be fruitful and multiply, and fill the earth." But this blessing is not merely a repetition of the first blessing. Something has changed because of the corruption of humankind. As God blesses Noah and his family, God also makes concessions to the violence that destroyed the earth. The original pristine state of creation, characterized by nonviolence, was embodied in the vegetarian lifestyle before the flood (see 1:29–30; W. Brown, *Ethos of the Cosmos*, 59). But now, according to the Priestly writer, God allows humans to eat the flesh of animals for the first time. This accommodation to human violence is like the Yahwist's record of God's forbearance in 8:22: God determines that humans cannot live by the divine will for nonviolence, so God determines to work with the violent creatures instead of destroying them. But God presents two imperatives that regulate and limit human violence. First, God declares that humans can consume only the flesh of an animal, not its blood. Blood represents life, and God is determined to sanctify and protect life, albeit with this allowance for meat eating. Second, God gives as a complement to the prohibition against eating the blood of animals an absolute law against the shedding of human blood: "Whoever sheds the blood of a human, by a human shall that person's blood be shed; for in his own image God made humankind" (9:6). This declaration highlights the seriousness of preserving life and acting as though life is holy, a gift from God, in whose image humans are made.

The Call of Abraham and the Prevention of Violence

At the juncture between the so-called primeval history in Genesis 1–11 and the story of Israel's ancestors in Genesis 12–50 comes a significant change that raises serious questions about violence.

In God's attempt to bless all humankind God introduces a new strategy. Into the failed human experiment God introduces Abraham and Sarah. God's attempt to stave off violence now centers on them.

The story of Genesis 1–11 is largely a story about God creating and attempting to bless the creation. But the story indicates that God's creatures rebel against the Creator at every turn, thus making God's efforts at order and blessing impossible. God in the beginning set an example of nonviolence, and God made human beings in God's image, presumably to imitate the Creator in caring for and managing the earth. Nevertheless, humans turn to violence anyway. The final narrative in Genesis 1–11 shows God's ultimate frustration with working to bring blessing on humankind through the whole human race (11:1–9).

Although the Babel story does not say those building the tower were acting violently, they show the attitudes at the root of violence: self-promotion and a heightened sense of autonomy. The speech by the residents of Babel hints that they are trying to take the place of God. When the residents of Babel determine to build a city they use the same plural imperative form of speech God used in creating humankind ("Come, let us"; 11:3, 4; see 1:26). But God responds to their action with identical speech, as though to establish the legitimate authority in the world. Indeed, God uses that same type of expression when determining to confuse their language (11:7). This expression has not occurred in Genesis since God's creation of humankind. The repetition of the language in 11:7 seems to indicate that God comes down to take an action that matches, in a negative way, the creation of human beings in 1:26–27. Thus the special role of humankind will be fulfilled in a way different from what God originally intended.

The next part of the story in Genesis is the call of Abraham. Although this story may seem like a completely new chapter in the account, and it appears to shift from primeval time to an historical period, the account of Abraham actually picks up where the tower of Babel account left off and has important implications for issues of violence. The blessing of God once bestowed on all humankind now is concentrated on this one man and his family. Two features of 12:1–3 indicate this shift in God's intentions. First, the blessing bestowed on the first humans is now given to Abraham. God said to Abraham, "I will bless you" (12:2), using the same word as in 1:28

43

("The LORD blessed them"; Heb. *bārak*). In later versions of the blessing the promise to "be fruitful" will also appear (17:6).

Second, the call of Abraham is framed as God's completely new and radical act, like God making and blessing the first humans. This is apparent in God's instructions to Abraham to leave his country, his kindred, and his father's house (Gen. 12:1). Modern Western readers can hardly conceive of the break God is here outlining for Abram. The three circles of associations—country, kindred, father's house—communicate an increasingly narrow field of relationships that gave a person in the ancient Near East his or her identity and security. Particularly the last, the household of the father (*bêt 'āb*) was *the* identifying mark of a person. The story of nearly every Old Testament figure is related directly to such identity and the inheritance that went along with it: Jacob tricks Esau out of his birthright, the sign of having first place in the household of the father; Joseph, though last in line for inheritance in the household of his father, is nevertheless favored, thus producing anger in his brothers. Hence God's call for Abraham to leave his father's house indicates God is giving him a new identity and a new purpose in the world. God is starting over with this man to work out the blessing for humankind God intended in the beginning.

The notion that Abraham bears uniquely the blessing of God and that God will work through Abraham and his descendants to prevent violence takes on much more concrete significance a few chapters later. In the story of God's destruction of Sodom God muses as to whether God should keep from Abraham what is about to happen to the city (18:17–18). God says, "No, for I have chosen him, that he may charge his children and his household after him to keep the way of the LORD by doing righteousness and justice; so that the LORD may bring about for Abraham what he has promised him" (18:19). The words "righteousness" (*sĕdāqâ*) and "justice" (*mišpāṭ*) appear rarely in Genesis, but they identify Abraham's purpose as that of defending the order of creation. "Righteousness" and "justice" are closely related words that denote that which promotes the life and well-being of all relationships humans have with one another and with the rest of creation (see Schmid, "Creation, Righteousness, and Salvation"). The Hebrew prophets use these words to call for economic justice, one important dimension of the effort against violence (e.g., Amos 5:24).

44

This perspective is crucial for understanding how and why God favored Abraham and Sarah. The election of this one couple and their descendants is sometimes understood as perhaps the greatest catalyst of violence. Indeed, it has encouraged some who identify with Abraham to understand themselves as people of special privilege. With that privilege they have abused others. But a careful reading of the Abraham story indicates that the opposite is intended (see Kaminsky, "Did Election Imply Mistreatment?"). As Hendrikus Berkhof rightly says, "Election is thus a favor and a mandate; and the mandate involves the calling to live from the love of this sovereign God in all areas of life. In the midst of the nations this gave Israel both an exceptional advantage and an exceptional burden" (*Christian Faith*, 249). The people of Abraham are chosen to be God's "treasured possession out of all the peoples" (Exod. 19:5), and through Abraham "all the families of the earth shall be blessed" (Gen. 12:3). This will mean first and foremost that Abraham will take the lead in preventing violence by promoting "righteousness and justice."

Conclusion

The creation stories that open the book of Genesis give a rather remarkable perspective on violence. Genesis 1:1–2:4a portrays God as one who creates without doing battle or engaging in conflict. This picture of God contrasts strikingly with the depiction of many ancient Near Eastern deities who were said to create by means of violent warfare. In light of this typical description of creation, the first picture of God in the Bible is noteworthy for its emphasis on God's nonviolent creative work. After the initial creation story many other passages will present God doing battle with cosmic enemies, much like the typical depiction of ancient gods did. But the presence of 1:1–2:4a at the beginning of the canon subordinates such accounts to the normative picture, expressed in the first pages of Scripture. Such a picture of God as nonviolent, in turn, directly affects a proper understanding of the image God placed on human beings that comes toward the end of the account.

In addition to the introductory role of the content of 1:1–2:4a and 2:4b–25, these opening stories of creation give a symbolic cast

45

to much of the violence in the rest of the Bible. As William Brown rightly says, the opening creation stories, by virtue of their place at the Bible's threshold, imbue "all other material, from historical narrative to law, with cosmic background" (*Ethos of the Cosmos*, 36). Hence it will become apparent that much of the Bible's description of violence and destruction is related directly to God's desire to maintain the proper order in creation. What is often understood as God's violence is actually God acting to protect the creation itself, or the creation, following the will of God, rising up in rebellion against those who would ruin it. Similar connections between creation and violence will become apparent in Scripture's presentation of the ban (the ritual slaughter of enemies) and other disturbing concepts. To these related accounts we now turn.

CHAPTER 2

"The LORD Is a Warrior"

In the last chapter I argued that the creation stories in Genesis 1 and 2 present God as open to the creation, as one who invites participation by the elements in the creative process. This view of God, in turn, has direct bearing on the understanding of humankind as made in "the image of God" (1:26–27). The absence of war and coercive action is at the center of the nature of God and of God's intention for humankind. With this picture of God and creation the book of Genesis sets the stage for the rest of the Bible. This will become apparent, among other places, in the exodus story. What may seem at first glance simply a story of liberation from slavery in which God battles an historical ruler, the pharaoh of Egypt, is actually an account of a contest between Pharaoh and the God who created Egypt. Pharaoh is the anticreator, the one who tries to undo the purpose of God that God began in Genesis 1. Thus the Egyptian king is largely a symbolic figure, and the story has an openness that defies historical limits.

Nevertheless, God's destructive activity takes a turn in the book of Exodus that demands further explanation. Here God is presented for the first time explicitly as a warrior. Exodus reports that God fought directly against Pharaoh and the Egyptians. For example, Exodus 14:25a recalls that when the Egyptians pursued the Israelites into the Red Sea (or Sea of Reeds), God "clogged their chariot wheels so that they turned with difficulty." The Egyptians then

47

respond by saying, "Let us flee from the Israelites, for the LORD is fighting for them against Egypt" (v. 25b). When the Israelites arrive safely on the other side of the sea they celebrate their deliverance in a song (15:1–18) in which they declare concerning their deliverer, "The LORD is a warrior; the LORD is his name" (v. 3). With this image of God, the second book of the canon seems to present a picture of God that contrasts strikingly with the picture in Genesis.

This image of God as warrior in large part led Marcion to complain that God in the Old Testament and parts of the New Testament is "desirous of war" (see Tertullian, *Against Marcion* I, 1.6). The description of God as warrior demands attention in any serious reading of the Bible. Although the church denounced Marcion for his view, Marcion was not wrong in his general observation about the appearance of God in the Old Testament. As Patrick Miller says, "the view of Yahweh as warrior can hardly be a peripheral matter in the effort to work out a biblical theology. Rather, it lies at the theological center and much of the traditional substance of God-talk when given content from an Old Testament perspective confronts one directly with the wars of Israel and the God who was active in them" (*Divine Warrior in Early Israel*, 7).

It is possible to conclude that the notion of God as warrior comes second in the canon to that of God as creator and is thus conditioned by the first portrait of God. It is also possible to separate the presentation of God as a warrior in the text from the *real* God. Such an approach would understand the text as a flawed work, a relic of the past that naturally presents God in ways that are imprecise and culturally conditioned. A careful analysis of the imagery, according to this view, will lead the thoughtful person to sort out unacceptable ideas, such as God as warrior, and to "think rightly" about God (on this approach see Seibert, *Disturbing Divine Behavior*, 5–6).

Although these two approaches are possible, neither seems particularly helpful theologically. While one cannot deny that biblical texts are culturally conditioned and that the image of God as warrior poses theological problems, the complete separation of the real God from the textually embodied God seems misguided. Such an approach also overlooks the potentially positive role this image 48   plays in Scripture and in Christian theology. Although all figurative language for God has limitations, when God is presented as a warrior God acts to correct and counteract oppression and injustice.

God is not "desirous of war," as Marcion said, but instead God engages in warfare to counteract the destructive forces at work in the world. In the discussion that follows, therefore, I do not try to reject or deny the label of God as warrior. Instead, I seek to discover why certain biblical texts include the imagery and how that imagery might actually speak against violence.

Exodus 15:1–18

The first occurrence of the idea that God is a warrior is in the so-called Song of the Sea in Exodus 15:1–18 (v. 3). The label is communicated in three words woodenly translated, "the LORD is a man of war" (*yhwh 'îš milḥāmâ*). The poem then proceeds to describe the Lord's warring activity: "the chariots of Pharaoh and his army he has thrown into the sea" (15:4a).

The Content of the Song

The Song of the Sea has two primary parts. Verses 1–10 celebrate the victory of God over Pharaoh and his army. Hence the first part harks back to the narrative in Exodus 14. This portion of the passages emphasizes two points about God's action. First, God expressed power directly in God's action against Pharaoh and his forces. For instance, verse 1b declares, "I will sing to the LORD, for he has triumphed gloriously; horse and rider he has thrown into the sea." Again in verse 4a the passage declares, "Pharaoh's chariots and his army he cast into the sea."

Second, the song shows God using the nonhuman world as an instrument in divine warfare. Statements to this effect punctuate the poem: "the floods covered them" (v. 5a); "at the blast of your nostrils the waters piled up, the floods stood in a heap; the deeps congealed in the heart of the sea" (v. 8); "you blew with your wind, the sea covered them" (v. 10a); "you stretched out your right hand, the earth swallowed them" (v. 12). After the poem ends a summary statement reiterates the point: "When the horses of Pharaoh with his chariots and his chariot drivers went into the sea, the LORD brought back the waters of the sea upon them; but the Israelites walked through the sea on dry ground" (v. 19). Thus in this concluding account of God's defeat of Pharaoh, Pharaoh's immediate

49

foe is the nonhuman world itself. The power of God is displayed mainly in God's ability to direct the elements against the Egyptian king. Hence the destructive, warring acts of God described here are closely related to the acts of God to preserve the creation presented in Genesis 1–11. As I will discuss more fully in chapter 3, Pharaoh has acted against the intentions of God to bring blessing to the creation through the Israelites. Exodus 15:1–18 shows that creation is under God's control.

Verses 11–18 then praise God for God's incomparable power (vv. 11–12) and God's steadfast love with which God led God's people to the holy mountain. This portion of the song looks forward to the rest of the book of Exodus in which the Israelites arrive at Mount Sinai and receive the law (Exod. 19–40). God's work as warrior thus provides a hinge between the two portions of the book and is indeed central to the message of the whole. God's fight against Pharaoh and the Egyptians is a key to Israel's freedom from bondage (Exod. 1–14) and Israel's being "planted" in the land of Canaan (Exod. 19–40).

The final portion of the Song of the Sea (15:11–18) gives important context to God's warlike activity described in verses 1–10. Verse 11 praises God with a series of questions, "LORD, who is like you among the gods? Who is like you, wonderful in holiness? Who can work miracles and mighty acts like yours?" The questions, however, are not about God's might in general. Rather, they address God's ability to keep the promises God made to God's people. As verse 13 states, "Faithful to your promise, you led the people you had rescued." God is not only caring and compassionate toward those enslaved in Egypt. God also is powerful enough to deliver on the promise of rescuing them. For that reason, those who oppose God's will (the Philistines, Edom, Moab, and people of Canaan) tremble with fear.

Verse 17 describes the ultimate goal of God's rescue of the Israelites. It is not simply to free them from oppression, but to "bring them in and plant them on your mountain." In other words, God desires to establish these people in the place where God also dwells. The notion of "planting" the Israelites on God's mountain anticipates worship in the Jerusalem temple, which will be central to the life and well-being of these people. It also hints that God is trying with the Israelites to restore paradise, since the Temple Mount is an Eden-like place (see Ps. 46; Ezek. 28:13–14). Exodus 15:18 sets all the descriptions of God using the natural world against Pharaoh in the proper context of God's kingship. The words "the LORD will reign forever and ever" speak of God's overarching role as universal sovereign. This point is essential in order to recognize properly the place of God's creative and warlike activity. God's chief identity is as one who rules the world. The creation can know the well-being God intends only when all God's creatures acknowledge God's rightful place as king. As already observed, God takes on the role of warrior when elements of the creation rebel against the intended order. In 15:1–18 "the LORD is a warrior" who fights against Pharaoh because Pharaoh tried to claim the role only God could occupy. The result was oppression and death. God's action against Pharaoh was thus an attempt to restore creation. In the next chapter I will observe that this is the real point of the plague narratives in Exodus 7–12. It is also the point, expressed more subtly, of 15:1–18, which culminates in the declaration, "the LORD reigns" (v. 18).

The Context in Exodus

As already noted, 15:1–18 plays an integral role in the book of Exodus. The larger literary and theological context of this book, therefore, provides guidance for understanding the first presentation of God as warrior. Any treatment of God's action as a "man of war" (v. 3) must be understood in this context. Three primary movements in this larger context seem important: (1) Israel cries to God; (2) God acts for Israel; (3) God's action for Israel attempts to establish justice.

Israel Cries to God

The victory song in 15:1–18, which celebrates God as warrior, is the final movement in Exodus 1–15, which began with Pharaoh oppressing the Israelites (Exod. 1–2) and the Israelites crying to God for help (3:7). The book begins with the Israelites in slavery, describes their condition, and states that the Egyptians "became ruthless in imposing tasks on the Israelites, and made their lives bitter with hard service in mortar and brick and in every kind of field labor. They were ruthless in all the tasks that they imposed on them" (1:13–14). The Song of the Sea is thus a hymnic response of thanksgiving for God's salvation, which was God's response to Israel's cry for deliverance.

Exodus 1–15 has a structure and movement seen in other parts of the Old Testament, specifically a pattern attested in the lament psalms of the Psalter. The pattern includes (1) a statement of distress, accompanied by complaints about being oppressed by enemies; (2) a plea to God for help; and finally (3) a song of praise for God's deliverance that assumes deliverance has indeed been granted (see Ps. 13 for an example of this pattern). Two points about this pattern are important. First, the psalmist's complaint often has a judicial basis. He or she is being accused falsely or is the victim of injustice, and no human authority is willing to hear the case. So the psalmist appeals to God, the ultimate judge. This may have occurred in a sanctuary or temple and in the presence of religious officials thought to have authority to seek God on behalf of one who suffers. Second, the concluding song of praise in such psalms was likely added after the psalmist received a hearing and was assured of protection or freedom. An act of salvation occurred between the plea and praise, though it is not recorded in the psalm.

This pattern in the Psalms identifies the psalmist in two very important ways that also applies to the Israelites in Exodus. (1) It identifies him or her as one who suffers unjustly at the hands of a cruel and evil enemy. The Psalter often characterizes enemies as "the wicked" and portrays them as those who refuse to acknowledge God's desires for the world (see Pss. 9–10). The psalmist, in turn, is called "righteous." This label does not denote moral perfection or moral superiority. Rather, it identifies the psalmist as dependent and pleading, one who turns to God when in trouble (see Creach, *Destiny of the Righteous*; and the larger discussion in chap. 7 below). (2) The psalmist's dependence on God is at root an openness that is critical for proper relationship with God.

God Acts for Israel

Exodus 15:1–18 also serves as the climax to the narrative's emphasis on God acting for Israel. The victory over Pharaoh is narrated in Exodus 14, and the meaning and ethical implications of the Song of the Sea may be discerned in part by paying attention to this narrative setting. The narrative emphasizes that God acted for Israel in a way that is enhanced in 15:1–18; for example, 14:25 noted that God "clogged their chariot wheels," and 14:27 declared that God "tossed the Egyptians into the sea"; so here in Exodus 15 God directly engages Israel's enemy. Particularly important are Moses' words to the Israelites when they realize they are hemmed in by Pharaoh: "The LORD will fight for you, and you have only to keep still" (14:14). The LORD fights because Israel cannot defend itself. Exodus 15:1–18 matches this emphasis on Israel's helplessness by not even mentioning Moses' role in the event, which is indirect even in the narrative. But in the Song of the Sea, God delivers Israel without even the mention of a human agent. The implications of this message are crucial. As Millard Lind says, "In the thought of the Song of the Sea Yahweh is involved in Israel's history by the fact that he *alone* is warrior" (*Yahweh Is a Warrior*, 51). The Passover Haggadah (the Jewish liturgy used during the Seder meal) also emphasizes this point. When recalling the story of the exodus it emphasizes that God acted without intermediaries:

> "I will go through the land of Egypt in that night": I, and not an angel. "I will smite all the first-born in the land of Egypt": I, and not a seraph. "And against all the gods of Egypt I will execute judgments": I, and not a messenger. "I am the Lord"; I am He, and no other.

Even the portion of the story that refers to Moses as the bearer of signs of God's power does not mention Moses directly—it mentions only the staff God gave him to display the miraculous signs (see Glatzer, *Passover Haggadah*, 37, 39).

It is possible that the image of God as warrior arose within the institution of holy war and thus was directly connected to the wars of Israel, as many scholars have argued (see Christensen, *War Oracle* 11–15). This assessment of the *origins* of the image of God as warrior may be correct, but it seems clear that the image remained in Scripture for a very different reason. Those who shaped the Pentateuch were exiles in Babylon, and, as such, they could not defend themselves. For them, the idea of God as warrior must have served two purposes. First, it would have given them hope that, despite having no recourse against enemies through military means, they had the ultimate defender on their side. Second, the notion of God as warrior served as part of the claim that their God was more powerful than the gods of Babylon and other oppressive peoples.

It is also crucial that the picture of God as warrior seems to include little or no recognition of earthly warriors who carry out God's intentions. Although some references to God's warfare mention other warriors (Isa. 13:4–5; Joel 3:9–10 [4:9–10 Heb.]), the warriors seem to be members of the divine council (Miller, "Divine Council"). The passages that do speak of human warriors typically speak of the warriors of the nations, marshaled by God to bring justice on earth. This may be the case in Jeremiah 51:27–28: "Raise a standard in the land, blow the trumpet among the nations; prepare the nations for war against her, summon against her the kingdoms, Ararat, Minni, and Ashkenaz; appoint a marshal against her, bring up horses like bristling locusts. Prepare the nations for war against her, the kings of the Medes, with their governors and deputies, and every land under their dominion." Obviously, this call to war is not a call to war in any sense we would recognize within history. Such portraits are probably intended to be apocalyptic in character, and the warriors called are heavenly warriors (Miller, "Divine Council," 104–5). The same use of the image of God as warrior appears prominently in the New Testament as well (see Mark 13:26; Rev. 19:11–16). John Howard Yoder suggests that the Exodus account of God fighting for Israel against Pharaoh and his army is paradigmatic of how the Divine Warrior theme appears in the Bible and should be applied to the Christian life. The Lord fights, but Israel does not (see Yoder, *Politics of Jesus*, 76–88).

Thus although the image of God as warrior poses problems for our understanding of God, it does not legitimate or encourage actual wars, and it may even nullify their legitimacy. This draws a striking contrast between Israel's use of the warrior image and Israel's neighbors' use of that image. Indeed, ancient Near Eastern kings typically used such imagery to support their own quest for power. The Bible, however, does not present God's warring activity to justify the earthly war efforts of Israel's kings. The earliest passages that portray God as warrior, such as Exodus 15:1–18, predate the Israelite monarchy in the opinion of most scholars (see Lind, *Yahweh Is a Warrior*, 47). Moreover, as I suggested in chapter 1, the two passages that clearly link God's warfare to the efforts of Israel's kings show Israel or its king in a state of utter helplessness, having been defeated and humiliated by enemies (Pss. 74; 89). In other words, the Divine Warrior fights for those who have no earthly warriors to defend them.

54

God Administers Justice

Exodus 15:1–18 presents God's action as a warrior specifically for the purpose of establishing justice. Marjorie O'Rourke Boyle makes the interesting suggestion that the language and imagery of Exodus 15:1–18 speak in important figurative ways about God judging the Egyptians. She sees two symbolic expressions that are particularly important in this regard ("Heart of the Sea"). The first such hint that the song means to present God's action as a matter of justice is the portrait of the nonhuman world as an instrument in the hands of God. Verse 8 describes God moving the waters of the sea with the blast of the divine nostrils. The result is that the waters of the sea stand upright:

> the waters piled up,
> the floods stood up in a heap;
> the deep congealed in the heart of the sea.

As Boyle points out, this verse is typically conflated with the narrative account of the sea dividing so the Israelites are able to pass through on dry ground (Exod. 14:21–25; "Heart of the Sea," 17–18). In Exodus 15, however, there is no record of the Israelites passing through the sea. The point is rather that the waters are in God's control and God uses them to cover Pharaoh and his army (v. 10).

The second hint that Exodus 15 is about God judging the Egyptians is the poem's emphasis on the Egyptians being overwhelmed with water and sinking into it (vv. 5, 10). This motif of water as the instrument of judgment is common in the ancient Near East. As Kyle McCarter points out, the cosmic river in Akkadian literature serves as a judge in legal cases (McCarter, "River Ordeal in Israelite Literature," 403–4). Exodus 15:1–18 emphasizes the Egyptian soldiers' being surrounded by water (vv. 4, 5, 10) and sinking in water. That the Egyptians appear as heavy objects that sink in the water is particularly interesting:

> Pharaoh's chariots and his army he cast into the sea;
> his picked officers were sunk in the Red Sea.
> The floods covered them;
> they went down into the depths like a stone.
>
> (vv. 4–5)

55

You blew with your wind, the sea covered them;
they sank like lead in the mighty waters.

(v. 10)

It is striking that these expressions emphasize the Egyptians going down into the waters because they are heavy, "like a stone" or "like lead." The emphasis here is not on death. To be sure, death is the result of their sinking in the waters of the sea. The song states twice that God destroyed the Egyptians: "your right hand, O LORD, shattered the enemy" (v. 6); "you sent out your fury, it consumed them like stubble" (v. 7). But most of the references in Exodus 15, and all the references to the Egyptians being covered by the sea, are to them being inundated or sinking: "were sunk in the Red Sea" (v. 4), "the floods covered them," "they went down like a stone" (v. 5), "the sea covered them," "they sank like lead" (v. 10).

The psalmists speak numerous times about "going down" to "the pit" or to Sheol as a sign of divine disapproval (Pss. 28:1; 30:3 [4 Heb.]; 55:15 [16 Heb.]). In such passages the issue is not death per se but judgment. For example, the psalmist in Psalm 55:15 (16 Heb.) pleads to God concerning one who is deceitful and untrue: "Let him go down to Sheol alive." In a similar way, Exodus 15 does not emphasize the death of the Egyptians as much as it focuses on the fact that they "went down" into the depths of the sea. Thus the image of God as warrior plays a positive role as this image is closely related to the picture of God as judge and arbiter of justice.

Within this set of ideas war seems to be one tool God used to settle legal arguments, thus as a *"legal* judgment of Yahweh made for the purpose of resolving a dispute between Israel and neighboring states" (Good, "Just War in Ancient Israel," 387). It would not seem an exaggeration to say that the Old Testament rests on a general assumption that God is intimately involved in warfare as a judge between the parties who have conflict. Second Chronicles 20 is another interesting case that highlights God's role as judge over against God's role as warrior. In this narrative it is Jehoshaphat who comes before God in a public assembly asking God to judge between Israel and its bellicose neighbors. The name Jehoshaphat itself means "Yahweh judges," a hint that God's role as judge is central to the story. At Israel's east is an assembly of forces prepared to march against Judean territory. Jehoshaphat then calls an assembly

in the Jerusalem temple and pleads to God with language suitable
for court:

> O LORD, God of our ancestors, are you not God in heaven? Do
> you not rule over all the kingdoms of the nations? In your hand
> are power and might, so that no one is able to withstand you. Did
> you not, O our God, drive out the inhabitants of this land before
> your people Israel, and give it forever to the descendants of your
> friend Abraham? They have lived in it, and in it have built you a
> sanctuary for your name, saying, "If disaster comes upon us, the
> sword, judgment, or pestilence, or famine, we will stand before
> this house, and before you, for your name is in this house, and
> cry to you in our distress, and you will hear and save." See now,
> the people of Ammon, Moab, and Mount Seir, whom you would
> not let Israel invade when they came from the land of Egypt,
> and whom they avoided and did not destroy—they reward us
> by coming to drive us out of your possession that you have given
> us to inherit. O our God, will you not execute judgment upon
> them? For we are powerless against this great multitude that is
> coming against us. We do not know what to do, but our eyes are
> on you.
>
> (2 Chr. 20:6–12)

Jehoshaphat appeals to God as universal sovereign, the one
who has responsibility for judging the world. Then he makes a case
against the enemies that threaten Israel. He specifically makes the
case that Israel obeyed God after the exodus from Egypt by not
challenging Ammon, Moab, and Edom. But now these same nations
are unjustly attacking God's people. Jehoshaphat finally appeals to
God as judge on the basis of this injustice and Israel's inability to
defend itself. In other words, 2 Chronicles 20 conceives the military
threat from Israel's neighbors as a legal dispute that only God can
arbitrate. The outcome of war is considered the legal decision that
God renders (see also Jephthah's prayer in Judg. 11:15–27; when
negotiating with the Ammonite king, Jephthah argues for Israel's
right to possess its land and calls on God to judge that right in the
context of the Ammonites trying to dispossess God's people; see
again Good, "Just War in Ancient Israel," 394–95).

This connection between the LORD's roles as judge and warrior
provides significant qualifications for the warlike imagery and language for God. It indicates at least that the label "warrior" for God

was not used lightly. It was also not used to argue for God's favor of Israel. In fact, in none of the examples discussed here does the text tout the Lord's love for Israel. Rather, each emphasizes that the actions of God were just because Israel's enemies violated an agreement or a standard of fairness.

Exodus 15 as an Antiwar Poem?

The discussion of Exodus 15:1–18 seems to indicate within the Bible a concern for the involvement of God's people in wars. It is sometimes assumed that reports of battles and military conflicts appear without any thought that such activity might be unjustified since Israel was the victim of the world's great empires (so Weippert, "Heiliger Krieg," 492). But this idea seems clearly to be wrong. Indeed, two very different points seem to be true: (1) Israel in its Scripture indeed felt the need to explore the validity of its involvement in individual wars; the examples shown above indicate the particular concern to show that Israel engaged in war to defend its own territory against illegitimate counterclaims to that territory; and especially (2) the Old Testament, with this guiding concern, in most cases subordinates the role of God as warrior to the role of God as arbiter of justice.

This relationship between God's role as warrior and God's role as judge does not remove all ethical dilemmas posed by the Bible's qualified acceptance of war. If Israel was challenged by an aggressive enemy, many texts suggest, Israel could engage in war and God would defend Israel against the aggressor. Perhaps the greatest problem is that such ideas are always open to misuse by those who are looking for an excuse to fight under the guise of justice. But the texts examined here will not allow such a reading if they are interpreted carefully in their contexts. They suggest rather that justice is God's business, and by extension war is as well. Some people of faith will surely want to keep God's hands clean and deny that God is involved in such dirty work. But the Bible seems to have the opposite view. By assigning war to God, as part of God's judicial actions, war is taken out of the hands of humans as a tool at their disposal. Any use of war for selfish purposes then becomes illegitimate. If this perspective is taken seriously it makes war extremely difficult to justify.

Does God Love the Egyptians Too?

We have noted that Exodus 15:1–18 appears in a context that begins with the Israelites crying out to God for deliverance (2:23; 3:7). The Song of the Sea, therefore, is essentially a song of thanksgiving and praise that God answered the prayers of the slaves. As also observed earlier, the celebration of God's defeat of Pharaoh has a theological and ethical legitimacy because of that setting. It belongs to those people who are victims of violence, not to those who perpetrate it. Nevertheless, when we ask about God's involvement in violence the question naturally arises, what about the Egyptians? Where is the record of their cries when their firstborn died and when their soldiers, however misled by Pharaoh, died on the shores of the Red Sea?

Although the book of Exodus does not deal directly with these questions, there is evidence that later biblical authors did, and certainly later Jewish interpretation expressed concern about this matter. In a famous midrash on Exodus 15:1–18, the Israelites, accompanied by the angels in heaven, see the Egyptian soldiers lying dead on the shores of the Red Sea and break out into cheers and song (the song of 15:1–18). But a voice from heaven thunders, "My children are drowning, and you want to sing songs?" (*Exodus Rabbah* 21:8).

This story may seem completely fanciful, having little to do with the actual story of the exodus and the celebratory song in Exodus 15:1–18. At least one passage, however, may indicate that such reflection indeed occurred within the Bible itself. Isaiah 19:18–25, which is part of Isaiah's oracle against Egypt (in a larger section of oracles against foreign nations), speaks of a future in which the Egyptians will come into fellowship with the people of Judah and worship Judah's God. The concluding verse indicates that God loves the Egyptians as God loves Israel: "the LORD of hosts has blessed, saying, 'Blessed be Egypt my people, and Assyria, the work of my hands, and Israel my heritage'" (v. 25). Earlier in the passage the oracle seems to allude to the exodus story: "The LORD will strike Egypt, striking and healing; they will return to the LORD, and he will listen to their supplications and heal them" (v. 22). The word "strike" here is the same word that appears in the narrative account of God bringing plagues on the Egyptians (*nāgap*). Specifically, the

59

term expresses God's striking Egypt with the plague of frogs in Exodus 8:2 (7:27 Heb.) and God striking down the firstborn in Egypt in Exodus 12:27. Thus it is tempting to connect Isaiah's declaration that God's action against Egypt amounts to both "striking and healing" to the story of God striking the Egyptians when they enslaved the Israelites. Whether or not this is what Isaiah intended, Isaiah's oracle against Egypt certainly testifies to a fuller appreciation for God's relationship to the enemy nation. The larger picture is that Egypt belongs to God as well and God will bring Egypt into God's will and purpose, even if by "striking" Egypt. This gives credence to the midrash's notion that the Egyptians lying dead on the shore of the Red Sea were indeed considered God's children. The death of these children, just like the death of any of God's rebellious creatures, was thus the cause of divine grief (see again Gen. 6:6–7).

Psalm 24

Psalm 24 is like Exodus 15:1–18 in its concern for who controls the world. The image of God as warrior in this psalm must be understood in the context of this question and concern. This psalm, however, presents God as warrior more clearly within God's role as creator. Thus the Divine Warrior is one who controls the world and maintains its order.

The psalm begins with the declaration that "the earth is the LORD's and everything in it" (v. 1). Then the psalm elaborates that God established the earth, evidence that God owns and controls it. The particular point of verse 2 is that God made the earth secure on the primeval waters ("founded it upon the seas/established it upon the waters"). Thus God mastered the forces that would threaten the habitable world and made it possible for human community to form. The image of God as warrior comes in verses 7–10, a section directly dependent on the claims of verses 1–2. This final section contains one of the most stirring proclamations of God's kingship in the Psalter. Verses 7–10 identify God as the "King of glory" and the "LORD of hosts." The latter title in particular is associated with the ark of the covenant. The term "hosts" can also be translated "armies," and indeed the ark is often associated with warfare. But "hosts/armies" here probably does not refer to human military forces. Rather, the word denotes the heavenly forces at God's command, those around his heavenly throne who do his bidding (Pss. 29:1–2; 82:1; 89:6–7 [7–8 Heb.]). The warfare that stands in the background of this psalm is God's defeat of chaos, which is implied in the opening verses of the psalm (24:1–2).

"King of glory" appears nowhere else in the Old Testament as a label for Israel's God. A similar label, "God of glory," however, does appear in Psalm 29:3 in a way that helps clarify the meaning of the expression in Psalm 24. Psalm 29 calls worshipers to ascribe glory to God in a cultic shout (vv. 1–2, 9). The ascription is made because the LORD has shown himself a mighty warrior by his defeat of the chaotic waters (v. 3). Hence both titles for God in verses 7–10 identify the one enthroned on the cherubim, who rules in Zion, as the one who also reigns over the world in its entirety.

The central portion of Psalm 24 reveals that the divine warfare celebrated in verses 1–2 and 7–10 intends not only to protect the creation in general but also to ensure justice among human beings in particular. To put it another way, God's reign over the world and the battle attributed to God as evidence of that reign sets boundaries for human behavior that make violence out of bounds. As James L. Mays says, the life described in verses 3–6 "is a life founded and established by the blessing and righteousness of the LORD in the midst of the chaos of evil" (*Psalms*, 124). Indeed, without God's battle against evil the human would have no hope of living in a world in which right prevailed over chaos and evil.

The central portion of Psalm 24 has prompted some scholars to label the work as an "entrance liturgy" (Gerstenberger, *Psalms, Part 1*, 117–19). Verses 3–6 contain a set of questions and responses concerning who may ascend God's holy hill to experience the reign of God. This section of the psalm indicates why the reign of God is so important and why it is sometimes described with military imagery. At stake is the welfare of those who acknowledge and give deference to God's reign and thus to the ideals of human community God intends. The main characteristic of those who "ascend the hill of the LORD" (v. 3a) is that they "seek the face of the God of Jacob" (v. 6). They live in humility before God and therefore relate to other people rightly; they have "clean hands and pure hearts" (v. 4a); they "do not lift up their souls to what is false, and do not swear deceitfully" (v. 4b). In other words, those who live this way work against

61

violence and oppression. God is their defender because God ultimately upholds and defends the order in which they live.

Thus one important purpose of the psalm is to present a place where and a people among whom one may know God's reign. The place is characterized by God's justice and equity. The people who are permitted to enter are given access because they seek to emulate and embody God's own righteousness.

On Zion, however, the Lord's ownership of the world and the stability and order of the cosmos God established on the watery chaos is made known. In the final four verses of the psalm the Lord's kingship on Zion is celebrated, thus bringing the praise of God as creator of the world to the specific identification of God as one who rules there (vv. 7–10).

The answers given in verses 4–6 portray people of ideal faith, those who trust in God's rule, in line with the proper response demanded of those on the holy mountain. Those approved to ascend the holy hill are those who align themselves with God's will and submit themselves to God's reign; as a result they know the blessings of God's reign on Zion; they "shall never be moved" (v. 5).

Psalm 24 clearly presents God as a mighty warrior, as one who has no rivals, and as one who controls the cosmos. This affirmation, coupled with a belief that this same God is loving and gracious and has good intentions for the world, is an important tenet of faith. It provides the basis of hope that evil and injustice will one day end. The righteous will rest in the protection of the King of glory. Psalm 24 was read by some early Christians as testimony to God's battle with and defeat of death through Christ. The *Gospel of Nicodemus* (a medieval document from Western Europe) reports in detail Jesus' descent into hell by using Psalm 24:7–10 to frame the narrative. This book reports that a cry went up in hell saying, "Remove, O princes, your gates, and be ye lift up, ye everlasting doors, and the King of glory shall come in" (V [XXI], 1; James, *Apocryphal New Testament,* 132 [Latin A]). Hell then sent Satan out to fight against the King of glory. But the multitude of saints heard of it and cried out again for hell to open its gates for the King of glory to come in (V, 2). Hell then asked "as if he knew it not: Who is the King of glory?" (V, 3). And David answered, "The Lord strong and mighty, the Lord mighty in battle, he is the King of glory" (V, 3; James, *Apocryphal New Testament,* 134). This reading is appropriate in that Psalm 24 presents God as a warrior who fights against the forces that would threaten life and well-being.

Psalm 46: God's Reign and the End of Warfare

The relationship God has to violence in Psalm 24 may be illuminated by Psalm 46, which also has a central concern for the experience of God's reign over the world on Mount Zion. Although God is neither called warrior nor described as doing battle in Psalm 46, the overall picture is the same as in Exodus 15 and Psalm 24, and Psalm 46 does describe in some detail God's relationship to warfare.

Psalm 46 opens with a declaration of trust in God, "our refuge and strength" (v. 1 [2 Heb.]). The psalmist declares that because of God's presence "we will not fear" (v. 2a [3a Heb.]). But then the psalmist sets the help God offers over against two dangers, the sea and the nations. The problem of the sea has already been discussed in relation to Psalm 24:1. In ancient near Eastern cosmology the earth was founded upon the sea and secured by the mountains that served as foundational pillars (Ps. 104:5). Natural disasters such as earthquakes and floods produced fear that the cosmic order would come undone. The psalmist is confident, however, that God is fully in control, that no earthly power can undo the order God established. The psalmist experiences this security in Zion, "the city of God, the holy habitation of the Most High" (v. 4 [5 Heb.]). It is not the city itself that gives such assurance; Zion is not impregnable. Rather, because of God's presence in Zion "it shall not be moved" (v. 5 [6 Heb.]).

The second danger the psalmist describes is the nations: "the nations are in an uproar; the kingdoms totter" (v. 6a [7a Heb.]). The psalm does not indicate whether this line refers specifically to rebellion against God (as in 2:1) or to political upheaval in general. The effect is the same, however; political unrest threatens the order and indeed the *shalom* God intends for humankind. The word *môt*, which refers to the nations' "tottering," is the same word used to speak of the mountains' "quaking" in verse 2 (3 Heb.); and the term that speaks of the nations being in an "uproar" is from the same root, *hmh*, that refers to the waters "roaring" in verse 3 (4 Heb.).   63
The raging and shaking of the nations, however, just as the shaking

of the mountains and the raging of the waters, are no match for God, who is "our refuge" (v. 7 [8 Heb.]).

The final stanza of Psalm 46 speaks about how God's reign relates to violence (vv. 8–11 [9–12 Heb.]). This section seems to address the nations directly with a series of imperatives: "Come, behold the works of the LORD; see what desolations he has brought on the earth" (v. 8 [9 Heb.]). The "desolations" mentioned here may at first seem to point to God's destructive actions as the Divine Warrior. A close reading of the verses that follow, however, seems to say just the opposite. Reference to the desolations of God lead directly to statements about God bringing peace to the world. Hence the word "desolations" (šammôt) was perhaps intended to be sarcastic. It is the nations who bring desolation through their wars, and God brings all of that to naught. In other words, the reference to desolation is, in essence, an indictment of the nations' attempts to control one another by violent means.

This becomes clear in verses 9 and 10 (10 and 11 Heb.). Verse 9 (10 Heb.) declares, "He makes wars cease to the end of the earth; he breaks the bow, and shatters the spear; he burns the shields with fire." This verse draws on the image of the ruler in the ancient Near East for whom warfare is crucial for protecting one's own people and for securing one's own land; God's works entail bringing war to an end. Unlike the picture such kings painted of themselves, however, God does not just bring peace for God's own people by defeating other people. Rather, God establishes peace as the norm in all the earth.

Verse 10 (11 Heb.) continues and clarifies this message with an order to the nations to cease fighting. Traditionally rendered "be still," the first expression in the verse is better translated "stop" or "let it go" (harpû). The word literally means "let drop." In some passages the word refers to the hands that hold weapons of war (2 Sam. 24:16 = 1 Chr. 21:15). In the context of Psalm 46 this imperative seems to order the nations to cease their dependence on warfare and destruction. Mays appropriately sums up the message of this verse: "Cease your warring! Stop your attacks! Leave off your vain attempts to subject history to your power. There is but one power exalted over the earth and nations. Only one is God—the one whose work is the destruction of weapons and whose help is the refuge of those who recognize that he is God" (Psalms, 184).

Thus the Divine Warrior does not destroy and hurt. Rather, here "God the warrior fights for peace" (McCann, "Book of Psalms," 866).

Isaiah 63:1–6

Isaiah 63:1–6 contains some of the most troubling imagery of any passage that speaks of God as warrior:

"Who is this that comes from Edom,
    from Bozrah in garments stained crimson?
Who is this so splendidly robed,
    marching in his great might?"

"It is I, announcing vindication,
    mighty to save."

"Why are your robes red,
    and your garments like theirs who tread the wine press?"
"I have trodden the wine press alone,
    and from the peoples no one was with me;
I trod them in my anger
    and trampled them in my wrath;
their juice spattered on my garments,
    and stained all my robes.
For the day of vengeance was in my heart,
    and the year for my redeeming work had come.
I looked, but there was no helper;
    I stared, but there was no one to sustain me;
so my own arm brought me victory,
    and my wrath sustained me.
I trampled down peoples in my anger,
    I crushed them in my wrath,
    and I poured out their lifeblood on the earth."

Although the word "warrior" does not appear here, the passage "describes the God of Israel as Divine Warrior on a bloody rampage, in the name of vengeance and vindication, against Edom, representative of the nations that had destroyed and humiliated captive Israel" (Hanson, *Isaiah 40–66*, 231). It depicts God wearing robes stained red, presumably with the blood of enemies who have been conquered. The passage also describes God's activity with several

65

terms that are associated with violence and destruction: vindication (v. 1), anger and wrath (vv. 3a, 6), and vengeance (v. 4).

It may be helpful to recognize first that the words "anger" and "wrath," words that appear frequently in the Old Testament and particularly in the prophetic books, have created for some the false idea that God in texts like Isaiah 63:1–6 is by nature an angry god who exacts harsh judgment on disobedient creatures as a first response (see Miller, *Way of the Lord*, 269). Two points about this language and imagery are important, however. First, each of the features of 63:1–6 just described is part of a picture of God as the Divine Warrior who comes to defend and save the oppressed. This is apparent in part by the fact that God's action is characterized as "redeeming work" (v. 4). The word "redeem" (*gā'al*) refers to the practice of a person buying a relative out of slavery, or of claiming the property of a dead relative in order to ensure the deceased property and the person's name are preserved for posterity (Ruth 4). In all cases, however, the redeemer acts on the part of one who is helpless to act for himself or herself. In 63:1–6 God "redeems" Israel.

Second, the nature of the warrior's saving deeds is characterized perhaps best by the word translated "vindication." The word is *ṣĕdāqâ,* most often translated "righteousness." Paired with the word "salvation" or "to save" (root *yš'*), it has the sense of a rescue that will restore the order God intended for the world. God comes here as warrior to announce a payback concerning those who had defeated Israel. But the word *ṣĕdāqâ* indicates that more is involved than simply God bringing retribution on Israel's enemies. As I indicated in the first chapter, "righteousness" is related closely to the notion of world order. It names the purpose of the world God intended. Thus the salvation God brings is meant to restore the harmony of the world, not just restore Israel's fortunes. This is clarified by the statement in verse 4 that his coming represents the "day of vengeance." "Vengeance" (*nāqām*) is not the seeking of revenge by an irrational God, as the term "vengeance" sometimes seems to imply. Rather, the word refers to something closer to a judicial action (see further chapter 7 below; Zenger, *God of Vengeance?*, 71).

This passage does not present the notion of God as warrior to support the warring efforts of human kings or warlords. Indeed, the passage is set historically when the people of Judah are in exile, having suffered the wrath of the mighty Babylonians. Edom,

Israel's neighbor and brother, participated in Jerusalem's fall and is presented here therefore as the symbol of oppression. Isaiah 63:1–6 portrays God fighting for the defeated who cannot fight for themselves.

The poem begins with a question, "Who is this who comes from Edom, from Bozrah in garments stained crimson? Who is this so splendidly robed, marching in his great might?" (v. 1a–b). The one who asks this question is probably to be understood as a lookout on a city wall who watches for anyone who approached the settlement. Seeing this one with bloodstained robes, the sentinel naturally asks about his identity and purpose. The warrior who approaches responds first concerning identity: "It is I, announcing vindication, mighty to save" (v. 1c).

The expression "day of vengeance" seems to apply to the punishment of Edom (v. 4a). It is important to note, however, that this "day" is paired with a reference to the "year for my redeeming work" (v. 4b). Therefore, the punishment of Edom is set in the larger context of Israel's salvation. It may be helpful to note how this same theme appears in Isaiah 34, a passage that also speaks of a "day of vengeance" against Edom that will bring salvation to Zion (34:8). In that passage the punishment meted out to Edom is like that given to Sodom and Gomorrah: "the streams of Edom shall be turned into pitch, and her soil into sulfur; her land shall become burning pitch" (v. 9; cf. Gen. 19:24–28). Like Sodom and Gomorrah, Edom will be turned into a wasteland.

Two points seem important concerning the presentation of Edom here: first, Edom here represents the nations that act against God's desire for the human community (Isa. 34:2, "For the LORD is enraged against all the nations"). Thus, as with so many other references to God acting destructively, the imagery is symbolic. God does not have a grudge against the nation called Edom or any other particular nation. Edom is vilified as an enemy and opponent of God (on the later use of Edom as a code word for Rome, see Aune, *Revelation 17–22*, 1050). Second, the passage uses such violent language because "Edom" acts against the very stability of the creation. The subtle comparison to Sodom and Gomorrah in Isaiah 34 suggests this, and 63:1–6 speaks of Edom the same way.

The sentinel then asks specifically why the warrior's robes are red, why they look like the garment of someone who has been treading grapes in the wine press (v. 2). The warrior answers with a metaphor that extends the image in the sentinel's question: "I have trodden the wine press alone, and from the people no one was with me; I trod them in my anger and trampled them in my wrath; their juice spattered on my garments, and stained all my robes" (v. 3). The implication seems to be that the red color comes from the blood of the nations that opposed Israel. But when verse 6 says, "I poured out their lifeblood," the word is not the typical word for "blood" but a term that appears only in this hymn and may simply extend the metaphor of the wine press (*nēṣaḥ*). This fits with the larger context of the poem. The poem does not describe a literal battle in which the blood of Israel's enemies stained the robes of real warriors. Rather, the poem represents hope that God will come and do the work that no human warrior has been able to do, to rescue Israel from its enemies. Verses 3–6 emphasize that God acted alone. No other nation was willing to participate in God's attempts to bring order back to the world; therefore, the nations were all trampled in the wine press of God's wrath (vv. 3b, 6).

The violent imagery of 63:1–6 must also be read in the larger context of Isaiah 62–64. Isaiah 62 proclaims salvation for Jerusalem that anticipates the hymn about the Divine Warrior in 63:1–6. For example, 62:6 portrays sentinels posted on the walls of Jerusalem who constantly remind the Lord of the work to be done to bring justice to the Holy City. The present arrangement of material suggests that these sentinels in 63:1–2 see the approach of the Divine Warrior and ask about his identity and purpose. Isaiah 62:8 promises a restored Jerusalem free from the threat of enemies: "The LORD has sworn by his right hand and by his mighty arm: I will not again give your grain to be food for your enemies, and foreigners shall not drink the wine for which you have labored." Then 62:11 proclaims, "Say to daughter Zion, 'See, your salvation comes; his reward is with him, and his recompense before him.'" The people shall be called "Redeemed of the LORD" (62:12). The Divine Warrior hymn then portrays God coming specifically to "redeem" Jerusalem (63:4) and to vindicate its people. Hence the picture of the Divine Warrior in 63:1–6 seems to present the realization of the promise in Isaiah 62.

The impression of the Divine Warrior and his actions for Israel changes, however, in light of the passage that follows the hymn in 63:1–6. Isaiah 63:7–64:12 presents a complaint that God has *not* come as a warrior and defeated Israel's enemies. Hence this larger section of Isaiah (62–64) is much like communal laments in the Psalms (see Pss. 74; 89). Such passages sometimes describe God's strength in terms of God battling and defeating enemies, but such descriptions merely set up the petition for God to act. Here the presentation of God as warrior in Isaiah 63:1–6 is the foundation for the complaint of Isaiah 64. The structure of Isaiah 62–64, therefore, is the opposite of the structure of Exodus 1–15. The two sections and their presentations of God as warrior are linked, however, by the fact that both speak to people who suffer at the hands of enemies.

The historical context of Isaiah 63:1–6 is also extremely important for discerning the poem's significance. Paul Hanson makes an essential point: "only those are in a position to judge who live in circumstances similar to sixth-century Israel's, circumstances in which the powers of evil seem to have defeated every human agency of justice and in which the only remaining hope seems to reside in God's direct intervention" (*Isaiah 40–66*, 234). Indeed, the extreme circumstances of defeat and domination have produced and give context to this passage. The extreme imagery of God as a conquering warrior is not only understandable, but perhaps necessary to express the theological conviction that God is really capable of saving Israel. As Brueggemann rightly says, "A 'nicer' god or a happier God might be preferred, but Israel entertains no romantic illusions about the vexed context of its life" (*Isaiah 40–66*, 226).

Given these observations on the original audience of 63:1–6, two final points seem pertinent. First, the original audience is incapable of responding directly to their oppressors. That is in part why 63:3 and 5 speak of the Lord acting alone. That point too is important because it sets Israel's God apart from others, particularly the Babylonian god Marduk, whose military conquests recounted in the great Babylonian creation myth served to legitimate the Babylonian monarchy's military campaigns.

Second, the desire of some contemporary faith communities to tone down the image of God presented in 63:1–6 may overlook the need for justice that gives rise to such imagery. Particularly faith communities made up largely of people who are politically and economically secure may miss the cry of the oppressed that lies behind the passage. Rather than wishing to alter the image, a better response might be to ask whether one's community of faith is part of the oppressive force against which the audience of 63:1–6 speaks. Put another way, the one who reads 63:1–6 might well ask if he or she stands with or against the actions of the God of this passage.

Finally, it is worth noting that 63:1–6 plays a prominent role in the New Testament portrait of Jesus. Revelation 19:11–16 presents a scene in which heaven is opened and a rider comes forth on a white horse. The rider, called "Faithful and True" (v. 11) and "The Word of God" (v. 13), is obviously Jesus. Yet the passage declares that "in righteousness he judges and makes war" (v. 11). As Revelation describes his warfare it draws heavily upon Isaiah 63:1–6. Jesus "is clothed in a robe dipped in blood" (v. 13), and he comes to "tread the wine press of the fury of the wrath of God the Almighty" (v. 15). As verse 11 makes clear, however, Jesus' engagement in war is bound up in his efforts to bring justice. The earthly opponents of God along with the beast and his followers will be judged and sentenced. Thus as David Aune says, "the emphasis here is on the *judicial* function of the Parousia" (*Revelation 17–22*, 1069). But the Divine Warrior image here does not change or tone down the imagery drawn from Isaiah 63:1–6. Indeed, Revelation 19's use of the warrior image is quite consistent with that in the Isaiah passage. In both cases the Divine Warrior comes to defend the powerless and set the world right for those who have been faithful to God's calling. Nevertheless, despite the fact that Jesus appears in Revelation 19:1–6 as a warrior, the dominant image of him in Revelation is as "a lamb having been slain" (Rev. 5:6). The final image of the divine warrior is of one who sacrifices himself, not one who kills others (see further chap. 8 below).

Necessity of the Divine Warrior

Throughout much of this chapter I have attempted to cast the notion of God as warrior in a light that makes it more understandable and acceptable. In so doing I have at times argued that this troubling picture of God should not evoke images of God acting destructively or violently. While these nuances are important, the last word should perhaps be that the image of the Divine Warrior is sorely needed, and we ought not attempt to rid ourselves of it. To do so would only increase the problem of violence because that

70

would deny God's crucial role as the one who has the desire and power to deal with violence. Indeed, to deny the notion of God as warrior would be to miss at least two crucial points.

First, God as warrior is meant to comfort those oppressed by the evil forces of the world. Therefore, many objections to God as warrior are bourgeois. From a perspective of power and wealth, it is easy to seek after a God who appears respectable, calm, and nonplussed by the rampant oppression in the world. But to take such a position is to stand with Pharaoh. For people who have power, however, the proper response to the claim that "the LORD is a warrior" (Exod. 15:3) is not denial but repentance. If we take this stand before God, we open ourselves to God's judgment of us; we allow God to call into question our participation in the injustice in the world. If we are oppressed, we may find in the warrior God one who stands with us in our oppression and fights against it, not one who stands idly by and allows it to continue. As Brueggemann says, "In a situation of victimization, one is not so worried about violence in the power of one's rescuer" ("Book of Exodus," 803).

Second, to confess "the LORD is a warrior" is to recognize the reality of evil and to claim that God is in conflict with evil in the world. Although Scripture insists the battle is certain to be God's, the persistence of evil requires a warrior God. Brueggemann is surely right when he declares that this battle is too great for us as human beings and that claiming God is a warrior is to claim that "God is for us" ("Book of Exodus," 803).

It is necessary, however, to qualify what it means that God is "for us" as a warrior. One of the problems often identified with the biblical picture of God as warrior is that it seems to carry with it the notion that God fights exclusively for Israel. God defeats enemies so Israel may live in peace, without threats from its neighbors. The goal of God's warfare seems to be reflected in the declaration that the result of God doing battle is that "Israel lives in safety, untroubled is Jacob's abode in a land of grain and wine, where the heavens drop down dew" (Deut. 33:28). Although this theme of God's protection for Israel is important and pervasive, it is not expressed in such a way that it advocates God only looks out for Israel. As God's chosen people, Israel benefits from this aspect of God's work when Israel is oppressed and defeated. But when Israel is unjust or disobedient, God can appear as a warrior against God's own people. Indeed, God also loves the nations.

71

In that regard, God's warlike activity may be categorized as one of two types of justice. There is retributive justice in which God punishes the forces opposed to life. But there is also restorative justice. God punishes in order to rehabilitate, bring back, and reestablish. This second type of justice is particularly apparent in later reflections on passages about the Divine Warrior. So, for example, Isaiah 19:22 insists God struck Egypt in an effort to heal Egypt as well as to defend Israel. The portrait of God as Divine Warrior, therefore, shows that God corrects and heals the world, even those in the world who oppose God's purpose and go against God's people.

CHAPTER 3

Enemies of God and Israel

Sodom, Pharaoh, and Amalek

In the last chapter we wrestled with the notion that God is a warrior, concluding that this image of God is the natural complement to the image of God as creator. Although Genesis 1:1–2:4a says God created the world without conflict and God declared the creation "very good" (1:31), as the story of God's creative work unfolds some creatures refuse to adhere to God's intended direction. Some of God's creatures even seem intent on being enemies of creation and thus enemies of God. When God engages these rebellious parts of the creation God inevitably becomes "destructive" in relation to these enemies in order to preserve the rest of creation. Thus the image of God as warrior is closely linked to the notion that God created and now sustains the world.

Part of the account of rebellious creation I have already discussed in the treatment of the flood story (Gen. 6–9). There the entire created order, or at least all human beings ("all flesh"), turn away from God's wishes. This turning away from God by "all flesh" in inextricably linked to the spreading of violence on earth. As Genesis 6:11–12 says, "Now the earth was corrupt in God's sight, and the earth was filled with violence. And God saw that the earth was corrupt; for all flesh had corrupted its way upon the earth."

In this chapter we look more closely at three specific enemies God opposes. The three enemies to be considered are the residents of Sodom (Gen. 18–19), the pharaoh in Exodus (Exod. 5–15), and

73

the people called Amalek, who attacked vulnerable Israel during the journey out of Egypt (Exod. 17:8–16). Each of these may be identified like the rebellious creatures in the flood story. Indeed, I shall argue that each of these is an image, a narrative symbol of total depravity, like "all flesh" in Genesis 6. In this sense, these three enemies are not *historical* figures in the narrow meaning of that word. Rather, they are symbols of evil, and the stories about them are emblematic of God's battle with evil.

Nevertheless, the portrait of enemies like those examined here, though emblematic of evil in general, grew out of evil experienced within history. As Joel Kaminsky points out, the treatment of these enemies "is an attempt to make some theological sense of recurring historical evils" (*Yet I Loved Jacob*, 116). Hence, this chapter addresses the point that these three enemies are so identified because of the way they oppose God's will as it is expressed in God's love and care for Abraham and his descendants. The identification of these three as enemies is closely bound to the notion that God chose Israel as the channel for disseminating blessing to the entire world.

Sodom and Gomorrah: Failure of Righteousness and Justice (Genesis 18–19)

One of the most fascinating, and arguably most misunderstood, stories in the Bible is the account of God's destruction of Sodom and Gomorrah. The story receives much attention because of the particular crime of the residents of Sodom. In turn, the complete destruction of these cities is often justified or questioned in connection with that crime. The account must be read in the larger context of the book of Genesis and of the whole Bible, however, to appreciate its portrayal of God's judgment.

The story of these two cities occurs at an important juncture in God's dealing with humankind, when God narrows the focus to the family of Abraham through whom all the families of the earth will be blessed (Gen. 12:3). Although the exact meaning of this shift is uncertain, Joseph Blenkinsopp is surely right that, "in the damaged postdiluvial world, powerful negative forces are at work against which Abraham is called by God to launch a new initiative and counterforce" ("Abraham as Paradigm," 233). One facet of that

74

counterforce seems to be Abraham's role in ensuring "righteousness" (*ṣĕdāqâ*) and "justice" (*mišpāṭ*) on earth (Gen. 18:19). This role brings Abraham in contact with the problem of the residents of Sodom and Gomorrah. At stake in maintenance of righteousness and justice is the safety of anyone who would sojourn in those cities. These terms seem to refer also to the stability of the world as a whole. The behavior of those who live in these two cities bears on the well-being of the entire created order.

The terms "righteousness" and "justice" have an important place in legal and judicial contexts. For example, when the psalmist calls on God to "hear a just [*ṣedeq*] cause" and to bring vindication (Ps. 17:1), the cry seems to be for a verdict of "innocent." But these terms connote much more than a legal decision of guilt or innocence. As H. H. Schmid argues, righteousness in the broadest context refers to the principle with which God created and ordered the world. It is similar to the Egyptian concept of *ma'at*, a principle of order in the universe that included both the stability of the physical world but also the right order of the moral world as well (see *Gerechtigheit als Weltordnung*, 66–67). Thus as Margaret Barker says in her book on creation and the environment, righteousness in the Old Testament is very similar to the idea of sustainability (*Creation*, 144). It refers to a force that unifies the world and human society, a force that promotes the well-being of the whole creation.

The broad meaning of righteousness and justice and their implications for the story of Sodom may be seen in Psalm 72. A prayer is offered for the king, that his reign might be characterized by God's righteousness and justice (v. 1). The prayer focuses on the monarch defending the cause of the poor (vv. 2, 4, 12–14). The main concern is that the king will ensure righteousness and justice: "May he judge your people with righteousness, and your poor with justice" (v. 2). Coupled with this wish for righteous rule is a wish for the land to produce abundantly: "May the mountains yield prosperity [*šālôm*] for the people, and the hills righteousness" (v. 3; my trans.). *Šālôm*, which signifies wholeness and "prosperity" in the fullest sense, is directly related to righteousness. The connection appears again in verse 7 as the prayer expresses the hope for righteousness to flourish and "peace" (*šālôm*) to abound (v. 7). Moreover, it expects the earth to abound with produce and give prosperity to the people if the king ensures righteousness (vv. 6, 16).

75

The concern for righteousness and justice is carefully woven into the story of Sodom and Gomorrah. The two cities are mentioned first by noting that the visitors to Abraham "looked toward Sodom" (Gen. 18:16), the first stage in a judicial inquiry that results in Sodom's destruction (see 18:22; 19:1; Fretheim, "Book of Genesis," 467). Then the Lord asks whether Abraham should be made privy to the imminent action against the cities (18:17). Abraham and his family have a special role in God's plans, particularly in establishing and maintaining righteousness and justice. Indeed, verse 19 suggests Abraham is the linchpin for righteousness and justice since he is the one through whom all the peoples of the earth are to be blessed. Abraham's actions are to be the polar opposite of the residents of Sodom and Gomorrah.

The sins of Sodom and Gomorrah are couched as injustice and oppression, a clear violation of principles of justice and righteousness. God declares to Abraham, "How great the outcry against Sodom and Gomorrah and how very grave their sin!" (v. 20) The term "outcry" is used elsewhere to describe the call of the oppressed to God (4:10; 27:34). Perhaps the best-known use of the term is in Exodus 2:23, which notes that Israel cried out in the midst of oppression in Egypt (see also Exod. 3:7, 9). In Genesis 18:20 the party that calls out to God is not identified. This verse may refer to oppressed residents of the city like Lot and his family or it may refer to visitors to the city, like the three messengers from the Lord in Genesis 19. It is also possible that the outcry is from the earth itself, which is polluted by the injustice of Sodom.

The text says nothing more specific about the injustice of these cities. A major clue appears, however, when the residents of the city identify Lot as an alien (19:9). The Hebrew word they use to describe Lot comes from the root *gûr*, meaning to sojourn or dwell in a land as a foreigner. In the law codes of Deuteronomy particularly, the treatment of such a person is a key to doing justice and upholding God's vision for society (Deut. 24:17–22). Throughout the story of Abraham, Abraham is identified by this term as well. Indeed, in Genesis 12–26 the treatment of and behavior by a resident alien seems to be a major point of delineation between Abraham and others. Abraham wanders from Mesopotamia through the land of Canaan as a stranger, a *gēr* (sojourner; 17:8; 23:4). Those who treat Abraham with kindness and cooperation are blessed (14:17–20). Those who threaten Abraham

76

experience disaster (12:17). Abraham, for his part, works for peace with those who live in the land. He does not try to take by force the land God promised him. Instead, he obtains land through legal processes (23:1–10) and offers the best pastures to Lot in order to prevent a land dispute (13:11b–12; see Blenkinsopp, "Abraham as Paradigm," 235). In light of this concern for the resident alien in the larger story and in the Old Testament in general, the fact that the residents of Sodom try to abuse Lot, the alien in their midst, is a major sign of their unrighteousness (19:9, "And they said, 'This fellow came here as an alien, and he would play the judge! Now we will deal worse with you than with them'").

The actual sins of Sodom displayed in the narrative focus on one particular act. When the men who had visited Abraham came to Lot at Sodom, the residents of the city called to Lot, "bring them out to us that we may know them" (19:5). This portion of the account is often taken to be a condemnation of homosexual activity. The larger context, however, suggests that the emphasis is on the injustice of abusing sojourners. The men who came to Lot were strangers and thus were to be offered hospitality and protection. The importance of this type of protection appears in Exodus 22:21, "You shall not wrong or oppress a resident alien, for you were aliens in the land of Egypt." Deuteronomy 10:19 takes this one step further by commanding, "you shall *love* the strangers," love being commanded otherwise only for God (see Nelson, *Deuteronomy*, 137). This concern for strangers may be due in part to the dangers associated with traveling in the ancient world. If a person was not traveling in a caravan, he or she risked being attacked and robbed (Luke 10:25–37; 2 Cor. 11:26). More certain, however, was the theological motivation: those who had been strangers in Egypt and were loved and protected by God should in turn love and protect the stranger in their midst. Lot did so offer, but the other residents of Sodom saw the vulnerable guests as merely victims to abuse.

Despite the horrendous sins of the residents of Sodom and Gomorrah, the question arises of the mercy of God. How could God destroy an entire city? Is it possible that every person in Sodom and Gomorrah acted unjustly? That is what the story says. The account emphasizes first that God would not destroy Sodom if righteous people were found there. Abraham's question is, "Will you sweep away the righteous with the wicked?" (18:23). Abraham bargains by reducing the number of required righteous at Sodom.

77

God responds each time with the assurance that Sodom will not be destroyed if the determined number of righteous people are found there. We should probably not take the number ten literally. That Abraham ends at ten should not suggest that God would destroy Sodom and let nine righteous perish. The point is that God will be gracious to the wicked for the sake of the righteous. Regardless of how rotten the wicked might be, they would be preserved for the sake of the few righteous who were left in the city. In the case of Sodom and Gomorrah, however, there were no righteous to be found.

The account of the sin itself also declares that no one in Sodom was just. Genesis 19:4 makes the point emphatic: "the men of the city, the men of Sodom, both young and old, all the people to the last man, surrounded the house." In other words, everyone in Sodom except Lot and his family participated in the injustice.

Given the connection between righteousness and justice in human society and the order and stability of the natural world—as Psalm 72 shows, for example—it should not be a surprise that the actions of Sodom and Gomorrah that bring their destruction also have an impact on the entire cosmos. One important connection between the themes of Genesis 6–9 and 18:16–19:29 is the notion that God's intentions in creation were violated and thus upset the cosmic order. As Terence Fretheim points out, the area of Sodom and Gomorrah was like a paradise before the residents of these cities acted so wickedly (*God and World*, 98). Indeed, 13:10 describes the territory as "well watered everywhere like the garden of God." Then the passage notes, "this was before the LORD had destroyed Sodom and Gomorrah." The actions of the wicked in these cities thus threaten the very order God established in creation. It is surely not a coincidence that when the cities are destroyed "what grew on the ground" is also listed among the victims (19:25). This is not to say that the story is about some mechanistic judgment built into the created order. It is important to recognize, however, that here the whole creation suffers because the people of Sodom and Gomorrah acted against the strangers in their midst. The moral corruption of those two towns created a crisis that was cosmic in scope. As in the account of the curse of the ground in Genesis 3, it seems the Sodom and Gomorrah story also recognizes that the social, moral, and geophysical spheres are intricately connected. As James Bruckner puts

78

it, in the story of Abraham "creational motifs subtly function to create a cosmology of relationship between the physical and moral orders" (*Implied Law*, 200). Thus when the moral order is violated as it is by the people of Sodom, the creation (the physical world) "convulses" in protest (ibid., 202).

Exodus, Oppression, and the Battle against Chaos

As the biblical narrative moves from Genesis to Exodus the peculiar role of Abraham and his descendants remains a central concern. In the Exodus story the main problem to be resolved is that an evil force opposes Abraham's seed and threatens to wipe them out, thus destroying God's plan to bring blessing to all creation. The forces that oppose God's people are two enemies characterized by their anticreation acts: Pharaoh and Amalek.

Pharaoh, the Anticreator

The opening of Exodus may seem to present the historical circumstances regarding a particular group of people: the sons of Jacob with their households went down to Egypt to dwell under the safety of their brother Joseph (Exod. 1:1–5); then Joseph and his generation died (1:6) as did the pharaoh who brought Joseph to power and welcomed Joseph's brothers and their families to Egypt (1:8). But the introduction to Israel's plight in Egypt also presents a key theological idea, that Israel is a people through whom God intends to bring blessings to all people on earth. Thus the battle God has with Pharaoh is intricately linked with God's election of Israel. As the focal point of creation, God's preservation of Israel is key to preserving the creation as a whole, to ensuring that "all the families of the earth shall be blessed" (Gen. 12:3). But as the central point of the creation Israel is also the special object of God's love and care. Israel is God's "son," as Exodus 4:22 says. Therefore, Israel's role should not be reduced simply to a service role, that is, to bring blessing to the world. Perhaps one could say that God's special love for Israel is a paradigm for God's love for all people or that God brings love to all through Israel, but the special place of Israel in the divine economy requires a distinct place to be

79

maintained for the descendants of Abraham (see Kaminsky, *Yet I Loved Jacob*, 84–85).

The charge to and blessings placed on all humankind in Genesis 1:28–30 are now concentrated in these people, as Exodus 1:7 indicates: "But the Israelites were fruitful and prolific; they multiplied and grew exceedingly strong, so that the land was filled with them." Indeed, this characterization of the Israelites recalls the blessing God gave to the first humans by including words that appear prominently in Genesis 1:28: *pārâ* ("be fruitful") and *rābâ* ("be many"; "be great"). Moreover, this verse also includes the Hebrew term *šāraṣ*, a word that appears in Genesis 1:20 and 21 to describe the teeming of animal life in the waters. By using the term with regard to humans here (and in Gen. 9:7), the narrator insists that God's intentions for the whole creation are coming to pass in the fruitfulness of the Israelites. This set of connections to the creation accounts in Genesis indicates that Pharaoh's actions against the Israelites are not simply political moves by a king to preserve his power. They are acts against the stability of the cosmos (Fretheim, "Plagues as Ecological Signs," 385).

The narrator hints at the cosmic significance of Pharaoh's actions when noting that "a new king arose over Egypt who did not know Joseph" (Exod. 1:8). This line could simply mean that the new pharaoh did not have a political connection to Jacob's son. But a few chapters later when Moses delivers to Pharaoh God's mandate that he release the Israelites, the Egyptian king responds with nearly identical language: "Who is the LORD, that I should heed him and let Israel go? I do not know the LORD" (5:2). Indeed, that Pharaoh did not "know the LORD" is reflected in the fact that he did not "know Joseph" (1:8). Although it is not certain that the previous pharaoh "knew the LORD," Jacob did bless him, and the Egyptian king supported God's work at least indirectly by protecting Joseph and his family (Gen. 47:7, 10).

Pharaoh exercised his claim to be the universal authority by attempting to rid the land of the Israelites. In so doing he showed that he was a force against life itself. This is particularly apparent in Pharaoh's attempt to kill the Israelite boys, an act that would effectively end the fruitfulness and proliferation of the descendants of Abraham (Exod. 1:15–22). Despite Pharaoh's anti-life actions, however, God continued to prosper the Israelites, and "the people

80

multiplied and became very strong" (1:20). In other words, Exodus sets up the conflict between God and Pharaoh as a conflict between God's creative and life-giving work in creation and Pharaoh's attempts to thwart that work. Egypt in general and Pharaoh in particular are symbols of death and disorder. Their oppression of the Israelites threatens to return "the entire cosmos to its pre-creation state" (Fretheim, "Plagues as Ecological Signs," 385). In trying to prevent God from bringing blessing to all creatures through the Israelites, Pharaoh puts himself in the place of God over the created order. Moses obliquely recognizes Pharaoh's false sense of authority when he confronts Pharaoh after the seventh plague, of thunder and hail (9:13–35). Pharaoh pleads with Moses to remove the plague. Moses obliges, noting that the cessation of thunder and hail will show that "the earth is the LORD's" (9:29)—not Pharaoh's.

This understanding of Pharaoh as anticreator is enhanced by his anonymity. The story does not identify Pharaoh as any particular historical figure. Although historians have often identified him as Ramesses II, there is little in the story itself to suggest that identity (see the discussion in Bright, *History of Israel*, 123). The name Rameses does appear in Exodus 1:11 as the name of one of the supply cities the Israelite slaves built. This points to the oppression of Egypt at a particular time. But the fact that Exodus does not name the pharaoh who ordered the building of the cities allows other oppressed people to claim the story as their own. Indeed, since the author could have named the pharaoh, there is reason to think his being unnamed is an important feature of the story. Ronald Hendel argues that the generic character of the ruler allowed people in later time periods to apply it to their experience with Egyptian aggression. The blank at the point of Pharaoh's name provides "a movable boundary of inclusion for those who share" the memory of the exodus ("Exodus in Biblical Memory," 604). But having Pharaoh nameless also allows him to appear as a representative of forces opposed to God, even as a paradigmatic or symbolic figure. As Martin Luther King Jr. wrote concerning the exodus account, "Egypt symbolized evil in the form of humiliating oppression, ungodly exploitation, and crushing domination" (*Strength to Love*, 73).

When we recognize these features of the story, we understand God's battle with the Egyptian king and his people properly as a story of God's defense of creation itself against the forces of chaos.

81

The Plagues as Reversal of Creation

In order to understand how Pharaoh's actions represent anticreation acts, it may be helpful to note generally that the number of plagues in Exodus seems to correspond to the number of divine utterances in the creation story in Genesis 1:1–2:4a (Zevit, "Priestly Redaction," 211). But more specifically there is a host of parallel language between the two stories, and the allusions to the creation account in the plague narratives are impressive. Hence, as Fretheim points out, the plagues are presented as "signs" of creation's rebellion against the Egyptians that point forward to a disastrous future for Pharaoh and his people ("Plagues as Ecological Signs," 387).

The notion that Egypt and Pharaoh represent chaos appears first in the plague narrative in Exodus 7:8–13, the story of Aaron's rod-turned-serpent swallowing the serpents of Pharaoh's magicians. Two key terms in the account make this clear. First, the word for "serpent" (*tannîn*) in some other texts refers to the mysterious creatures of the sea that represent disorder and chaos. For example, Psalm 74:13 uses the term to refer to the chaos dragons God defeated to demonstrate mastery over the cosmos. This seems to indicate that the first show of power in the contest with Pharaoh implies the Egyptian king is an agent of chaos, the recalcitrant force that works against God's attempts to establish order (Fretheim, "Plagues as Ecological Signs," 388). Pharaoh is depicted as commander of the forces of disorder, forces that would destroy and diminish life.

Second, the word for "swallow" (*bāla'*) hints at the way creation will strike back at Pharaoh. The term is unusual in that it appears only here (Exod. 7:12) and in the Song of the Sea: "You stretched out your right hand, the earth swallowed them" (15:12). In the case of the word "swallow," the point is that the elements (in this case the underworld) fight against the Egyptians at God's command. Hence the reference to Aaron's rod swallowing the rods of the magicians anticipates the victory song in Exodus 15. But it will be the nonhuman world that acts against Pharaoh to indicate that the battle is really between Pharaoh and God (with the agency of creation), not Pharaoh and the people of Israel. As Moses promised the Israelites, "The LORD will fight for you, and you have only to keep still" (14:14). Although the Israelites are victims of Pharaoh,

God uses elements of the natural world, not an Israelite army, to provide salvation.

Another example of a plague that expresses creation themes is the plague of flies recorded in 8:20–32 (16–28 Heb.). Moses promises Pharaoh that the Egyptians will be completely overwhelmed by swarms of flies. The flies will fill the Egyptian houses and will be everywhere the Egyptians live. But the flies will not reach the Israelites. The two peoples will be separated, and that will be a sign to Pharaoh of God's power (v. 23 [19 Heb.]). The narrative reporting the appearance of the flies, however, makes the remarkable statement that "in all of Egypt the land was ruined because of the flies" (v. 24 [20 Heb.]). Hence Fretheim rightly notes, "Such language seems too strong for a fly infestation!" ("Plagues as Ecological Signs," 389). The word "ruined" (*šāḥat*), however, may be a clue to what this description means for the onslaught of the plague of flies. The same word appears in Genesis 6:11–12 in reference to the state of the earth as a result of the violence of God's creatures. Exodus 8:24 may intend to say therefore that Pharaoh's actions against Israel caused the land to be ruined just as the violence of God's creatures caused the land to be ruined before the flood.

As a "sign," a portent of future disaster, the flies also have a particular significance. As Fretheim points out, Exodus 8:31 (27 Heb.) emphasizes that when God removed the flies "not one remained." The same expression appears again in 14:28, which says not one of the Egyptians who pursued the Israelites at the Red Sea remained (Fretheim, "Plagues as Ecological Signs," 389–90). In both cases the totality of God's action points to God's power over the forces of chaos.

The other plague accounts contain similar references to the battle between God and the forces of chaos. For example, the plague of locusts (10:3–20) describes a wind from the Lord that blew over the land of Egypt bringing the insects that devour vegetation (v. 13). What is described seems to be the reverse of what God did in Genesis 1 when God's spirit or wind blew over the waters to bring forth life. The word for "wind" (*rûaḥ*) is the same word that appears in Genesis 1:2, and the description of vegetation destroyed by locusts is similar to the description of plants created by God in the beginning: green plants (*'ēśeb*) and the fruit of the trees (*pĕrî hā'ēṣ*, Exod. 10:15; Gen. 1:11–13). So what God established in Genesis 1 by divine invitation is now destroyed by the onslaught of locusts.

83

But perhaps the most striking parallel is the account of darkness that preceded the death of the firstborn. Genesis 1:2–4 reports that God's first act in creation was to separate light from darkness, to make a pattern of darkness and light as the first sign of the order of the cosmos. In Exodus 10:21–29, however, the separation of light and darkness is reversed. As a result, the Egyptians dwelled in total darkness, though the Israelites "had light where they lived" (v. 23). Whether this meant the Israelites had light all the time or simply that the separation of light and darkness did not cease is uncertain. What is clear, however, is that the darkness upon the Egyptians amounted to a return to the precreation state of chaos. For this reason the plague of darkness is the most serious sign prior to the death of the firstborn. It signifies the return to chaos prior to God calling forth light in Genesis 1:2. Hence the conditions God established in creation to make life possible are, for Pharaoh and the Egyptians, removed.

The symbolic importance of the darkness plague in the exodus story appears also in Psalm 105. This psalm recalls major events in Israel's history, recording a slightly different version of the plague account. One obvious difference is that it places the darkness first among the plagues: "He sent darkness, and made the land dark; they rebelled against his words" (v. 28). Although no rationale is given for placing the plague of darkness first, it clearly separated the Israelites from the Egyptians. Some ancient authors interpreted the onset of darkness as an invasion from the abode of the dead (see Wis. 17:14; *Exodus Rabbah* 14:2). In other words, they thought the place of chaotic unrest, the place where ordered life was not possible, invaded the space God intended for life and order.

The plague of darkness, with its inherent connection to the forces of death and the underworld, appropriately anticipates the final plague. God's last move against Pharaoh is in fact an invasion of the abode of the dead:

> At midnight the LORD struck down all the firstborn in the land of Egypt, from the firstborn of Pharaoh who sat on his throne to the firstborn of the prisoner who was in the dungeon, and all the firstborn of the livestock. Pharaoh arose in the night, he and all his officials and all the Egyptians; and there was a loud cry in Egypt, for there was not a house without someone dead.
>
> (Exod. 12:29–30)

This is not really a plague like all the others. The other disastrous events have been "signs," as already noted. As signs, the onslaught of blood, frogs, flies, boils, hail, and darkness all point forward to the final catastrophic event. The final event, however, is really the final result of creation reversing course. As Fretheim puts it, "It is a kind of flood story in one corner of the world, that corner where God's creational purposes were beginning to be realized" ("Plagues as Ecological Signs," 394). This characterization is crucial for understanding the meaning of the death of the firstborn. We should recognize that the story is about justice. When Exodus 11:6 says there will be a "loud cry" (*ṣĕʿāqâ gĕdōlâ*) that goes up from the Egyptians, it likely alludes to the cry of the oppressed slaves in 3:7. The tables have now turned and justice is meted out, measure for measure. Nevertheless, what happens during the final plague is perhaps more about God's protection of the Israelites from chaos than about God's destruction of the Egyptians. One sign of this is the contrast of the circumstances of the Egyptians and the Israelites on the night the death angel passes through Egypt. Concerning the Egyptians, every firstborn will die (11:5) and there will be a loud cry throughout the land (v. 6). But concerning the Israelites, they will not be harmed; in fact, not even a dog will growl at them or their livestock (v. 7).

The comment that "not a dog shall growl at any of the Israelites" (v. 7) seems to enhance the idea that creation rebels against Pharaoh and the Egyptians, but God is protecting the Israelites from chaos. Some ancient Near Eastern peoples (mainly the Egyptians and Persians) cherished dogs as pets, but the Old Testament seldom speaks of dogs positively. Rather, dogs in the Old Testament typically symbolize threatening and demonic forces from which humans seek deliverance by God (Ps. 22:20 [21 Heb.]; see Wapnish and Hesse, "Pampered Pooches or Plain Pariahs?," 75). Moreover, the description of the dog's growl seems clearly to suggest a threat to the Israelites (see the same language in Josh. 10:21). The dogs, which patrolled the outskirts of villages looking for something to devour, would be silenced and tamed for the Israelites (Ps. 59:6, 14 [7, 15 Heb.]). It is interesting also that the dog will not threaten the Israelites or their livestock. It may be the case, therefore, that Exodus 11:7 paints the picture of the plagues moving Egypt back to a state of existence characterized by the disorder that prevailed before creation (Gen. 1:1–2), while the Israelites are kept safe. For

85

the Israelites during the night of death, all will be at peace; the lion will lie down with the lamb; no predator, human or animal, will harm them.

Hardening Pharaoh's Heart

Despite the image of Pharaoh as the anticreator, the question can still arise as to God's justice in dealing with the Egyptian king. One difficult aspect of the exodus story in this regard is the theme of hardening Pharaoh's heart. The problem is that at certain points in the narrative God says, "I will harden his heart" (e.g., 4:21), or it is reported that "the LORD hardened Pharaoh's heart, and he would not let the Israelites go" (e.g., 10:20). The issue is one of divine causality in relation to the punishment of Pharaoh and the Egyptians. If God caused Pharaoh to continue to oppress the Israelites, can God be just in the punishment of Israel's oppressors?

One way of trying to solve the problem is to show that the verbs that refer to the hardening of Pharaoh's heart appear in different forms, many of which do not indicate that God did the hardening. Some of the verbs are intransitive and say only that Pharaoh's heart "was hardened" (7:13; 8:19 [15 Heb.]). Exodus 7:22 contains such a statement and takes the onus off the Lord by following with, "he would not listen to them; as the LORD had said." Other verb forms have God as the subject and communicate the notion that God hardened Pharaoh's heart. Scholars have typically assigned these varied statements to different authors and sources. Some have assumed that the references to God hardening Pharaoh's heart belong to only one source that now is balanced by the presence of other sources. Or it is noted that one source seems to include both types of statements, that Pharaoh's heart hardened (7:13) and alternatively that God hardened Pharaoh's heart (4:21; 14:4). But the identification of such sources does not resolve the problem. In fact, according to one scholar's analysis, the final editor of Exodus used verbs exclusively that state the Lord hardened Pharaoh's heart (Friedman, *Bible with Sources Revealed*, 125–142). Whether this is correct or not, one of the final sections of Exodus in which these statements occur ends with a flourish of statements that "the LORD hardened Pharaoh's heart" (10:20, 27; 11:10; see also 14:4).

Brevard Childs points out that in nearly every case the hardening of Pharaoh's heart appears in conjunction with a sign (in the

86

form of one of the plagues) that has been performed (see 7:13; *Book of Exodus*, 170–75). Thus a plague appears as a sign to Pharaoh; in response, Pharaoh's heart is hardened. For example, in Exodus 8:16–18 (12–14 Heb.) Aaron strikes the dust of the ground and it turns into gnats that cover the land of Egypt. The Egyptian magicians identify this act as a sign from God ("This is the finger of God"). Nevertheless, "Pharaoh's heart was hardened, and he would not listen to them, just as the LORD had said" (8:19 [15 Heb.]). Two points about this order are important. First, the hardened heart of Pharaoh does not produce the plagues; rather, it represents Pharaoh's failure to see the plagues' significance (as the hardening comes after). In the case of the Priestly writer, who says that the Lord hardened Pharaoh's heart, the hardened heart is the reason for plagues to continue or be multiplied. But as Childs says, "The motif has been consistently over-interpreted by supposing that it arose from a profoundly theological reflection and seeing it as a problem of free will and predestination" (*Book of Exodus*, 174).

A few additional observations are necessary. That both God and Pharaoh are subjects of the verbs for hardening seems important. The blend of the two types of statements indicates that Pharaoh is not a helpless pawn. He makes his own decisions regarding the Israelites. Moreover, as he indicates at the beginning of Exodus, Pharaoh's ruthless treatment of the Israelites is to preserve his own power and to act as one above the intentions of God (1:10, 16, 22). But just as Pharaoh is not powerless, he also cannot act against God forever. The statements that God hardened Pharaoh's heart hints at this point. As the final occurrence of these statements indicates, God hardens Pharaoh's heart "so that I will gain glory for myself over Pharaoh and all his army; and the Egyptians shall know that I am the LORD" (14:4). The context here is Pharaoh's observation of the Israelites wandering in the land and his determination that they are defenseless against him (14:1–3). God does not force Pharaoh to pursue the Israelites; he allows Pharaoh to pursue his own desire for power and glory. So it may be that God's very being creates the hardening of Pharaoh's heart; that is, God confronts Pharaoh with his evil and Pharaoh, who is obsessed with gaining power and glory for himself, cannot but defy God. God declares that through the encounter with Pharaoh everyone will know that "I am the LORD" (14:4). Since Pharaoh is overtaken by his own desire for control, however, he does not recognize who

God is. With that failure to recognize God's sovereignty, Pharaoh naturally uses violence in the attempt to maintain his own control over his world.

War with Amalek

The exodus from Egypt is often conceived as beginning with Pharaoh's oppression of the Israelites (Exod. 1:8–14) and ending with Pharaoh's defeat at the Red Sea (15:1–18). But after the celebration in 15:1–18 the Israelites face another enemy who would cut them off: Amalek.

Deuteronomy remembers the attack as unprovoked and unjust. It is terrorist-like: "Remember what Amalek did to you on your journey out of Egypt, how he attacked you on the way, when you were faint and weary, and struck down all who lagged behind you" (Deut. 25:17–18a). As with the injustice of Sodom and Gomorrah, however, the actions of Amalek threaten the very balance of the cosmos because they attempt to overturn the purpose of God. Thus the writer of Deuteronomy makes the judgment concerning Amalek that "he did not fear God" (25:18b).

Given the cosmic significance of such injustice it is not surprising that the story of Amalek has symbolic dimensions. A notable part of Amalek's figurative importance is the connection to the wilderness. Whereas Pharaoh's threat appears in concert with the threat of the sea (and in a sense is defeated with the help of the sea, particularly in Exod. 15), Amalek appears when the Israelites are facing the untamed desert. Immediately after the Israelites escape from the Egyptians at the Red Sea they enter the wilderness and begin to experience harsh realities: shortages of water (15:22–27; 17:1–8) and food (chap. 16). Then Amalek "came and fought with Israel" (17:8). The symbolic importance of Amalek is more subtle than the confrontation with Pharaoh, but very much at the heart of the narrative.

In ancient Near Eastern cosmology the symbolism here is clear: Egypt represented the threat of unruly waters; Amalek represents the threat of the lifeless desert. As Othmar Keel says, "Because the desert could not yet be mastered with fast, safe means of transportation, it, like the sea, was not a place of romantic associations, but rather a region of danger and death" (*Symbolism of the Biblical*

World, 76). Amalek is a personification of this life-threatening "un-world" just as the Egyptians are symbolic of the waters of chaos (Stern, *Biblical Ḥerem*, 173).

The dual threat of sea and desert is expressed in texts and artwork from the ancient Near East. For instance, in a well-known Egyptian sarcophagus relief the earth is depicted as a disc surrounded by a mysterious watery region. The main dwelling place of human beings is in the center of the earth, while the edge of the earth is marked by two jackals, animals thought to guard the realm of the dead (see Keel, *Symbolism of the Biblical World*, 37–39). It is surely not a coincidence that when the psalmist complains of being near death, with chaos and evil all around, the complaint includes images of being overwhelmed by water (Ps. 42:7 [8 Heb.]) or wandering in a wasteland (Ps. 63:1 [2 Heb.]; 107:4–5).

With the understanding of Amalek just outlined, it is clear that the battle with this desert foe is cosmic in scope and emblematic in character. Although the Amalekites may have been a real historical people and a real historical foe of the Israelites, Amalek in Exodus 17:8–15 is a prototypical enemy that represents the forces of evil. As the desert setting suggests, Amalek stands for the chaotic wilderness just as Pharaoh represents the chaotic waters of the sea.

The Legacy of Amalek: 1 Samuel 15 and Beyond

One of the most troubling parts of the Amalek story comes when the Amalekites reappear in 1 Samuel 15. This story is one of two accounts of Saul's failure that causes the Lord to reject him as king (for the first, see 1 Sam. 13:2–15a). The chapter begins with Samuel commanding Saul to "go and attack Amalek, and utterly destroy all that they have; do not spare them, but kill both man and woman, child and infant, ox and sheep, camel and donkey" (v. 3). At the heart of the command is the practice of the ban (Hebrew root *ḥrm*). We will examine this practice further in chapter 4. For now suffice it to say that the ban involved the ritual slaughter of all the spoils of battle. The narrative reports that Saul indeed won the battle against Amalek, but he took their king Agag along with the choice sheep and cattle and brought them to Gilgal and put under the ban only the worthless animals (vv. 8–9). According to the story, therefore, Saul's failure is that he did not completely put the Amalekites under the ban.

89

Samuel's command to put the Amalekites under the ban seems to advocate something like what would be termed genocide today. Indeed, one reason the story is so chilling is that some Christians have used it to advocate the destruction of entire populations of people deemed a hindrance to their place in the world. Most famously, the Puritan preacher Cotton Mather promoted the genocide of Native Americans by calling them "Amalek" and calling for vengeance "against the Amalek that is now annoying Israel in the Wilderness" (see Bainton, *Christian Attitudes Toward War*, 167–69). That is not what the story suggests, however, or at least it does not easily support such an idea. In the discussion below I will suggest that 1 Samuel 15 continues to present Amalek as a symbolic figure and therefore does not advocate the destruction of real people.

Amalek and the Prophetic Critique of Saul

The first reason for reading a story like 1 Samuel 15 symbolically is that the story was preserved long after the "event" it recalls in order to call into question the validity of Saul's kingship. Parts of the Samuel story seem to show knowledge of an actual battle with a people called Amalek during the reign of Saul, as the summary in 1 Samuel 14:48 indicates: "He [Saul] did valiantly, and struck down the Amalekites, and rescued Israel out of the hands of those who plundered them." Regardless of the historical events that stand behind the Amalek stories, however, the account in present form is the result of those stories being reworked to show Saul's disobedience to the prophetic word expressed by Samuel (see McCarter, *I Samuel*, 269–70). In other words, the story in 1 Samuel 15 is part of a prophetic critique of Saul that intends to set Saul over against David, the ideal king. As McCarter states, "Whatever the antiquity of the tradition of Saul's Amalekite campaign, it comes to us wholly as a part of the prophetic reworking of the Saul materials" (ibid., 270). Indeed, the account as it appears in 1 Samuel now marks a pivotal point in the story at which God rejects Saul and chooses David as king over Israel.

90 The particular focus of the critique draws from the larger concern in the Deuteronomistic History for the Israelites to separate from the Canaanites. Concerning the practice of placing an enemy under the ban, the story in 1 Samuel is part of a larger concern for

separating from the people of the land, a concern in which *ḥērem* is paramount. In Deuteronomy and Joshua the practice seems perhaps the overriding concern. As Douglas Earl observes, the symbolical character of the ban is evident in Joshua in the difference between two genres—narratives and speeches—in Joshua 23 and 24. Both narratives and speeches in these chapters have separation from the residents of the land as the highest concern. In the narratives the ban is the chief means by which this is accomplished. In the speeches in which Joshua directs the people on how to keep themselves pure, however, the ban is not mentioned (Earl, *Reading Joshua as Christian Scripture*, 204). Thus the ban seems to be part of a "narrative world" that is not intended to carry over into the real world and to take shape as real actions against enemies. As Paul Ricoeur says, such a narrative creates its own world and invites readers into it that they may be transformed or shaped by that world. Written for this purpose, the story does not simply report an event or occurrence; rather, it *redescribes* reality (Ricoeur, "Narrative Function," 194–95). Saul's encounter with the Amalekites thus must be read in that light.

Amalek and the Praise of David

Just as the Amalek story in 1 Samuel 15 is a critique of Saul, it also points forward to the affirmation of David. It may be helpful to consider one historical period that possibly produced the story or at least saw its development into the form that now appears in the Old Testament. The account of Saul's failure to comply with the prophetic mandate to place the Amalekites under the ban would likely have been of great interest in the seventh century BCE during the reign of Josiah (d. 609 BCE). Josiah ruled the kingdom of Judah when the mighty Assyrian Empire was waning in power. The Assyrians had destroyed Israel (the northern kingdom) a century earlier (722 BCE), but now their decline left a vacuum of power that allowed Josiah to revive memories of the golden age of David and Solomon. Part of Josiah's program was a set of religious reforms associated with the values expressed in Deuteronomy: the people of God would live in a land promised to Israel's ancestors; they would worship this God alone (Deut. 6:5), in one place God would choose (Deut. 12), and the king would serve as the primary example of religious faithfulness for the people (Deut. 16:14–20). The book of

91

Deuteronomy and the so-called Deuteronomistic History, the history of Israel in the land (Joshua through Kings), were largely compiled during Josiah's reign. In this literary complex David serves the primary example of faithfulness to God. As Israel Finkelstein and Neil Silberman state:

> According to the Deuteronomistic History, the pious David was the first to stop the cycle of idolatry (by the people of Israel) and divine retribution (by YHWH). Thanks to his devotion, faithfulness, and righteousness, YHWH helped him to complete the unfinished job of Joshua—namely to conquer the rest of the promised land and establish a glorious empire over all the vast territories that had been promised to Abraham.
>
> (*Bible Unearthed*, 144)

For the Israelites in the time of Josiah the story in 1 Samuel 15 would not have served as a mandate to put enemies under the ban. Rather, it would have provided a dramatic narrative portrait of what it meant to be devoted exclusively to the Lord.

In the context of this larger portrait of Amalek, Saul's failure to eradicate Amalek indicates his unfaithfulness to God's order and purpose. A closer reading of 1 Samuel 15 also shows that the real focus is not on Saul's failure to practice *ḥērem* but on Saul's failure to fear God above all else and therefore to strive to discern the will of God. Instead, Saul has allowed the people to shape his actions. When confronted with the fact that he did not carry out the prophet's command, Saul confesses, "I have sinned; for I have transgressed the commandment of the LORD and your words, because I feared the people and obeyed their voice" (v. 24; see McGinnis, "Swimming with the Divine Tide," 254–55).

That 1 Samuel 15 is about Saul's religious faithfulness in a broader sense is confirmed by the contrast between Saul and David. When David appears as a rival to Saul he fights against and opposes the Amalekites on several key occasions. When he is banished by Saul and forms a mercenary band in the wilderness, he raids the camps of the Amalekites (1 Sam. 27:8–12). Later the Amalekites capture two of David's wives; David defeats them and recovers his wives (1 Sam. 30); finally, and perhaps most importantly, David kills an Amalekite who comes claiming to have killed Saul (2 Sam. 1:11–16), "the LORD's anointed." The messenger's claim provides the primary clue to Amalek's identity: he is the one who opposes the

Lord and tries to thwart divine intentions (see Ps. 2:1–2). The irony of 2 Samuel 1:11–16 is that the Amalekite thought David desired the death of the Lord's anointed as he did. But David is portrayed as virtuous precisely because he did not pretend to take the place of God. When David killed the Amalekite messenger, therefore, he was essentially defending the world against evil. Hence it is appropriate that David identified the Amalekites as "the enemies of the LORD" (1 Sam. 30:26).

Whatever "history" lies behind the story in 1 Samuel 15, that history is now used for a larger religious purpose. The Amalekites do not represent so much real historical foes as the forces of disorder that threaten to undo God's creation. Thus the promise to eradicate the memory of Amalek must be understood against the backdrop of order and chaos; God's opposition to Amalek is related closely to and is symbolic of God's work to establish order in creation.

Esther's Use of Amalek and the Problem of Genocide

The symbolic nature of the story of Amalek in 1 Samuel 15 seems to be confirmed by the oblique references to the account in the book of Esther. The story of Esther has some resemblance to historical narrative, but it contains so many historical inaccuracies, contradictions, and exaggerations that it has more the character of a cartoon than history (Levenson, *Esther*, 23). The story narrates the survival of the Jewish people in the Diaspora through the heroic efforts of its lead character. The characters are indeed cartoonish: Esther, a beautiful Jewish girl in exile, marries the king of Persia and eventually saves her people from extermination; Esther's cousin Mordecai was a palace official who coached Esther on all the right political moves that eventually made it possible to save the exiled Israelites; and Haman, the personification of evil, thought of nothing but how to kill Mordecai and his people.

The book of Esther paints Haman with the story in 1 Samuel 15 in mind. Mordecai is identified as a descendant of Kish of the tribe of Benjamin (Esth. 2:5). Although the Kish mentioned here is not clearly the father of Saul (1 Sam. 9:1), the connection is intriguing. What is certain, however, is that Mordecai is from the same Israelite tribe as Saul. Haman is introduced as "the Agagite, the enemy of the Jews" (Esth. 3:1). In other words, Haman comes from the same stock as the Amalekite king in 1 Samuel 15. Thus

93

the conflict between Mordecai and Haman recalls the old rivalry of their ancestors (see Clines, *Esther Scroll*, 43–44). As Kenneth Craig says, "By mentioning that Haman is a descendant of Agag on five occasions and establishing that Mordecai is a descendant of Saul early in the story, the author places 1 Samuel 15 in the background of the unfolding plot in Esther" (*Reading Esther*, 114; see the five references in Esth. 3:1, 10; 8:5; 9:10, 24).

Moreover, that Haman is wholly possessed by evil intent suggests the emblematic character of the conflict. Haman alone opposes the Jews and plots to wipe the exiles from Jerusalem off the earth. When Mordecai refuses to do obeisance to Haman, Haman "plotted to destroy all the Jews, the people of Mordecai, throughout the whole kingdom of Ahasuerus" (Esth. 3:6). Clearly Haman has more than a grudge. He is like the pharaoh of the exodus who desires to wipe out the descendants of Abraham completely. Portrayed with this singular obsession, Haman appears as a storybook figure rather than a real person.

These features of the Esther story suggest that the author reads the conflict between the leading characters in 1 Samuel 15 as a trope for the battle between good and evil. This explains why a government official in Persia (Haman) would be identified as a descendant of an Amalekite king (Agag) who was killed by an Israelite prophet more than four hundred years earlier!

Amalek and the Call to Nonviolence

If the stories about and references to Amalek in the Old Testament are to be read figuratively, then such a reading of these passages provides important guidance about how stories like 1 Samuel 15 are appropriated to the life of faith. Ironically they become stories about the battle *against* violence, not justifications of it. Hans Andreas Tanner notes that the initial account of Amalek in Exodus 17 communicates the notion that Israel cannot be overcome by military forces (*Amalek*, 71). But just as Israel cannot be overcome by military might, so also Israel does not ultimately overcome its enemies with such use of force. In Exodus 17:8–13, indeed, "Joshua defeated Amalek and his people with the sword" (v. 13), but the victory depended on Moses holding up his hands until the battle was complete. The uplifted hands seem to be a gesture of prayer, and thus the battle depends on God's presence and aid, not

94

on Israel's military action. This is indicated by the fact that when Moses becomes tired and his hands fall, Israel begins to lose the battle (v. 12). The story is about Israel relying on God for protection.

These features of the Amalek story have rightly influenced some Jewish interpreters to see in the account testimony to God's work for justice and order, not a justification for violence. For example, some have noticed that the action God orders Moses to perform at the end of the battle with Amalek in Exodus 17 is not total annihilation of a people. Rather, God commands Moses to *write*, not take up the sword: "Write this as a reminder in a book and recite it in the hearing of Joshua" (v. 14). A prominent strain of Jewish exegesis has focused on this point. The enormously influential modern rabbinic commentator Samson Raphael Hirsch (1808–1888) observed that Amalek sought greatness with the sword and thus represented the violent forces of humankind. The call of the people of Abraham, he said, was to fight against such armed power with moral force, without arms. This is why the text emphasizes writing. "The war against Amalek is waged with the book" (Sagi, "Punishment of Amalek," 333). A close reading of the Exodus passage shows that such a reading is a faithful rendering of the content of the passage. Indeed, although the previous section (Exod. 17:8–13) says the Israelites fought against and defeated Amalek, it does not say Amalek was destroyed. In fact, the word rendered "defeated" (*ḥālaš*) might be better translated "overwhelmed" (as in NJPS). Moreover, verses 14–16 emphasize the written declaration of God's opposition to Amalek. Hirsch's interpretation of the passage and his understanding of how Israel should respond to an enemy like Amalek undoubtedly reflects the powerless and vulnerable state of the Jews in his time. That circumstance matches the defenseless state of the Israelites when the book of Exodus, and the Amalek story, reached its final form.

Another feature of the Amalek texts that leads away from a focus on violence is the content of what Moses wrote: "I will utterly blot out the *remembrance* of Amalek from under heaven" (v. 14). If the author wished to say that the people called Amalek would be physically annihilated it could be said in a much simpler and straightforward way. This leads Hirsch again to conclude that the passage is not about an attack upon Amalek: "'I will utterly blot out the remembrance of Amalek,' not Amalek, but its remembrance and glory" (*Pentateuch*, vol. 2, 171). Another Jewish interpreter

95

identifies the "remembrance" of Amalek here as a memory that encourages a way of relating to and controlling others through violence (Sagi, "Punishment of Amalek," 334). Those who interpret the passage this way are certainly right that the Old Testament remembers Amalek's treatment of Israel in the wilderness and promises the end of that memory. The real battle, they aver, is between the sword (Amalek's chosen weapon) and the word (the instrument of God through God's people).

The particular language of these first references to Amalek creates at least the possibility that the Old Testament is not speaking about the literal annihilation of a group of people. Rather, it seems concerned that Israel remove from their memory and consciousness the prominence of Amalek's action against them. Amalek has come to represent the power of brute force and violence, so often used against the weak and powerless. Amalek represents self-centered and self-aggrandizing actions that oppose the purpose of God and lead to violence.

Throughout much of this chapter I have downplayed the historical reality of the "enemies of God" like Sodom, Pharaoh, and Amalek. As I close the discussion, however, it seems important to raise the historical issue again in order to recognize that enemies like those presented in the texts noted here are problems precisely because real evil and real violence are a constant threat to the world. The insightful reflections of Hirsch on the Amalek narratives provide helpful directives against taking up arms in the name of God. He was surely right in his assessment of how the Amalek stories should be appropriated, as opposed to the reading promulgated by Cotton Mather. Nevertheless, it is important to remember that about half a century after Hirsch rendered his assessment of the Amalek texts, a force arose in the world that attempted to do what Haman, the descendant of Agag, tried to do to the Jews in exile. The result was that six million Jews died. This reality, in turn, makes understandable other parts of the Bible that seem to permit violence in defense of the powerless and vulnerable.

CHAPTER 4

"You Shall Utterly Destroy Them"

The Ban and Conquest

There is perhaps no part of the Bible more directly associated with the problem of violence than the story of Israel's conquest of Canaan and its description of Israel placing residents of the land "under the ban." The story appears in Joshua 1–12, but Exodus (17:8–16), Numbers (13; 21:1–3, 21–35; 31; 32; 33:50–56), and Deuteronomy (1:1–4:43; 7; 20) anticipate the taking of the land, and the narrative books that follow Joshua present its completion (see especially Judg. 1–3; 1 Sam. 15). Therefore, this story cannot be dismissed as a minor part of the Old Testament. Moreover, when we recognize that the New Testament also assumes the validity of this story (see Acts 7:45; Heb. 4:8; 11:30, 31; 13:5; Jas. 2:25), we must consider it a foundational part of the larger biblical canon as well.

The main issue with the conquest account is that it seems to describe and advocate what modern people would call war crimes. In his famous work *The Age of Reason*, Thomas Paine sums up the problem this way, commenting specifically on the book of Joshua: "There are matters in that book, said to be done by the *express command* of God, that are as shocking to humanity and to every idea we have of moral justice as anything done by Robespierre, by Carrier, by Joseph le Bon, in France, by the English Government in the East Indies, or by any other assassin in modern times" (104). Indeed, this portion of Scripture may seem to represent the worst impulses of humankind, dressed up as an expression of the divine will. And

97

if God really did order the conquest and the ban, then God appears brutal and inhumane to all but God's own chosen people. How can God's order to "utterly destroy" (Deut. 7:2) the Canaanites and to possess their land be considered part of Christian Scripture?

The historical circumstances of the writing of Deuteronomy and the conquest account are important factors to help gain a purchase on this difficult question. Although the books are set in the time of Moses and Joshua (perhaps the twelfth century BCE), they were composed much later when there were no Canaanites in the land to conquer or place under a ban. Indeed, as noted in the introduction and again in chapter 3, the first draft of the conquest narrative and its foundational principles in Deuteronomy likely date to the time of King Josiah in the late seventh century BCE. During that time Josiah instituted religious reforms aimed at purging the worship of Yahweh of elements of the worship of Baal, Molech, and other gods (2 Kgs. 23:4–20). Josiah removed pagan sanctuaries, banned cultic practices influenced by the worship of other gods, and banished priests who promoted such acts. His reform was an inner religious purification. The story of placing the people of the land under the ban seems to have served this reform movement largely as an emblem of purification, but was not meant to be taken literally. Although this does not remove the difficulty of the story completely, it does affect the way the story is read and appropriated to the life of faith.

It is also important to keep in view the circumstances that existed when Deuteronomy and the conquest story reached their present canonical form. The perspective of the canon is shaped by Israel's defeat and exile, events that occurred less than fifty years after Josiah's attempts at reform (587 BCE). Thus the accounts of warfare promote neither Israel's identity as warlike people nor participation in violence as a sacred act. Indeed, from the perspective of the final telling of such stories, Israel is incapable of any such military or violent activity.

These historical considerations may help explain why accounts of Israel's warfare are in some ways quite distinct from other battle stories from the ancient Near East. Such extrabiblical stories were composed by powerful kings who tried to legitimate their own power and military aggressiveness. For example, Assyrian king Tiglath-pileser (1114–1076 BCE) asserted concerning an expedition into Syria and Palestine, "At the command of my Lord Ashur

98

I was a conqueror . . . from beyond the Lower Zab River to the Upper Sea which (lies towards) the West" (Pritchard, *Ancient Near Eastern Texts*, 275). Biblical texts that describe war and conquest, however, are third-person accounts that highlight God's role in fighting and winning victory. Human agents often have little part in the actual victory, and the accounts themselves are testimonies to God's power and God's willingness to fight for those who are not capable of fighting for themselves. The question about such stories then is, what does it mean theologically that God fought for God's people? What does it say about God and what, in turn, does it mean for Israel?

In this chapter I will treat the general problem of God ordering Israel to conquer the land of Canaan. I will address the issue from various perspectives but will focus on the notion that God favors certain people—Israel in this case—to the detriment of others. I will suggest that a close reading of Joshua 1–12 does not actually support such an idea. This is evident from the fact that Joshua 1–12 presents some Canaanites who not only are preserved but are presented as models of faith as well. The chapter begins with the more specific problem of the ban. Concerning this subject I will suggest that the command for Israel to "utterly destroy" the Canaanites (Deut. 7:1–5) does not actually call for the killing of others. Instead, the ban serves as a metaphor for complete devotion to God. This way of interpreting the ban was suggested by some of the earliest Jewish and Christian interpreters. It has largely been dismissed in the modern period. The discussion here will attempt to show, however, that the symbolic readings of texts like Deuteronomy 7:1–5 are much closer to the plain sense of the text than many modern interpreters have recognized.

The Problem of the Ban

In Deuteronomy 7:2 Moses gives the Israelites strict instructions about how to treat the people in the land of Canaan: "when the LORD your God gives them over to you and you defeat them, then you must utterly destroy them. Make no covenant with them and show them no mercy." The Hebrew verb *ḥāram* means "to devote to destruction" and the noun that derives from it (*ḥērem*) is used to denote persons or objects as "devoted things" (that is, set apart

99

for destruction). When this language appears within stories about Israel's wars, it refers to the complete destruction of the enemy and all their possessions that might otherwise be captured as spoils of victory.

One problem with the reference in Deuteronomy 7:2 is that the practice of the ban does not have the same character as in some other passages. The brief story in Numbers 21:1–3 reveals at least two important features of this practice that illustrate the problem. First, the story seems to indicate that originally the ban was imposed as part of a vow meant to gain God's help in battle. The idea seems to be that by giving up all spoils of war, Israel acknowledged that God was the real force behind the victory and thus the true owner of all that was conquered. Hence in such cases the practice of *ḥērem* seems to be a sacred ceremony closely related to sacrifice (note that in 1 Sam. 15:21 the devoted things are burned as an offering, though 1 Sam. 15 at other points draws a distinction between the devoted things and things to be sacrificed).

It is perhaps significant that two texts outside the Bible that describe this practice both report the establishment of a worship site after the enemy is "utterly destroyed" (Monroe, "Israelite, Moabite and Sabaean War-ḥerem Traditions," 335). The best-known text is the Moabite Stone, a ninth-century victory monument erected by Mesha, king of Moab. Mesha records his victories and reports that he placed certain Israelites under the ban in gratitude for winning the battle. Then he establishes a worship place. The second text dates to roughly the same time period and describes a similar practice by an Arabic tribe in the southern Arabian desert. What these texts indicate is that the practice of the ban is ultimately a religious act. It is precisely its religious character that makes it most reprehensible.

Second, the practice of the ban in these texts seems ad hoc. It is invoked on certain occasions when an army calls on God for help. Numbers 21:1–3 reports:

100

When the Canaanite, the king of Arad, who lived in the Negeb, heard that Israel was coming by the way of Atharim, he fought against Israel and took some of them captive. Then Israel made a vow to the LORD and said, "If you will indeed give this people into our hands, then we will utterly destroy their towns."

The LORD listened to the voice of Israel, and handed over the Canaanites; and they utterly destroyed them and their towns; so the place was called Hormah.

Here God does not order the practice. Instead, Israel of its own accord promises to "utterly destroy" the towns they attack. Although Numbers 21:1–3 implies God approved Israel's actions, there is no indication that God urged the Israelites to practice the ban. In Deuteronomy 7:1–5, however, the practice of the ban has a significantly different character. Here the destruction of the Canaanites is identified as a crucial event that ensures Israel's proper moral action. The Canaanites are presented as morally deficient, and they must be destroyed so Israel will not be tempted by them (Deut. 7:1–5). Concerning this presentation of the ban, Walter Brueggemann states, "The basis of *ḥērem* is not that Israel should not possess, but that Israel should not be seduced" (*Revelation and Violence*, 70). Thus with this emphasis on moral purity through separation from the Canaanites comes a different understanding of the ban than what appears in Numbers 21:1–3 and the texts outside the Bible. In Deuteronomic tradition the practice is not Israel's choice, not an ad hoc decision as in Numbers 21:1–3, but the command of God to be applied whenever the Israelites encounter residents of Canaan. Indeed, the ban in Deuteronomy is a precondition for Israel to occupy the land (Deut. 7:2) and the ultimate sign of religious purity while living in the land (Deut. 7:3–4).

Origen's Allegory and the Canaanite Within

One interesting interpretation of the ban and the conquest story that may help Christians who struggle with the problem of violence is Origen's allegorical reading of this portion of the Bible. Origen (b. 185 CE) believed that the ultimate goal of biblical interpretation was to unite the believer with Christ. He believed specifically that reading Scripture was like participating in a sacrament, and Scripture itself was an extension of the incarnation. Given that understanding of the Bible, Origen thought every portion of the Bible had some contribution to make to the life of faith. Moved by the conviction that Scripture has an essential unity, Origen taught that every text consisted of a literal aspect (the letter) and a spiritual

101

aspect. The spiritual aspect was the key to the Christian life. With these assumptions, what spiritual benefit could one find in the story of the conquest and, especially, in the command to annihilate all residents of Canaan?

Origen asserted that the entire account of Israel's conquest of Canaan was a figurative account of the battle with temptations, part of the Christian's effort not to be "conformed to this world" (Rom. 12:2). He saw this meaning of the story from the very first account of the appearance of Joshua in the Old Testament. Joshua is introduced in Exodus 17:9 as the military leader Moses appointed to battle Amalek. This introduction of Moses' successor has several important features for Origen. Since Origen was reading from the Greek version of the Old Testament, Joshua's name was written as *Iēsous* (Jesus). This provided the starting point for thinking of Joshua's actions as a figure of what Jesus would later do, a connection the author of Hebrews had already made explicit (Heb. 4:1–11). Origen noticed further that Joshua is here simply called by his name and not identified as "the son of Nun," as he is later in the biblical narrative (Exod. 33:11). Hence Origen argued that "Jesus" in Exodus 17:9 is obviously meant to be understood as the Son of God, not as Moses' young assistant. That, in turn, made it quite important that "Jesus" appears first in the Bible as the leader of God's army (fighting Amalek in Exod. 17:9–13). It can only mean, Origen asserted, that the battle referred to here is a spiritual battle (Origen, *Homilies on Joshua*, 26–33).

Origen takes this connection of Joshua to Jesus and fills out his reading of the conquest story as a trope of the spiritual life. Jericho (Josh. 6) is a metaphor for the present age, to be overcome by the kingdom of God. The city of Ai (Josh. 7–8) represents the chaos of life and sin Jesus overcame on the cross. Most importantly, the order to place under the ban all the residents of the land is not an injunction to kill other human beings. Rather, it is a figurative way of saying that the Christian must purge the self of all that would hinder pure devotion to God. Indeed, Origen said, "within us are the Canaanites; within us are the Perizzites; here [within] are the Jebusites" (Origen, *Homilies on Joshua*, 34).

Some early Jewish interpreters of Deuteronomy 7:1–5 also suggested that the passage does not say what it seems on a surface reading to say. In contrast to Origen, however, these exegetes focused on the language of the text itself, not on the symbolic value of the language. Their proposals focus on a portion of 7:2: "and when the LORD your God gives them over to you and you defeat them, then you must utterly destroy them. Make no covenant with them and show them no mercy." Jewish exegetes were particularly interested in the section of the verse that the NRSV translates "show them no mercy" (*lōʾ těḥānnēm*). One interpretation that appears in the Babylonian Talmud comes from a rabbi named Yossi. He declared that the verb does not derive from the verbal root *ḥānan*, "to show mercy" but from *ḥānâ*, "to encamp." Hence the idea is not that Israel should not show mercy to the residents of Canaan, but that they should not "encamp" near them (see the ambiguous translation of NJPS, "give them no quarter" which could render either verbal root). The rabbinic literature includes other theories about this verb as well, all intended to mitigate the offense of what seems to be an order to kill all the Canaanites. For example, one interpretation is that the verb is from *ḥnm* ("to be free") and has the sense, "do not give them free gifts." Another takes the verb at the end of verse 2 to relate to a word for beauty (*ḥēn*). It was understood as a prohibition against declaring beautiful the heathen residents of the land (see Hoffman, "Deuteronomistic Concept of Herem," 197). What all of these interpretations have in common is a commitment to reading 7:1–5 as something other than an order to kill the residents of Canaan.

But even if these interpretations are potentially helpful to people of faith, many modern interpreters have nonetheless denounced them as efforts to cover up the text's true message. Indeed, it may seem that Origen's allegorical interpretation and the rabbinical reading of Deuteronomy 7:1–5 were simply attempts to keep up the appearances of the text by means of fanciful and imaginative denials of what the text seems to plainly say. Speaking against Origen's interpretation specifically, John J. Collins says, "Allegorical interpretation of the kind practiced in antiquity is hardly viable in the modern world. It is all very well to say that the Canaanites that we should root out are vice and sinfulness, but we still have texts that speak rather clearly of slaughtering human beings" (*Does the Bible Justify Violence?*, 29–30). If Origen's allegory denies what the text "rather clearly" says by spiritualizing it, Jewish interpretations like those cited above may seem to strain at the text so as to make the words themselves say something that in fact they do not say.

Another way to approach the problem therefore is to highlight the many passages in Deuteronomy that reflect humanitarian sensibilities (Deut. 15; 21:10–14; 24:17–18). In light of such texts the command to put all the Canaanites under the ban seems quite out of character. Therefore, some have suggested that the commands that are more compassionate toward foreigners should be considered normative and should trump texts like Deuteronomy 7:1–5 (see Collins, *Does the Bible Justify Violence?*, 28–30).

It seems premature, however, to dismiss Origen's allegorical interpretation as arbitrary or as a cover-up. Indeed, a close reading of Deuteronomy 7:1–5 and Joshua 1–12 seems to support these ethically sensitive readings much more than modern scholars have typically recognized. In other words, Origen and early Jewish interpreters present interpretations that are much closer to the plain sense of the text than has often been perceived. To that point we now turn.

A Closer Look at Deuteronomy 7:1–5

To come to terms with the ban in Deuteronomy 7:1–5 it is important to notice that this passage seems to be patterned after Exodus 23:20–33, a text likely written earlier but with the same concern for how to live in the land of Canaan (Fishbane, *Biblical Interpretation in Ancient Israel*, 200–201). While the Exodus text speaks emphatically about living and worshiping in a pure manner, Deuteronomy 7:1–5 speaks of this specifically in terms of placing the residents under the ban. They both begin with declarations that God will deliver the land and its inhabitants to the Israelites (Exod. 23:20–23, 28–31; Deut. 7:1), followed by instructions to remain separate from those living in land (Exod. 23:32; Deut. 7:2) and to demolish their sacred objects (Exod. 23:24; Deut. 7:5). Moreover, some of the language in the two passages is identical. For example, both texts instruct Israel not to make covenants with the people of the land (Exod. 23:32; Deut. 7:2). But although the Exodus passage speaks in strong language about Israel destroying the Canaanite *objects of worship* ("you shall utterly demolish them," v. 24; Heb. *ḥārēs tĕḥārĕsēm*), it does not say explicitly that Israel should obliterate the *people of the land*. Deuteronomy 7:1–5 does make this explicit. Moreover, Deuteronomy 7:2 uses an expression that is grammatically identical to the one in Exodus 23:24, but with the language of the ban: *haḥărēm taḥărîm* ("you shall utterly destroy them"; included in both passages is an infinitive form, followed by a verb from the same root, a common way for Hebrew to express the certainty or intensity of an action). So, on the face of it, Deuteronomy seems extremely harsh and seems to have hardened the text from which it draws.

Second, as already noted, the command to place the Canaanites under the ban is absolute in Deuteronomy 7:2 (and in 20:10–20), whereas in other texts it is assumed that the ban is not always applied to an enemy but done only as part of a vow during warfare (Num. 21:1–3; cf. Judg. 2:1–5). In other words, the other examples of the ban show Israel placing an enemy under the ban voluntarily as a way of showing allegiance to God. In Deuteronomy 7:2, however, the ban is something ordered by God. This may indicate that Deuteronomy has made the occupation of the land even more brutal than a conquest. There are signs, however, that the ban has become a symbol for religious fidelity, not a literal command to kill people.

The Ban and Complete Devotion to God

In support of the idea that the ban in Deuteronomy 7:2 is not a literal order to annihilate the Canaanites, R. W. L. Moberly offers an interesting suggestion: the order to "utterly destroy" the residents of the land should be read as an extension of the command to "love the Lord your God with all your heart, and with all your soul, and with all your might" (6:5). Hence Moberly essentially supports Origen's allegorical interpretation but he does so from a close reading of the text, not an appeal to allegory (note that Origen's allegory was spun from a close reading of the text as well). Moberly argues that the ban in Deuteronomy is "a metaphor for religious fidelity" that does not involve the taking of life (Moberly, "Toward an Interpretation," 135).

Moberly's understanding of the ban rests on the fact that the first appearance of *ḥērem* in Deuteronomy comes just after the chapter that contains the Shema (Deut. 6:4–9). The Shema begins (v. 4) with a command for Israel to "hear" that the Lord is the sole object of Israel's devotion ("the Lord is our God, the Lord alone"). Then it gives the well-known injunction to "love the Lord your God with all your heart, with all your soul, and with all your might" (v. 5).

The remainder of the chapter elaborates on how Israel is to inculcate this exclusive love of Yahweh (vv. 6–9) and how such love is the
proper response to God rescuing Israel from slavery (vv. 10–25).
As the passage offers this extended explanation of Israel's love of
God, it presents separation from the gods of the people living in the
land as the main practice of faith. Hence 6:4–25 insists that Israel
live out its love of God by obedience to Moses' commands, and
those commands are, as Jesus said, summed up in the injunction to
be completely devoted to this and only this God (Matt. 22:36–40;
Mark 12:28–34; cf. Luke 10:25–28).

Moberly then argues that Deuteronomy 7:1–5 is essentially an
explanation and expansion of 6:10–25. That is, it describes what it
means for Israel not to "forget" the Lord (6:12) by following "the
gods of the peoples who are around you" (6:14). Hence the *hērem*
law is part of this larger concern to show an exclusive love of God,
the Lord who brought Israel out of Egypt. Indeed, the verse immediately after the discussion of the ban puts it in those terms: "For
you are a people holy to the LORD your God; the LORD your God
has chosen you out of all the peoples on earth to be his people,
his treasured possession" (7:6). The law of the ban expresses the
extreme requirements of both loving the one God and being the
people chosen by that God. In the expression of that ideal, Israel's
relationship with those living in the land is crucial, and herein lies
the primary problem: 7:1–2 puts this in terms of making the residents of the land *hērem*, devoted to destruction. So, on the face of
it, exclusive love of God seems to produce the notion that Israel is
superior to the residents of Canaan and thus encourages violent
action against the residents of the land.

Deuteronomy 7:3–5, however, explains what *hērem* means
in two stipulations, neither of which involves taking life. The first
stipulation is a statement against intermarriage (vv. 3–4). Marrying
those living in the land would lead to religious unfaithfulness. The
second stipulation is to destroy the sacred objects of the residents
of Canaan: "break down their altars, smash their pillars, hew down
their sacred poles, and burn their idols with fire" (v. 5). As Moberly
notes, "These stipulations not only make no mention of the taking of life, but the first of them presupposed that life is not taken
(for, to put it crudely, corpses do not raise the temptation of marriage)" ("Toward an Interpretation," 135). Indeed, the only things

"devoted to destruction" are the religious objects associated with the worship of foreign deities.

The connection between loving Yahweh with all heart, soul, and might and destroying sacred objects is strengthened by the fact that the two are connected in the account of Josiah's reform in 2 Kings 23. Josiah is described with language nearly identical to that in the Shema: "Before him there was no king like him, who turned to the Lord with all his heart, with all his soul, with all his might, according to all the law of Moses" (v. 25). His actions that caused him to be seen as the embodiment of the Shema are precisely the destruction of sacred objects and sanctuaries associated with heterodox religious practices. Moberly notes that Josiah's actions included the slaughter of priests on the altars of the high places (v. 20). This does not disprove the point, however, since "the overwhelming emphasis in the account of the reform is on the destruction of religious objects and desecration of the locations of such objects" ("Toward an Interpretation," 137). The *ḥērem* that Josiah practices does not seem to be identified with taking life; or at least the taking of life is peripheral to the reform efforts as they are described in 2 Kings 23. It is the desire to worship other gods that is to be wiped out.

It is telling that the figure of Joshua is painted with remarkable similarity to King Josiah. Indeed, Richard Nelson makes a convincing case that the figure of Josiah and the elements of his religious reform were the primary inspiration for the portrait of Joshua ("Josiah in Joshua"). This lends further support to the idea that the ban in Deuteronomy and Joshua was not a literal description of what the Israelites did to the Canaanites. Rather, it was a figurative description of what it means to be devoted to God completely.

Origen's Interpretation and the Plain Sense of the Text

What this reading suggests is that God (according to Deuteronomy) did *not* order Israel to ritually annihilate the residents of Canaan. To be sure, the language of the ban is still present and the language itself remains troubling. But the language must be read as figurative, as an emblem of something higher and nobler, however reprehensible the background of the figure might be. Therefore, this reading of Deuteronomy 7:1–5 also suggests that Origen's allegorical interpretation and early Jewish interpretations of 7:2 were not as far from the "plain sense of the text" as many modern scholars have thought. Indeed, it is much closer to what 7:1–5 actually says than most modern interpreters who insist on a literal reading of the command to place under the ban the residents of Canaan. Since the command to place the residents of the land under the ban is illustrated by further commands to avoid intermarriage and to destroy sacred objects of alien religions, it seems that *ḥērem* really does signal a concern not to "be conformed to this world" (Rom. 12:2), just as Origen said.

Origen did not present a detailed discussion of the subtleties in Deuteronomy 7:1–5 that have been mentioned here, so it is impossible to know if he noticed these details. It does seem, however, that he recognized the purpose of these texts dealing with the ban, namely, to engender a deeper and purer faith. Also, Origen's insistence that the Old Testament could not be encouraging bloodshed (because it must be consistent with the teachings of Jesus) is essentially right as well. What once was a reprehensible practice (apparently) of Israel (and some other ancient Near Eastern peoples), close to "ethnic cleansing," was transformed into a metaphor of spiritual purity. Again, this becomes clearer when we recognize that the commandments to place conquered people under the ban (and the narratives about such actions) are part of a story likely written in first draft in the late seventh century during the religious reform of King Josiah (622 BCE). Josiah was not dealing with Canaanites in the land, but with his own people, who often practiced the worship of their God with elements of the worship of Baal and other deities (2 Kgs. 23). Hence Origen's allegory really does capture the meaning of the text, a meaning that points away from violence and bloodshed.

Deuteronomy 20:10–20

If Deuteronomy 7:1–5 uses the ban metaphorically, it still leaves the question of how to interpret 20:10–18, which may seem more difficult. This passage is part of a larger set of regulations on how to wage war during the conquest and occupation (20:1–20). It opens with an order for the Israelites to offer terms of peace when they approach a town (v. 10). If a town does not accept the terms, the Israelites are then to follow certain procedures in besieging and defeating it (vv. 11–14). This initial order concerning peaceful surrender would seem to lessen the offense of the ban. The end of the passage, however, seems to distinguish between towns far away (towns not part of the inheritance God gave the Israelites) and towns nearby (that are part of the inheritance; vv. 15–18). For those towns nearby, the order seems to be unconditionally to place everything under the ban: "But as for the towns of these peoples that the LORD your God is giving you as an inheritance, you must not let anything that breathes remain alive" (v. 16).

Although 20:10–18 seems to give straightforward instructions to put under the ban "anything that breathes," a closer reading of the passage indicates something different. Norbert Lohfink offers three key insights in this regard. First, when read carefully in its context, 20:10–20 does present the ban during the conquest as a last resort, as an act that came only after offering terms of peace and those terms being refused. In Moses' opening speech in Deuteronomy 2 he recalled how the Israelites sent messengers to King Sihon of Heshbon with terms of peace (2:26–30). Moreover, the terms Moses offered were not for surrender; he requested merely for Sihon to allow the Israelites to pass through the land without conflict and to be able to buy food and drink from Sihon's people (vv. 27–28). In like fashion, Deuteronomy 20:10 opens the instructions with a blanket order to offer terms of peace. Later in the summary of the conquest in Joshua 11:19 this procedure seems to be assumed: "There was not a town that made peace with the Israelites, except the Hivites, the inhabitants of Gibeon." The implication of these passages is that the Israelites were to offer peaceful terms of surrender to every town, not just those far away (Lohfink, "חָרַם *ḥāram*," 197).

Second, as already noted, the historical circumstances of the writing of Deuteronomy 20:10–20 would seem to indicate that Deuteronomy and Joshua were written largely during the time of Josiah (622–609 BCE). The memory of the conquest of the land and the religious ideals that Moses ordered the Israelites to follow provided a foundation for his religious reforms. The instructions about placing towns under the ban, however, are limited to the time of conquest. The people to be annihilated—the Hittites and Amorites, the Canaanites and the Perizzites, the Hivites and the Jebusites (v. 17)—no longer existed at the time of Josiah. Thus, as Lohfink says, "The war law in Dt. 20:10–18 also limits the *ḥērem* strictly to the situation of the occupation and the inhabitants of the

\mised land. For later periods and other peoples, different rules
\ly. In principle, then, the very law that appears to demand the
.~*rem in fact forbids it in the case of those to whom the law is actually addressed" ("חָרַם *hāram*," 197).

As Miller rightly says further, such laws "belong to particular
times and places. In later times and new contexts, the community
takes up the commandment afresh, listening to what it has learned
from its application along the trajectory and learning from that how
to live by the commandment in a later time" (*Ten Commandments*,
238). That the ban is part of a story of the past (the time of Joshua),
but not part of the present (the time of Josiah), further suggests that
the ban in the conquest story is an emblem of religious fidelity, not
justification for killing people.

Finally, it is important to note that the passage as a whole shows
great concern for how warfare is conducted and contains important
prohibitions meant to preserve life and prevent wanton destruction. Thus as Miller says, "The protection of life is not partial but
comprehensive" (*Ten Commandments*, 238). Evidence of this concern is found particularly in verses 19–20, which prohibit cutting
down fruit trees in order to build siege works. The law precluding
felling trees that produce food sets off sharply Israel's participation
in war from that of Assyria. Artwork depicts the Assyrians destroying vineyards and fruit trees even after a siege was completed. One
reason for this practice seems to have been simply to show power
and dominance. The Israelites, however, were to approach the land
of promise more humbly by recognizing that the Lord alone gives
victory (Deut. 20:4). To do so would mean to treat all life as a gift
from God.

Ethical Significance of the Sublimation of the Ban

The texts in which the ban has taken on symbolic rather than literal meaning do not prescribe what stance should be taken to the
violent acts associated with *ḥērem*. What seems clear, however, is
that the way the ban appears in Deuteronomy 7:1–5 simply will not
allow the practice of the ban to be replicated in the name of the
Old Testament God in the form of genocide or other such practices.
110 Another important reason violence like that described in the
ḥērem law should be rejected comes from other texts in the Old
Testament, and some important ones in Deuteronomy. Many have

charged that monotheism, the exclusive worship of one God—like that described in the Old Testament—naturally leads to violence (see Schwartz, *Curse of Cain*). That such often has been the experience is true enough. This experience, however, is due to human misappropriation of biblical faith, not to the faith itself. As I will show in the following discussion, the conquest story portrays Israel as the unworthy recipient of God's grace whose favoritism before God is predicated on humility and gratitude. The residents of Canaan who bow before Israel's God, being perhaps more aware of their precarious place before God than the Israelites, become in this story the model of faith. Hence the story does not encourage—indeed, will not permit—elitism or self-congratulation.

In an essay on the First Commandment Miller shows how the larger witness of the Old Testament makes this point as well. While the command to worship only one God may lead to the destruction of those who do not so worship, Miller says, "In the Commandments one finds an implicit critique of such a way of responding" (*God You Have*, 17). Indeed, Miller points out that the first half of the Decalogue, dominated by the command to faithfulness to God, is complemented by the second table of commands that focus on how one treats one's neighbor. "Neighbor" is a theological category that gets defined in the legal codes of the Old Testament to include the resident alien or stranger. For example, Leviticus 19:18 commands the Israelites concerning their own people, "you shall love you neighbor as yourself," thus identifying the neighbor as kin. But as the chapter progresses another command appears with the same language and sentence structure, "you shall love the alien as yourself" (Lev. 19:34). Jesus makes clear the necessary openness to the identity of the neighbor in the parable of the Good Samaritan. The neighbor may indeed be someone who worships in ways differently from us. Therefore, the Commandments, the larger canon, and the story of Israel's conquest of Canaan resist and discourage the temptation to violence against those who do not worship the one God, even as these texts insist on purity of worship from God's people.

On Not Rejecting the Ban: A Final Word

If the ban is indeed a metaphor for spiritual purity and devotion to God, it must still be handled carefully. That some very fine biblical scholars read Deuteronomy 7:2 as a clear command to slaughter people is evidence enough that even more lay readers will take it the same way. Moreover, the history of Puritans in North America, with their identification of Native Americans as "Amalek," should give pause to anyone who uses this language. It has inspired unspeakable horrors. Nevertheless, if treated properly the tradition of the ban has potential to speak to people of faith in at least two very constructive ways.

First, the language communicates the idea that some religious practices are not permissible if faith is to have a meaningful impact on the life of the believer. As Solomon Schechter says, it is the role of true religion "just as much to teach the world that there are false gods as to bring it nearer to the true one" (*Aspects of Rabbinic Theology*, 77). But as the idols are revealed any honest person must surely recognize that idols are expressions of one's self-interests and selfish ambitions. Are there any more readily apparent idols than nation and personal wealth? If these idols are clearly recognized, then the ban will have its proper place, to purify the believer of all things that would tempt him or her to worship other gods but will not lead to violence.

Second, if the language of the ban accomplishes that purpose it will also bring the believer nearer to God, and any close reading of the biblical text will reveal that the true God is "merciful and gracious, slow to anger, and abounding in steadfast love and faithfulness" (Exod. 34:6; see again Moberly, "Toward an Interpretation," 144).

The Conquest of Canaan

Even if the ban is not taken literally, we still must come to terms with the notion that Israel conquered the land of another people and possessed it for their own. Such action seems characteristic of empires, the like of which the Bible typically speaks against. Is this simply a prejudice on the part of the authors of the conquest story? Is this essentially a double standard?

Conquest, Exile, and Israel's Dependence on God

112

In order to address the question of how people of faith today should appropriate the story of Israel's conquest, it is necessary to consider the historical accuracy of Joshua 1–12 and the possible reasons Israel told this story and included it in the larger narrative of God's care for them. Concerning the first issue, Joshua 1–12 gives the impression that the Israelites marched into Canaan and summarily conquered the whole land. Thus 11:23 concludes the account of Israel's sweep through the land: "So Joshua took the whole land, according to all that the LORD had spoken to Moses; and Joshua gave it for an inheritance to Israel according to their tribal allotments. And the land had rest from war" (Josh. 12 then gives a summary of kings conquered). This gives the impression that Joshua's army was akin to the great military forces of the ancient world; indeed, it sounds as though Israel rivals the major empires of the ancient Near East (for example, the Assyrians, Babylonians, and Egyptians) in military might. The historical reality, however, was likely quite different. Immediately after the grand claim that Joshua "took the whole land," 13:1 states that "much of the land still remained to be possessed" (v. 1; see Judg. 3:1–6). The book of Judges begins with the same point and describes how the various tribes worked to secure control of their territories (Judg. 1:1–3:6). Archaeological evidence corroborates this portrait of the Israelites' limited control of the land. It suggests that Israel's domain was limited to the hill country, the least desirable areas, until much later in its history (Mazar, *Archaeology*, 329–38). In other words, the story in Joshua 1–12 is idealized. It does not reflect what Joshua's army in the Late Bronze Age (1550–1200 BCE) actually accomplished.

The realization that Joshua 1–12 is an aggrandized account raises the question of why Israel would have told such a story. The answer is difficult in part because the account of the conquest likely developed over a long time and was told, in whole or part, in different periods of Israel's history. As already noted, the first writing of the story was likely in the seventh century BCE during the reign of Josiah. Josiah sponsored the writing of the first draft of the history in order to support his religious and political reforms that focused mainly on purifying worship and limiting the cult to the Jerusalem temple. The story came into its final form while Israel was in exile in Babylon. In other words, the story of Israel's sweeping conquest of Canaan was told by people who themselves had no land and who were powerless before the great empires of their day.

This situation of powerlessness may help explain how the boundaries of the land to be conquered were conceived and presented.

113

There are numerous descriptions of these boundaries in the Old Testament, each of which has its own logic and theological reasoning. There are, however, two main types of verbal maps of the land. One type emphasizes the Jordan River as the eastern boundary of the land; the other type conceives the land as stretching all the way to the Euphrates (Josh. 1:4). The latter type seems to envision Israel as a power like Babylon, the nation that saw its own boundaries defined by the Euphrates; thus Israel is the area "Beyond the River" (Ezra 7:21; 8:36). The point of the more extensive way of "mapping" the land is not that Israel is powerful enough to conquer people living in the land of Canaan, let alone territory hundreds of miles to the east; rather, the point is that Israel, empowered by God, is equal to the mighty Babylonians, who dominated the world at the time. Of course, this was never the case "on the ground." But it shows how a weak and threatened people expressed their theological conviction that in God's eyes it was indeed part of the power structure built into the cosmos.

The other type of verbal map, which presents the Jordan as the border of the land, may be even more helpful for understanding the biblical story of conquest. The clue to the significance of this type of map is likely found outside the Bible in the treaty between the Egyptian pharaoh Ramesses II and the king of the Hittites (in modern Anatolia, Turkey) in 1270 BCE. For some lengthy periods, including the time just before the historical period in which the story of Exodus was set, Egypt was the controlling power in Canaan. The territory the Egyptians agreed by treaty with the Hittites to possess was essentially the territory described in Numbers 34, which has the Jordan as its eastern boundary. Interestingly, this map is described in the context of Israel's relationship to Egypt. Indeed, Numbers 33 described Israel's journey from Egypt, having just been freed from bondage there. Now in Numbers 34 Moses outlines the land the Israelites "inherited" (v. 2) or attained "by lot" (v. 13). The implication of this particular map, given its eastern border at the Jordan and the context in the book of Numbers, is that Israel received the land as reparation for its years in slavery in Egypt (Havrelock, "Two Maps of Israel's Land," 661–62). In other words, the writer has in mind not so much that Israel will conquer those living in the land as that Israel rightly receives the land of Canaan as payment for its hard service. Canaan, which once belonged to Egypt, is now Egypt's payment to Israel for Israel's years of servitude.

When Israel's precarious place in world politics is recognized, another feature of Joshua 1–12 perhaps becomes more apparent: the story of Israel conquering Canaan actually focuses on God's action, not on Israel's. The installation of Joshua that begins the story (1:1–9) makes this clear. This passage, in which God commissions Joshua to lead Israel into Canaan, consists almost entirely of divine promises concerning the land: "the land that I am giving to them" (v. 1); "every place that the sole of your foot will tread upon I have given to you" (v. 3); "I will not fail you or forsake you" (v. 5); "the LORD your God is with you wherever you go" (v. 9). The first battle is introduced by a story of the appearance of the "commander of the army of the LORD" (5:14). Moreover, the battle of Jericho resembles a liturgical celebration much more than a military campaign. In fact, Joshua 6 hardly reports any recognizable military action. Instead, it depicts Joshua and his "army" relying completely on God's action (see further Creach, *Joshua*, 61–63).

The historical setting of Israel's account of the conquest of Canaan and the theological character of the story just described provide important direction for anyone who desires to identify with the account. The reality that the Israel who created Joshua 1–12 was actually a conquered people gives an important perspective on the telling of the story. Indeed, the account should be read as a liberating story for those who are oppressed, not as a triumphant account of conquest by a dominant force. As such, the story urges reliance on God, not on military action. To be sure, such a reading of the story could simply shift the focus of violence from Israel to God, which may not ultimately help attenuate violence among God's people today. But another implication is probably closer to the story's intended impact: When Israel reflected on its history—particularly in exile—it ultimately declared the futility of using weapons to accomplish the purposes for which God established them (Lind, "Concept of Political Power"). Or as John Howard Yoder aptly put it, "Confidence in YHWH is an alternative to the self-determining use of Israel's own military resources in the defense of their existence as God's people" (*Politics of Jesus*, 83). In other words, the conquest story presents a stance toward warfare and military action much like that expressed in Psalm 20:7 (8 Heb.): "Some take pride in chariots, and some in horses, but our pride is in the name of the LORD our God."

Ethical Concerns within the Story

The perspective on the conquest just presented comes from considering what lies behind the story. But there are signs within the story itself that those who put the story together seem to be quite concerned about the violence of the conquest.

The Conquest as a Defensive Action

One such sign is the presentation of the conquest as a largely defensive action by Israel and the residents of Gibeon, its covenant partner, against the attacks of the kings of the land. This perspective is evident in a series of five comments (Josh. 2:9–11; 5:1; 9:1–2; 10:1–5; 11:1–5) that tie together the individual stories of the conquest into a unified narrative. Each of the five editorial summaries reports the Canaanite reaction to Israel's presence in the land. Each of these statements notes that (a) the people in the land "heard" of the Israelites' presence, and then each statement describes (b) the Canaanite response. Most important for the ethical question, these statements show a definite progression. The first summary statement acknowledges that "all the inhabitants of the land melt in fear" (2:9) and that the people of the land had "no courage" because of the Israelites (see 2:9–11; 5:1). As the story progresses, however, the residents of the land plan for war against Joshua's army (9:1–2; 11:1–5) and against the Gibeonites who are allied with him (10:1–5; see Stone, "Ethical and Apologetic Tendencies"; Creach, *Joshua*, 13, 17). In the final editorial summary the Canaanite kings "came out, with all their troops, a great army, in number like the sand on the seashore, with very many horses and chariots" (11:5). Hence Joshua 9–11, which contains the most extensive description of Israel's slaughter of the Canaanites, depicts the entire Israelite action, after the defeat of Jericho and Ai, as a response to Canaanite aggression and as a defense of the Gibeonites, with whom Israel is bound in covenant (Josh. 9:3–27). This part of the story shows Joshua and his army moving from south to north, conquering everything. These transitional statements serve as the "structural backbone" of this part of the book. As Lawson Stone observes, "It is therefore enormously significant that they construe the *entire military campaign after Ai as a defensive reaction*" (Stone, "Ethical and Apologetic Tendencies," 33).

This reading of the story is further affirmed by the concluding statement in 11:19: "There was not a town that made peace with the Israelites, except the Hivites, the inhabitants of Gibeon; all were taken in battle." This statement is quite curious if indeed the story intends to say that Israel from the beginning planned to place under the ban all residents of the land. It sounds rather that there was a chance for all those in the land to make peace, but the kings, led by Adoni-zedek of Jerusalem (10:1), refused to do so. This is precisely how the Jerusalem Talmud treats 11:19. It reports that the spies Joshua sent to Jericho offered the Canaanites a chance to evacuate or make peace (*Shebi'it* 10.1 [16b]; see Hoffman, "Deuteronomistic Concept of Herem," 197). Such an interpretation may reflect the relative helplessness of Palestinian Jews in the fourth century (the time of the compilation of the Jerusalem Talmud) and their eagerness to make peace with their neighbors. But that circumstance mirrors the situation of those who put Joshua in its final form, as verse 19 indicates. Verse 20 then suggests that the Canaanite kings' refusal to surrender put them in company with the pharaoh of the exodus whose hardened heart led to his defeat and death (Exod. 10:20; 14:4).

The exact place of Joshua 2:9–11; 5:1; 9:1–2; 10:1–5; and 11:1–5 in the editorial process of the book of Joshua is not certain (for example, see Noth, *Deuteronomistic History*, 28, for the idea that these statements are part of an intermediate phase of development; there is currently little agreement on such editorial stages, however). Nevertheless, this much is clear: these statements cast the stories of the conquest in a light perhaps not shared by the original storytellers. The editorial summaries almost deny that Israel acquired the land through aggressive military action; rather, they suggest that the Israelites defended themselves and their covenant partners (the Gibeonites) against Canaanite aggression. Hence those who brought the larger story together from its constituent parts seem quite concerned from an ethical perspective about the means by which Israel came into possession of the land.

117

The Canaanites as Models of Faith

Given that Joshua 1–12 depicts the Canaanite kings as oppressive and unjust, it may seem odd that it portrays ordinary residents of Canaan as models of faith, as people who recognize the power of Israel's God and submit to his authority. This aspect of the story, however, is extremely important. Indeed, it will not allow a simple identification of the Israelites as virtuous and objects of God's blessings with the Canaanites as objects of God's wrath. Any application of the conquest story must, in turn, consider that the true witnesses to God's action may be outside one's own group and outside one's own understanding of what is acceptable to God. In sum, this feature of the story makes a point similar to Acts 10:15, "What God has made clean, you must not call profane."

Two prominent groups of Canaanites are said to have survived the Israelite attack and continued to live in Israel's midst after the conquest: Rahab the harlot and those in her house, and the Gibeonites. The very presence of these two groups illustrates further that the ban in Joshua was not actually carried out according to the strict rules laid out in Deuteronomy 7:1–5 and 20:10–20 (which, as we observed above, is not a law to be taken literally in that passage either). But their presence is more than just an amelioration of the ban. Indeed, the way they are presented in the story seems to undermine the notion that the Israelites as a people are "pure" as opposed to the Canaanites from whom they are to be separated. At least these two groups of Canaanites appear as idealized characters and provide the example Israel is to follow. The implications of such an idea for the application of the conquest story are profound. Indeed, if some of the residents of the land are presented as exemplars of faith rather than reprobates, it turns on their head any attempts to apply the story according to ethnic, nationalistic, or in-group interests.

At first glance it may seem that Rahab is anything but obedient and could not possibly serve as a model of faith. She is identified as a prostitute, and her house serves as cover for the two spies Joshua commissions to gain information about Jericho (Josh. 2:1). Sexual innuendo permeates the story and is a driving force in its plot. The name Rahab itself may be intended to evoke seductive and provocative images. The Semitic root *rḥb*, which means "to open" (and giving rise to noun forms that mean "open place" or "broad place"), is

118

used in Ugaritic epic material to refer to female genitalia. Likewise, the same term is often associated with sexual impropriety in the Old Testament (Isa. 57:8; Ezek. 16:24, 31). This evidence leads Ellen Davis to suggest that the name was "an old soldier's joke" ("Critical Traditioning," 743). However, if this association with Rahab's name is accurate, the humor is ironic. As Davis also points out, the story does not focus on Rahab as a "broad," though it may be a crudely humorous element. Regardless, the story certainly emphasizes her wits. She is the most savvy character in the story. She thwarts the efforts of the king to capture the spies, and she maneuvers the spies into an oath that will protect her and her family. Moreover, of all the characters in Joshua 2, Rahab is the most keenly aware of the Lord's sovereignty, and she confesses that knowledge in classic Deuteronomic language. Rahab is a sympathetic character indeed.

At the heart of the Rahab story is a speech (Josh. 2:9–13) in which Rahab pays tribute to Israel's God. To be sure, her oration serves largely to explain the risk she has taken to protect the two spies and to bargain for her life. Nevertheless, the words of this foreign woman are striking in the way they attest to the power and identity of the Lord. Her discourse consists of two parts. In verses 9–11 Rahab makes a confident statement of faith:

> I know that [*kî*] the LORD has given you the land, and that [*kî*] dread of you has fallen on us, and that [*kî*] all the inhabitants of the land melt in fear before you. Indeed [*kî*] we have heard how ['*ăšer*] the LORD dried up the water of the Red Sea before you when you came out of Egypt, and what ['*ăšer*] you did to the two kings of the Amorites that ['*ăšer*] were beyond the Jordan, to Sihon and Og, whom ['*ăšer*] you utterly destroyed. As soon as we heard it, our hearts failed, and there was no courage left in any of us because of you. The LORD your God is indeed [*kî*] God in heaven above and on earth below.

In verses 12–13 she pleads for safety for herself and her family when the city is attacked. The confessional portion of Rahab's speech (vv. 9–11) concerns the Canaanites' fearful reaction to the Israelite entry into the land. It is built upon Rahab's opening declaration, "I know" (v. 9a). Then the content of what she "knows" about the inhabitants' state of mind is presented in three consecutive and similarly structured lines in verse 9, each introduced by the same Hebrew particle (*kî*) translated "that." This gives a certain

119

cadence and structure to Rahab's statement: "I know *that* the LORD has given you the land, and *that* dread of you has fallen on us, and *that* all the inhabitants of the land melt in fear before you."

The second portion of the confession (vv. 10–11) is also ordered by a prominent verb, "we heard," which appears at the beginning of verses 10 and 11. Moreover, these verses begin and end with lines introduced by the same Hebrew particle that dominates verse 9. This little word in verses 10 and 11 is probably intended as an intensive marker; therefore, it may be appropriate to translate it differently than most English translations: "*Indeed*, we heard . . ." (v. 10a); ". . . *indeed* , the LORD your God is God in heaven above and on earth below" (v. 11b). Verse 10 contains a concatenation of clauses that makes emphatic Rahab's awareness of the Lord's power and control over Canaan. The rhetorical force comes by Rahab expressing what she heard in three similarly structured clauses, each introduced by a repeated *ʾăšer* particle, which might be "how" or "what": "*how* the LORD dried up the water of the Red Sea before you when you came out of Egypt" (v. 10a); "*what* you did to the two kings of the Amorites that were beyond the Jordan" (v. 10bα); "*how* you put them [the Amorite kings] under the ban" (v. 10bβ; NRSV: "whom you utterly destroyed").

Rahab's speech in Joshua 2:9–11 is remarkable in that Rahab, in good Deuteronomic parlance, acknowledges that Israel's God is the true owner of the land and has chosen to assign the territory to Israel. Much of the rest of Rahab's speech also draws its vocabulary from Deuteronomy. Her reference to the Canaanites melting in fear is reminiscent of Moses' recollection of his people's response to their spies' report ("Our kindred have made our hearts melt," Deut. 1:28; Josh. 2:9, 11), and it also confirms Moses' prediction that the Canaanites would have "dread and fear" because Israel entered the land (Deut. 2:25). When Rahab speaks of the two Amorite kings, Sihon and Og, being defeated by the Israelites, she raises a subject that serves as part of the temporal setting for Moses' first speech in Deuteronomy (Deut. 1:4) and constitutes a significant part of that speech (see also Num. 21:21–35). In this portion of her confession Rahab says Israel "utterly destroyed" Sihon and Og (Josh. 2:10). Hence in her dealings with the spies Rahab seeks an exemption from this practice.

120

The importance of Rahab's confession in Joshua 2:9–11 is illustrated by the way early Jewish and Christian interpreters spoke of her. In rabbinical tradition Rahab married Joshua and thirty of Israel's prophets came from her lineage (see references in Ginzberg, *Legends of the Jews*, 4:5; 6:171). Similarly, Matthew 1:5 names Rahab as the mother of Boaz and hence as an ancestor of Jesus. Although the text itself never actually says that she devoted herself to the Lord (she refers to Yahweh as "your God"), Rahab does recognize Israel's God as the universal sovereign, the one who is in control of all territory and who has power to allot it to whomever he chooses. Whether she identifies personally with Israel's God is not as important in the story as the fact that she properly identified the Lord as the power to whom she should bow. This recognition sets her apart from all other Canaanites except the residents of Gibeon (Josh. 9). But equally important, the way Rahab is contrasted with the Israelite spies suggests she is more in tune to what God was doing in Canaan than the Israelite invaders. Hence she becomes a model for Israel as well.

The Gibeonites are formed from the same mold as Rahab in that they manipulate their way into the covenant community. They are like Rahab and other characters in Israel's past who use trickery in order to gain something they would otherwise be denied. Approaching the Israelites in disguise, pretending to be from a distant land, the Gibeonites convince Joshua's representatives to enter a covenant. The upshot of the story is that they, like Rahab, are preserved because they outwit the Israelites. As a result, they gain a place in the community of faith, even though they should be destroyed according to stipulations about the ban (Deut. 20:10–20). But the Gibeonites seem to value and seek a covenant with Israel's God, a covenant that the Israelites have but take for granted. Therefore, the narrative seems to suggest that the reader should admire and empathize with the Gibeonites because of their covenant desire. They are rewarded by being allowed to live among the Israelites. They are given what seems to be a lower status as "hewers of wood and drawers of water" for the Israelites (Josh. 9:21). Nevertheless, this imposition of lower status does not seem overly punitive, if we heed the psalmist's passionate declaration: "For a day in your courts is better than a thousand elsewhere. I would rather be a doorkeeper in the house of my God than live in the tents of wickedness" (Ps. 84:10 [11 Heb.]).

121

The story clues the reader to the fact that the residents of Gibeon are like Rahab and should be classified with her. They are distinct from the other residents of the land in that they acknowl-edge the power of Israel's God and prudently seek exemption from the ban. Indeed, the Gibeonites, who heard "what Joshua had done to Jericho and Ai" (9:3) and then "acted with cunning" (9:4), are like Rahab, who, upon hearing what God had done for Israel, connived her way into an agreement with the Israelite spies. In contrast to the other Canaanites in 9:1–2; 10:1–5; and 11:1–5, the Gibeonites, like Rahab, acknowledge Israel's success as due to the action of Israel's God, not simply to military prowess. The outline of the Gibeonites' speech in 9:9–10 is strikingly similar to that of Rahab's confession in 2:9–11. Like Rahab, they recognize that it was the Lord who was displacing the people of Canaan (2:9; 9:9); they "heard a report of him," not of Joshua's army, just as Rahab heard that "the LORD has given you the land" (2:9). The Gibeonites' own speech indicates they heard of God's liberating action in Egypt (9:9) and of what he did to Sihon and Og east of the Jordan (2:10; 9:10), and responded in fearful submission.

According to the larger biblical story, the pact would pay long-term dividends to the Gibeonites. Second Samuel 21:1–14 reports that Saul tried to wipe out the Gibeonites, but David took up their cause to avenge the bloodguilt on Saul's house. The passage centers on the treaty Joshua's people made with the Gibeonites to allow them to live among the Israelites. Saul breached this covenant. In response, David handed over seven of Saul's sons to be impaled at the town of Gibeon, thus ending the house of Saul (2 Sam. 21:6, 9).

Some have concluded that the stories of Rahab and the Gibeon-ites are primarily etiological. That is, their purpose is to explain some present reality (the presence of Canaanites who remain in the land) by means of stories from the past. Furthermore, on a literary level, these stories prepare the way for Judges 2–16, which nar-rates how the indigenous population of Canaan became a snare for Israel. The problem with this interpretation, however, is that the text never indicates that these redeemed Canaanites (Rahab and the Gibeonites) pose any threat to Israel. On the contrary, they are viewed quite positively. Both Rahab and the Gibeonites acknowl-edge Israel's God as the supreme power, the creator and primary mover in the world. Their confessions of belief in God's might and their ultimate dependence on him for salvation are exemplary (Josh. 2:9–13; 9:9, 24). Therefore, it seems better to conclude that these stories are included not to explain the Canaanite survival in

122

the land so much as to mitigate ideas about Israel's exclusive virtue. Indeed, they represent many Israelites, and, to judge from Joshua 9, they represent a rather positive element within Israelite society. Perhaps those who recognize their precarious place before Israel's God more readily acknowledge their dependence on God's mercy. Hence the main point that grows out of the stories of Rahab and the Gibeonites may be that certainty of one's own righteousness is really the opposite of righteousness. Only those who approach God in humility, as these Canaanites did, will find God's favor.

What Does the Conquest Story Teach Us?

In light of the metaphorical interpretation of the ban discussed above, and in light of the surprisingly inclusive conquest story just examined, it seems the conquest story has much more to teach the contemporary community of faith than often assumed. If the conquest story is read as a flat historical report that centers on the order to place the Canaanites under the ban (and treating the command as literal), then the account is just a difficult portion of Scripture to overcome. But the story is much more insightful and sensitive and therefore has potential to shape those who read it in line with the gospel. There are at least three prominent lessons in the conquest story, none of which involves dominating or killing other people.

First, by presenting the conquest as purely the action of God, the story urges complete dependence on God. This may seem simply to shift the responsibility for violence from humans to God. But it seems rather to identify warfare as something outside human prerogative. The claim that God fights for Israel puts the responsibility for righting the world completely in God's hands.

The ban serves as a primary symbol for religious devotion and reliance on God. The language of the ban is troubling, to be sure, but a careful consideration of what the extreme devotion means should encourage the believer away from violence, not toward it. Indeed, if the God of Exodus and Deuteronomy is followed, the primary quality of God to be observed will be God's mercy and compassion, arguably the most recurrent descriptors of the Lord (Exod. 34:6).

Second, this perspective on the role of humans and God in warfare also implicitly critiques the kind of royal power built on violence that ancient Near Eastern kings often displayed. As noted already,

123

the conquest story is a narrative about God acting for Israel, not a boastful account of Israel's leaders regarding their accomplishments. The kind of autonomy some kings expressed in their victory boasts is the root of violence. Recognizing God as the only legitimate authority produces humility and nonviolence.

Third, the role of characters like Rahab and the Gibeonites in the conquest story suggests that those outside the community of faith often recognize the power of God more than many within the community. The survival of these two in Joshua 1–12 mitigates the story's emphasis on Israelite superiority. The Canaanites are obviously not morally bereft, and therefore they are not destroyed (thus apparently contradicting Deut. 9:4–5). Instead, these two Canaanite characters are models of faith, concerning whom Israel is implicitly called to imitate.

CHAPTER 5

Judges' Use of Violence

Perhaps more than any other biblical book, the plot and development of Judges turns on reports of violence. War, torture, domestic abuse, and rape are all integral to the story. The book poses problems, however, not simply because of the prominence of violence in the narrative, but because it does not explicitly condemn the violence it presents. A casual reading of Judges, therefore, might lead to the conclusion that it gives tacit approval of violence or at least presents violent acts without concern for their horrors. This is particularly true of violence against women, which is one of the most troubling aspects of violence in the Judges account.

In this chapter I will suggest that Judges does not in fact condone violence; to the contrary, violence appears primarily as a sign that Israel lost its way in relationship to God, that God's people failed to recognize God's reign over their lives and they subsequently spiraled downward into violent chaos. To make this point, however, four dimensions of the subject are crucial. First, I will suggest that violence done to women particularly symbolizes Israel's deterioration and downfall. Some feminist scholars have found in Judges a primary source of misogyny. This criticism often centers on the fact that Judges seems ambiguous about violence toward women. It presents the various kinds of mistreatment without any explicit statement against them. Hence this is often taken as tacit

125

approval of the atrocities presented, or at best as a lack of concern about them. I will argue, however, that, far from overlooking violence against women, Judges uses the declining status of women and the violence done to women to represent the downfall of Israel as a whole. Thus Judges does not overlook the violence done to women, but offers a strong if subtle critique of it. This will be discussed in more detail in the next section.

Second, when Judges does condone violence (and it almost certainly does at points), it does so because violence serves the larger purpose of liberation. It is helpful to remember, however, that the final form of the book comes from the perspective of exiles who are in no position to use violence for this purpose. Therefore, the approval of violence for liberation should not be considered the primary dimension. It appears in Judges as part of a story world in which violence serves to free oppressed people. Even in this narrative world some judges meet with disapproval in this regard. Some use violence for selfish reasons. But those who use violence "appropriately" appear as the saviors of the underdog. Such persons operate by cunning, deception, and physical violence because these are their only means of survival.

A third point, closely related to the second, is that some of the judges who have major flaws in character and judgment retain some value because they resist the evil of oppressors. Indeed, with some of the judges, the book holds up their resistance efforts as praiseworthy while also highlighting their major flaws.

Finally, some of the violence is presented with humor and works on the level of story but is probably not meant to be taken literally. Although there may be no true comedy in Judges, some of the narratives do seem intent on producing laughter. For example, the story of Ehud is similar to burlesque with its ridiculing caricature of the enemy, King Eglon of Moab (Judg. 3:12–30). But some of the humor in Judges should be recognized as tragic irony. This is particularly apparent in the story of Samson, who has great promise with a divine endorsement, but who gets caught in his own web of desire and weakness for the wrong women. Thus the story of Judges recognizes that many characters are flawed and deserve the laughter they receive. The laughter sometimes releases fear as the enemy is portrayed as a buffoon (as in the case of Eglon). In other cases the laughter is close to tears as Israel recognizes the tragic flaws of its own heroes (as in the case of Samson).

Overview of Issues for Interpretation

Israel's Deterioration into Violence and the Structure of Judges

Violence plays a crucial role in the overall movement and plot of Judges. This is apparent in at least two literary features of the book. First, Israel's experience in the land is presented in terms of a recurring pattern of apostasy, defeat, and deliverance (2:11–19). The judges appear in this pattern as a divine gift of leadership to help Israel. Thus the book receives its name from the statement in Judges 2:16 that when Israel suffered at the hands of enemies "the LORD raised up judges [*šōpĕṭîm*], who delivered them out of the power of those who plundered them," and from the central role of those said to have "judged" Israel (Hebrew verb *šāpaṭ*; 2:7; 15:20; 16:31). Violence thus appears as part of the inevitable struggle between the Israelites and those who live in the land as the judges fight against Israel's oppressors. But the cycle of events is not just a recurring pattern in which violence regularly appears. As the book unfolds it becomes apparent that the cycle of rebellion, oppression, and salvation serve the larger picture of Israel in a downward spiral of lawlessness and violence.

Second, the final five chapters of the book are held together by the repeated note that "in those days there was no king in Israel; all the people did what was right in their own eyes" (17:6; 21:25; and a shorter version in 18:1; 19:1). The meaning of this recurring comment is uncertain. Some scholars propose that Judges portrays Israel's violence in the period of the judges in order to prepare the reader for the Davidic monarchy (introduced in Samuel) with the implication that if David had only been king, Israel would have lived in order and stability without such rampant violence. The monarchy would have ensured order and civility (Brettler, "Book of Judges," 417–18).

But Judges' understanding of monarchy is not that simple, and the formula concerning the lack of a king in Israel was probably intended to carry a much deeper theological meaning. Some of the judges are portrayed as heroic and honorable, but they do not take up the mantle of kingship. The one figure who declares himself king (Abimelech; Judg. 9) is sharply criticized for the ruthless means by which he gains power. The note that Israel had no king

127

seems to have a more subtle meaning that is related to God's role as sovereign. That is, the largest problem Judges seems to narrate is that Israel does not recognize the King it does have, namely, the God who delivered Israel to the land (see 8:3; Klein, *Triumph of Irony*, 14–15). The primary message, therefore, seems to be that "when God's justice, righteousness, and peace are not established for all, then violence is the natural result" (McCann, *Judges*, 21).

Violence and the Role of Women in Judges

Although Judges has rightly received attention because of its portrayal of the mistreatment of women (chiefly in Judg. 11 and 19–21), the notion that Judges is misogynist seems inadequate for two reasons. First, the society portrayed in Judges featured more complex roles for men and women than often recognized. The term *patriarchy* is sometimes used to describe ancient Israelite society's organization around the power of males. Patriarchy, by its very nature, is seen as a system that perpetuates violence against women. Certain stories in Judges seem to confirm this impression (see the discussion of Judg. 19 below). But as Carol Meyers has shown, *patriarchy* is too simple a term for this society, especially in the period portrayed in Judges. Women's roles were, to be sure, associated largely with domestic affairs (see the character of Jael in Judg. 4–5), and men occupied more formal public roles (particularly in the priesthood). But women and men were interdependent, and women often had significant influence even if it was not formalized politically. Life in ancient Israelite society centered in the home, where women sometimes had quite significant authority. In turn, women could exert power outside the home in political, legal, and military matters (Meyers, *Discovering Eve*, 43). This seems to have been true particularly in the settlement period when there was no centralized authority, that is, no monarchy. Susan Niditch is probably right when she says the prominent role of women is due in part to the liminal time in which Judges is set (*Book of Judges*, 41).

Second, the portrayal of violence against women, graphic as it is, should not be taken as tacit approval. Indeed, the deterioration of Israel in Judges seems especially marked by the declining status of and violence done to women. Moreover, the movement of Judges, from the promise of life in the land to chaos and violence, may be plotted in large part by the women who appear in the book.

128

This is significant in part because of the symbolic role women play in this book and in the Old Testament as a whole: women represent all those who do not possess great power; and, as such, women represent Israel, who is small and powerless among the nations (see Frymer-Kensky, *Studies in Bible*, 174–75).

The vulnerable plight of women in Judges may be observed by comparing women at the beginning of the book to those in subsequent sections of the narrative. In the opening chapter Caleb's daughter Achsah appears as a favored and prosperous woman. She seeks a blessing of land from her father and he grants it (1:14–15). Specifically she asks for an area called Gulloth-mayim, which means "basins of water" (1:15). In a land where water was at a premium, and survival of towns often depended on capturing and storing water in cisterns, owning land with a water source would have been a sign of power and influence (on the role of water see Meyers, *Discovering Eve*, 50, 54–55). Thus the book of Judges begins with this striking portrait of a woman who possesses watered land.

In the chapters that follow, other prominent women enter the narrative. Deborah appears early in the cycle of judges as one of the most influential leaders in Israel (chaps. 4–5). Although identified as "the wife of Lappidoth" (see further the discussion below), she has a role that extends far beyond the domestic realm. Within the story of Deborah another woman, Jael, kills the villain Sisera (4:21–22; 5:26–27). Jael, like Deborah, is associated with household activities. The book introduces Jael in relation to her tent and refers to her as the wife of Heber. It is worth noting, however, that the tent in 4:17 is identified with Jael, not her husband. Clearly she exerts significant power within the tent and that power alters the military and political situation outside the tent. Similarly, an unnamed woman kills Abimelech in Judges 9:53.

As the book progresses, however, women suffer abuse at the hands of men. This circumstance reaches a high point in Judges 19 when the men of Gibeah rape and murder a Levite's concubine (19:22–30). The story shows all the main characters contributing to the violence against the woman. As the story subtly communicates, however, the tragic situation is due directly to the Levite's treatment of the woman as one of secondary concern, and the other characters also show no thoughtfulness in the regard. By the end of the book, Israel traffics in women in an effort to restore the tribe of Benjamin (chap. 21). In other words, the violent treatment of

129

women in Judges seems the primary illustration of how Israel has lost its way during a time when "there was no king in Israel."

The Canaanites as Forces of Death

As already noted, warfare and physical assault also play a positive role in Judges in that these are means for ridding the land of a primary menace, the Canaanites. The book of Judges begins with a concern that dominates large portions of the book: the Canaanites occupy much of the land God promised to the Israelites. Judges 1:1 reports, "After the death of Joshua, the Israelites inquired of the LORD, 'Who shall go up first for us against the Canaanites, to fight against them?'" In the rest of chapter 1 the Canaanites are mentioned thirteen times more, along with related groups such as the Perizzites (v. 5), the Jebusites (v. 21), and the Amorites (v. 34; for the particular groups see Niditch, *Judges*, 38–39). The content and tone of the chapter make clear that removing the Canaanites is a major part of the theological agenda of Judges.

The negative understanding of the Canaanites may seem an outright approval of violence. In dealing with this theological ideal of ridding the land of the Canaanites, however, it is important to keep two points in mind. First, at the time Judges was likely composed there were no Canaanites in the land. The origin of the stories in Judges was likely in the period from about 1200 to 1020 BCE, when the Israelites struggled against powerful forces in the Canaanite city-state system; but as noted in the last chapter, this book, along with Joshua through 2 Kings, was likely the product of authors working in the late seventh century during the reforms of Josiah (see Niditch, *Judges*, 10–11). These books expressed religious ideals Josiah tried to implement, ideals found in the book of Deuteronomy. At the center of those ideals is the notion that the Israelites should keep apart from the religious practices of those living in the land (see Deut. 7). The Canaanites are therefore a primary symbol in the narrative of what Israel should root out in order to maintain faithfulness to God.

Second, as a symbol of evil and disorder, the Canaanites in Judges largely represent forces of death, forces that oppose God's intentions for the well-being of those in the land. J. Clinton McCann rightly compares the Canaanites at the beginning of Judges to Pharaoh in the book of Exodus. He notes in that regard, "God's

130

opposition to the Canaanites should not be understood to mean God's hatred of a particular people; rather, it indicates God's opposition to that way of life that was based on injustice and unrighteousness that consequently resulted in deadly oppression" (McCann, *Judges*, 19). In other words, "Canaanite" in Judges is a code word for the kind of society that works against God's intentions for shalom. Thus the charge for the Israelites to drive the Canaanites out of the land is really a charge to establish justice and to reject the death-producing society the Canaanites represent.

The nature of Canaanite wickedness may be understood more fully by considering the ideals presented in Deuteronomy, to which Judges looks for its theological direction. Deuteronomy 9:4–5 emphasizes the wickedness of the Canaanites as the reason God brought the Israelites in to occupy the land: "do not say to yourself, 'It is because of my righteousness that the LORD has brought me in to occupy this land'; it is rather because of the wickedness of these nations that the LORD is dispossessing them before you" (9:4). The passage does not specify the exact nature of the "wickedness" of the Canaanites. It does describe them, however, as having "great cities, fortified to the heavens" (9:1). Although the Bible does not say explicitly that cities are bearers of wickedness, there are no cities that are unambiguously good either. The first city in Genesis 4:17 is built by Cain, who had murdered his brother. The Old Testament portrays Babylon as a source of arrogance (Gen. 11:1–9). Further, cities were signs of concentrated and centralized power, which was often oppressive; and entry into the promised land is marked by the destruction of the world's oldest city, Jericho. Jericho was not a prize to be possessed, but something to be destroyed completely (Josh. 6). The Israelite kings were warned against the temptation of developing such a society fueled by their own wealth and military might, which was found in cities (Deut. 17:16–17). Although Jerusalem will eventually appear as a city God chose for expressing the divine will, the Old Testament makes clear that it was built by the Jebusites and only later used by God for divine purposes (Josh. 15:63; see Schneidau, *Sacred Discontent*, 5–6).

This picture of the Canaanites has important nuances that identify them with violence. The biblical portrait of the Canaanites suggests they rely on their own might to control others and to build their society. Judges 1:1–7 gives evidence of this concern. The book begins by reporting that Judah defeated and captured King

131

Adoni-bezek. Joshua 10 earlier reported that this king organized a coalition of five kings who launched an unprovoked attack on the Gibeonites (who had made peace with the Israelites in Josh. 9). A related group in Joshua 11 is characterized the same way with emphasis on their use of "horses and chariots" (11:4). This portrait of Adoni-bezek and the kings associated with him suggests he headed a military organization that ruled with brute force. Deuteronomy states emphatically that Israel is to be governed differently. Its king is not to acquire horses and is not to rely on military might (Deut. 17:16), but is to be led by torah, by God's instruction given through Moses ("he shall read in it all the days of his life, so that he may learn to fear the LORD his God"; Deut. 17:19; cf. Josh. 1:7–8). The capture of Adoni-bezek at the beginning of Judges therefore signals the rejection of the use of royal power to control a population (though one must still contend with the treatment of Adoni-bezek described in Judg. 1:6).

The Judges

Othniel (Judges 3:7–11)

The first judge, Othniel, sets the stage for the rest of the judges. The brief account of Othniel identifies him in two important ways. First, Othniel appears as an answer to the dilemma of the Israelites when they are in the clutches of a ruthless enemy. Indeed, this seems to be the intended role of Israel's judges. Othniel, the first judge (3:9–11), is paradigmatic of this type of leader. The spirit of the Lord comes over him and enables him to lead Israel to victory over its oppressors (Niditch, *Judges*, 56).Thus the pattern introduced in Judges 2 appears here: the Israelites worshiped other gods; God sold them into the hands of their enemies; the Israelites cried out to the Lord and God gave them Othniel to deliver them out of the hands of their enemies (3:7–9; cf. 2:11–23).

Second, the enemy Othniel overcomes appears as an almost cartoonish symbol of evil. His name is Cushan-rishathaim, which means "Cushan of the Double Wickedness" (McCann, *Judges*, 23). The author here uses a touch of humor that appears frequently in Judges. The label given to Cushan unmasks the powerful king so as to alleviate the audience's fears of him. The humor with which

132

some of the stories were told was a way of denying the authority of such forces, and this seems to be the case with the description of Othniel's nemesis (McCann, *Judges*, 23). This is true also of the next judge, Ehud.

Ehud (Judges 3:12–30)

The first judge after Othniel is an assassin named Ehud who accomplishes his mission by deception and cunning. The account of Ehud in Judges 3:12–30 does not explicitly glorify or approve Ehud's violent actions. There are subtle hints in the story, however, that this judge is considered a hero and is justified in killing the Moabite king. One tacit sign of approval is that the storyteller uses humor to craft the narrative. The account contains "elements of satire, suspense, and humor that probably reflect a previous history of oral storytelling" (Olson, "Book of Judges," 770). The humor of the Ehud story turns attention away from the violence itself and the actual outcome of violence. As Noël Carrol rightly says of such storytelling, "Within the comic frame, though injury, pain, and death are often elements of a joke, we are not supposed to dwell on them, especially in terms of their real or human weight or consequences" ("Horror and Humor," 158). This description of the use of comedy in Judges 3:12–30 rings true because the humor is often like burlesque. It satirizes the enemy so he hardly appears like a real historical figure. Thus, as the Ehud story reveals, the humor of the account tells us not to focus on the death of Eglon and its gruesome details as a tragic event.

The humor of the story is closely related to its theology in relation to violence. Indeed, as the discussion below will note, part of the humor of the story is the portrayal of King Eglon of Moab, whose portly physique symbolizes the wealth and privilege of the Moabites (see 3:21). The comedy of the story of Ehud centers on the physical condition of Eglon of Moab. Judges 3:17 says Eglon was "a very fat [*bārî'*] man." That description then drives part of the plot, especially the part that occurs in the king's bathroom. The humor particularly communicates something of the character of Eglon. *Fat* here is both a description of Eglon's physical appearance and a statement about his opulent lifestyle. In a time before processed foods, only the most wealthy could afford to be overweight. Eglon therefore is the supreme "fat cat," a wealthy and arrogant

133

enemy who stands in sharp contrast with the Israelites whom he lords over.

The story unfolds with Ehud acting with cunning to outsmart the king's security forces. As a left-handed man, Ehud conceals his dagger on his right thigh and thus gets into the king's presence with the weapon. Then, after the official meeting with Eglon, Ehud asks for a private audience with the king, presumably to give information about an unfaithful vassal. But when Eglon dismisses the other attendants, Ehud assassinates him. That Eglon lay dead in his "cool roof chamber" (3:20)—a reference to his private bathroom—contributes to the humor, for when Eglon's servants return they are embarrassed to inquire about his well-being, thinking perhaps he was simply "relieving himself" for a long time (3:25).

The story of Ehud concludes with him rallying the Israelites against Moab, thus giving the land "rest" for eighty years (vv. 26–30). The reference in 3:29 to the ten thousand Moabite soldiers all being "strong" could also mean "fat" (*šāmēn*; see the use of this word in v. 22 ["fat closed around the blade"] and see Hab. 1:16, where this word is paired with *bārî*, the term used to describe Eglon in v. 17). Hence the entire Moabite army is like King Eglon. This portrait enhances the idea that underdog Israel triumphs over a more wealthy and powerful enemy.

Deborah (Judges 4–5)

An important part of the Deborah story is that she leads Israel in ways that may seem to the modern reader to defy typical gender roles. In turn, the portrait of Deborah contributes to the larger movement of Judges in which the status of women mirrors the spiritual health of Israel as a whole.

Deborah's leadership includes the roles of prophet and judge. She is identified with a tree where the Israelites seek her for "judgment" (*mišpāṭ*). They come for "decisions" (as NJPS renders), that is, for divine judgment, which she gives by virtue of her role as mediator between God and humans (the basic role of prophet). The label "mother" for Deborah refers to her authority and may apply to her prophetic identity, just as Elijah and Elisha were called "father" (2 Kgs. 2:1–2; 13:14). It therefore is interesting that Judges 4:4 identifies her as the "wife of Lappidoth." This expression could also be translated, "woman of Lappidoth" (thus identifying her with a place rather than with a husband) or perhaps "woman of fire" (*lappîdôt* means "torches"). If understood this way, the focus is on Deborah's charisma. She is a fiery figure, like Elijah one chosen by God and endowed with extraordinary gifts. Whether this is the intention of the label or not, Deborah is a prime example of a woman in the settlement period who exerted significant influence beyond the domestic realm.

The story of Deborah begins with Israel in the clutches of a warmonger. Jabin represents the use of force characteristic of Canaanite kings Israel is to reject when it settles in the land. Deborah is, in turn, the instrument of God's deliverance from such forces. Like the leadership of Othniel and Ehud, Deborah's leadership also represents an effort to free the Israelites from oppression. According to Judges 4:3, when Deborah came to power King Jabin of Canaan had "oppressed the Israelites cruelly twenty years." Judges 4:3 says specifically that Jabin's forces were formidable because they had "nine hundred chariots of iron."

Another sign that Deborah and her forces are liberators is that the Israelite troops are presented as militia fighters, summoned when needed, and pitted against a standing army led by Sisera. This is particularly apparent in the song in Judges 5. For example, throughout verses 10–13 there are hints that the Israelites are outside the typical power structures. They dwell in rural areas outside the power of cities; hence they march "down to the gates" (that is, to walled settlements), not from them (v. 11b; see also v. 13b, "they marched down for him [that is, for God] against the mighty" [NRSV translates "for him" from the Greek version; Hebrew has "they marched down for me," perhaps a reference to their action on Deborah's behalf).

When one considers the presentation of violence and the narrative's apparent approval of it, it is important to recognize that Judges 5 speaks of Deborah's victory over Sisera as God's doing, not the result of superior strategy or military tactics. Chapter 5 is a song that recalls the victory of chapter 4 and attributes the victory to God (see the same pattern of victory hymn following narrative in Exod. 15). The song is addressed to God ("to the LORD I will sing," v. 3); twice the singer calls for participants to "bless the LORD" (vv. 2, 9); and the victory is cast as the outcome of God's mighty rule over cosmic forces (vv. 4–5). Even when human agents such as Deborah appear, the hymn recognizes that heavenly forces assured

135

the victory. Verse 20 declares, "The stars fought from heaven, from their courses they fought against Sisera."

Judges 4:12–16 portrays Barak, Deborah's general, routing the forces of Sisera. Sisera escapes on foot while Barak pursues Sisera's chariots in another direction. Sisera's retreat to the "tent of Jael, wife of Heber the Kenite" (or "a woman of the Kenite community") assumes a world dominated by tribal chieftains (v. 17). Sisera believes Heber is sympathetic to him, and Jael gives that impression by welcoming Sisera into the tent (v. 18). Jael here is portrayed in language that suggests either a mother who dotes over a child (Sisera) or a lover, or perhaps as an ambiguous mix of the two. She extends hospitality to Sisera by giving him milk to drink when he asked only for water (v. 18). The milk causes him to sleep. When he falls asleep beneath the cover Jael placed over him, she approaches him "softly" (stealthily; v. 21). She then takes in her hands a tent stake and mallet and drives the stake through Sisera's temple.

Jael is known for the gruesome manner in which she killed Sisera. Both the narrative in chapter 4 and the poem in chapter 5 report this event. Judges 5:24–27 recounts how Jael killed Sisera, albeit with strikingly different details than 4:17–24. Judges 5:24 pronounces blessing on Jael in a poetic line that begins and ends with the expression, "May you be blessed" (*tĕbōrak*; NRSV "Most blessed"). The identifying expression, "wife of Heber the Kenite," could also be translated, "woman of the company of the Kenites." The poetry of verses 25–27 suggests a very different sequence of events than those in the narrative in 4:19–21. The parallel expressions in 5:25, "he asked water"/"she gave milk"/"curds in a lordly bowl" may suggest (as does the prose narrative) that she provided something more than requested. The poetry here heightens and intensifies the statement of what she provided (note that the substance provided becomes richer and more calorie-laden as the poetic line moves from start to finish), a common technique in Hebrew poetry (see, e.g., Ps. 51:5 [7 Heb.]). Similarly, Judges 5:26 states that Jael hit Sisera with a blunt object, probably while he consumed what she had given him. Tent pegs could be substantial (Isa. 33:20) and might well have been an object tent dwellers would have grabbed in an act of self-defense (as some have proposed, Jael might have been fending off a rape). At any rate, the parallel expressions, "her hand to the tent peg"/"her right hand to the workmen's mallet," do not suggest two objects used to kill Sisera. Rather,

136

Jael simply picked up a common item available in the tent. This picture of the event is confirmed by verse 27, which indicates Sisera fell at Jael's feet after she hit him (see again Halpern, "Resourceful Israelite Historian").

The song's penultimate section (vv. 28–30) portrays Sisera's mother waiting for her son to return from battle with the spoil. Sisera's mother receives attention in a way the family of enemies rarely do in such stories, a fact that reveals her importance. She is presented as the mirror opposite of Deborah (and Jael). Both are "mothers," but Deborah represents the oppressed Israelites (as charismatic prophet and warrior), while Sisera's mother is the picture of aristocracy. But further, the queen mother in the ancient Near East typically had other formal roles in which she participated in and enhanced the rule of her son. She was typically a chief counselor within the palace. The appearance of Sisera's mother gazing out the window probably also suggests she represented the main female deity in support of the king's rule. Indeed, numerous Canaanite ivory carvings with depictions of women looking out the window have been discovered and the woman in each case seems to represent the goddess Asherah (see the discussion of Ackerman, *Warrior, Dancer, Seductress, Queen*, 155–60). Hence Sisera's mother not only held power over others by virtue of the rule of her son but probably also represented the religious faith that promoted a way of life characterized by oppression and death.

This understanding of Sisera's mother is borne out by the response she and her attendants make to Sisera's delay in returning from battle. As she waits for the return of her son, she wonders, "Why is his chariot so long in coming?" (v. 28). Her attendants answer consistent with the expectations of a queen: "Are they not finding and dividing the spoil?—A girl or two for every man; spoil of dyed stuffs for Sisera" (v. 30). But the answer reveals an attitude toward those conquered that is to be rejected. That is, she and her attendants think of the Israelite women simply as spoils of battle, objects to be possessed. The term (euphemistically) translated "girl" is crude; it literally means "womb" (*reḥem*). The queen and those around her are so used to Sisera and his army capturing women as spoil that they speak of them only as sex objects possessed by conquerors. This portrait of the queen mother again draws a sharp contrast between powerful and weak, urban and rural (Niditch, *Judges*, 82). Perhaps most important, it marks a difference

137

between Canaanite and Israelite. Deuteronomy 21:10–14 stipulates that female captives cannot be treated as chattel. They are given time to mourn their dead and they cannot be held as slaves or sold for money. For Sisera's mother, however, such women are just "wombs."

The attitude of Sisera's mother to those captured in battle may help explain why Judges 4–5 justifies and even glorifies the actions of Deborah and Jael. These women, like the judges before them, are used to free the Israelites from forces that view people as prizes, as commodities to be possessed or traded. The attitude toward the women captured in war, however, presages what eventually becomes of Israel in the book of Judges—their moral deterioration leads to a similar devaluation of women in chapters 17–21.

Jephthah and the Sacrifice of His Daughter (Judges 11:29–40)

The story of Jephthah is like a Greek tragedy. Jephthah begins with nothing, but he works his way into power and wealth by means of his military and negotiating skills. He uses those skills too readily, however, by "negotiating" with God and thereby loses his most prized possession, his daughter.

As the son of a prostitute who is rejected by his half-brothers (11:1–3), Jephthah is denied any claim to inheritance, a key to wealth and financial success in the ancient Near East. Hence the story of Jephthah is similar to the story of Abimelech (Judg. 9) and of David (1 Sam. 16:1–13), who was forced to find wealth and position apart from the resources of the household of the father (David being the youngest of seven sons, thus virtually assured of inheriting nothing). Jephthah gathers around him others who were similarly disadvantaged economically, and they "went raiding," that is, they became essentially mercenaries or guerrilla fighters (again, like David [1 Sam. 22:2], as well as Jeroboam [2 Chr. 13:6–7] and Abimelech [Judg. 9:4]). Eventually Jephthah wins the support of the elders of Gilead, and he then leads them successfully against the Ammonites. He shows himself particularly adept at negotiation. At issue was Israel's possession of traditional Ammonite territory. Jephthah adroitly argues that the Israelites took possession of such territory during the exodus only because the kings who lived there

138

launched unprovoked attacks on them (11:12–28). In response to such unprovoked attacks God gave Israel the land.

But despite Jephthah's successful beginning, his story turns tragic when he makes a vow to enlist God's help in his battle with the Ammonites. Jephthah pledges to sacrifice "whoever comes out of the doors of my house" (11:31). The first one to emerge from the house is his daughter, his only child. Thus Jephthah, who had worked so hard to overcome his lack of inheritance, now has no one to inherit what he has gained.

The story is told largely from the perspective of Jephthah's loss (shaped by Jephthah's need for an heir). As many modern interpreters point out, however, it is important also to focus on the daughter and her loss.

Jephthah's making of a vow in itself is not unusual. Numbers 21:1–3, for example, tells of the Israelites making a vow to God in order to seek God's help in battle. What is unusual is the open-ended nature of Jephthah's vow. The expression, "whoever comes out" could be translated just as accurately "*whatever* comes out." Thus it is possible to speculate that Jephthah assumed a domestic animal would come out of the house. The first floor of houses in this period typically had a central courtyard where domestic animals were kept and a second floor that served as the family's domestic quarters. It was possible that the one "coming out" of the house would be a sheep or goat. But the courtyard was also used for cooking and other domestic chores and would have been a typical workplace for women. Therefore, it should also not be a surprise that Jephthah's daughter emerged first. The openness of the vow again points to the tragic nature of the story. As Judges 12:35 itself shows, Jephthah did not intend to sacrifice his daughter: "When he saw her, he tore his clothes, and said, 'Alas, my daughter! You have brought me very low.'" But by forming the vow the way he did, he bound himself to such an act unintentionally.

The daughter came out specifically to meet her father "with timbrels and with dancing" (11:34a), which would not be unexpected. Women had a particular role as leaders in victory celebrations (see the same expression, "with timbrels and dancing," in Exod. 15:20). When Saul's army returned victorious the women of the villages met them with celebrative songs (1 Sam. 18:6–7). Jephthah in turn lamentably keeps his vow.

The story of Jephthah's daughter has important parallels to Genesis 22:1–19. Jephthah's daughter is called the "only child" (*yĕḥîdâ*; Judg. 11:34), as Isaac is also identified (Gen. 22:2, 12, 16). As Phyllis Trible points out, a voice from heaven directed Abraham not to sacrifice Isaac, but in Judges 11:34–40 God is silent (*Texts of Terror*, 102). The narrator also allows the event to unfold without comment. This has led some to conclude that God and the narrator favor the sacrifice of the daughter. This seems an unfair burden to place on the Judges passage, however, for two reasons. First, the story of the sacrifice of Jephthah's daughter seems not to be about God or God's take on the sacrifice of this child or any child. Rather, the story is about Jephthah and his failure. This is important unless we are to conclude that every passage in the Bible makes some point about who God is or how God acts (or fails to act). Again, the comparison to Greek tragedy is apt. Although Jephthah has all that is necessary to succeed, he has a fatal flaw that finally undoes him and his daughter. Indeed, after working his way into power and wealth by means of military and negotiating skills, Jephthah oversteps his bounds ("negotiating" with God) by making his vow. Trible astutely illuminates this feature of the story. She notes that Jephthah's bargaining words to the elders of Gilead shows that he "uses" God to get power, but he does not really serve God: "If you bring me home again to fight with the Ammonites, and the LORD gives them over to me, I will be your head" (11:9). As Trible notes concerning these words, "the deity who is useful in the bargaining process has no part in the aftermath of victory" (*Texts of Terror*, 95).

In so doing he ensures that his own property, and his name, will not be passed on. The emphasis on his daughter being his "only" child suggests that this point is primary. Also, Jephthah's comment to his daughter when he sees her coming out of his house should be understood in this light ("Alas, my daughter! You have brought me very low; you have become the cause of great trouble to me"; 11:35aβ). His "great trouble" refers to the loss of his progeny. The label of the daughter as the only child is probably due to common ideas about child sacrifice. Where this horrifying practice existed, it was based on the notion that the one who sacrificed a child was giving the very best, the most meaningful thing (the "only"), to the deity (see Levenson, *Death and Resurrection*, 47). In the case of Jephthah, as of Abraham, the sacrifice of the child does not mean the child is not valued. To the contrary, the child is most precious.

Second, the striking parallels between Judges 11 and Genesis 22 might better suggest readings other than one that sees God favoring the sacrifice. It is worth noting that the story ends with the daughter taking initiative: she responds to her father with a request to go for two months with her friends to "bewail" her "virginity" (11:37). After Jephthah granted the request (11:38a), she went (11:38b). When she returns, she gives herself over to the vow (11:39a). Because of the character of the daughter presented briefly here, this story became a paradigm for Jewish and Christian martyrology (see C. Brown, *No Longer Be Silent*, 94). This use of the story was inspired in part by the interpretation of Pseudo-Philo (or *Liber antiquitatum biblicarum*), a Jewish work dating to the first century CE. In Pseudo-Philo the daughter speaks even more. As she does she refers specifically to the sacrifice of Isaac and identifies her own role as a sacrifice (*L.A.B.* 40:2). Hence the daughter is held up as a model of self-sacrifice for the good of the community. Indeed, in these later reflections the daughter symbolizes Jerusalem, which remains precious to God when destroyed by the enemy. In turn, God affirms the daughter, but God criticizes Jephthah and censures him for his vow (see C. Brown, *No Longer Be Silent*, 98–99). This interpretation reads into the account much that is not clearly there. It does follow some hints in the narrative, however, more clearly than the modern, blanket critique of the story. The daughter does appear as an active and ideal character; Jephthah, on the other hand, is a tragic figure who oversteps his bounds in relation to God and suffers a horrible consequence.

To the last point it should be added that the story of Jephthah's daughter presents a complex picture of the role and status of women. The story particularly emphasizes the relationship between father and daughter. But the relationship between the two is not a caricature of father-daughter relations in what is sometimes labeled "patriarchal" social structures. It should be noted, for example, that the centrality of the theme of inheritance implies a higher status for a daughter than might be expected. Only sons were to inherit property (Deut. 21:17), but the inheritance could be passed on to daughters if there were no sons (see the story of the daughters of Zelophehad in Num. 27; 36; Josh. 17:3–8; see also the special case of Job 42:15). Here her role as heir to Jephthah's property provides the crux for the story. The daughter also appears as an actor in the story, not just as a victim of her father's vow. Although she acquiesces to her father's vow, nevertheless she expresses her opinion, makes a request of her father, and creates the ritual that is passed on to the daughters in Israel. In the end the story does not really highlight male privilege or leadership. Rather, it shows Jephthah's weakness and the daughter's faithfulness.

Samson (Judges 13–16)

Samson is a much more ambiguous figure than the judges who went before him. The announcement of his birth is filled with promise that he will be a devout and effective deliverer. Samson's battles with the Philistines shape his "public" life. His life is framed by the Philistine conflict (13:1; 16:23–30) and against them Samson acts to deliverer Israel. Despite the potentially positive value of the Samson story, he also embodies much of what is wrong with Israel in the book of Judges. Samson's career as Israel's deliverer continues the worst impulses of previous judges. Gideon and Jephthah at times were given over to revenge and settling personal vendettas (8:4–9, 13–17; 12:1–6), and Samson is consumed with such acts (14:19; 15:7, 14–17; 16:28–30). Hence Samson's career punctuates the period of decline that is the period of the judges, and it anticipates the complete lawlessness with which the book ends.

Samson's relationship with women is perhaps the most important driving force in the narrative, and his failure in this regard symbolizes Israel's failures on a larger level. Samson sleeps with a prostitute (zônâ; 16:1–3), just as Israel "prostituted" itself with foreign gods (the same root is used in 2:17 and 8:33). In this regard Samson contrasts with Othniel, the first and model judge, in that Othniel married an Israelite woman from a devout family (1:11–15). But Samson has a string of bad relationships with foreign women that lead to his downfall. Specifically, Samson attaches himself to women who have little capacity (or in some cases, opportunity) for faithfulness, to either Samson or his God, and the women's unfaithfulness seems to increase as the story progresses. The best chance Samson has for covenant fidelity is to follow the lead of his mother, who accepts the nazirite requirements for her son even while he is in the womb (Judg. 13:3–7). But instead Samson goes after women who lead him to destruction. The account concludes with the story of Delilah, who betrays Samson into the hands of the Philistines (Judg. 16). As McCann says, "Everyone, including the

142

reader, knows what Delilah is doing, except Samson, who is incredibly and ridiculously clueless" (*Judges*, 24). The result, of course, is that Samson is captured and eventually dies for his reckless behavior, even if his last act is cast as heroic (16:23–31). Although there is no direct comment about the meaning of this tragic humor, it is possible Samson represents Israel in its inability to recognize the source of life. Instead, Israel in Judges continually attaches itself to practices that lead to violence and destruction.

The account of Samson's birth in chapter 13 raises great expectations for him to deliver Israel. The first story of Samson as an adult, however, immediately shatters those expectations. Samson marries a Philistine woman in violation of covenant regulations (Deut. 7:3–4). In route to and during his wedding he breaks one, and possibly two, of his nazirite vows: he eats honey that is unclean because it is from the carcass of a dead animal (Judg. 13:4; 14:9); and his proximity to the vineyards (14:5) and the seven feast days (14:12) may hint that he drank wine as well. Throughout chapters 14 and 15 Samson seeks vindication on the Philistines who have wronged him, thus misusing his physical strength. Despite the selfish motivation of these acts, however, the story still claims that God uses them to bring about Israel's deliverance (14:4).

Samson is born in Zorah, a town on the border between Israelite and Philistine territory. The account in chapters 14–15 turns on issues especially pertinent to residents of such an area. The covenant God established with Israel demanded separation from the people of the land, with particular emphasis on avoidance of marriage contracts with them (2:2; Deut. 7:3–4). Samson's first act is to request his father and mother to arrange a marriage with a Philistine woman at Timnah, another town on the border between Philistine and Judahite territory. Recognizing the covenantal implications, his parents suggest marriage to an Israelite woman. Like many other accounts in Judges, the author here also uses humor by noting the parents' denunciation of the Philistines as uncircumcised (Judg. 14:3) and by portraying Samson as a spoiled brat. Samson insists, "Get her for me, because she pleases me" (v. 3; see v. 2).

Samson's marriage to the woman from Timnah begins a series of relationships with women that mark his own decline and that parallel the decline of Israel throughout the book of Judges. When Samson declares, "she pleases me" (*hî' yāšěrâ bě'ênāy*), the word translated "please" is from the same root as the word translated

143

"what seemed right" in the refrain that structures the final portion of the book, "all the people did what was right in their own eyes" (17:6; 21:25; see parallel words, *hayyāšār bĕʿênāyw*). Samson's declaration for the Philistine wife, therefore, echoes the narrator's judgment on Israel's behavior. As the story of Samson unfolds, it seems the women in his life have less and less capacity to be faithful to him. In each subsequent relationship Samson shows a decreasing capacity for religious faithfulness, just as Israel throughout Judges falls away from God's intentions for them.

A significant feature of Samson's wedding feast is the assignment of thirty Philistine companions for the Israelite groom. This act has potential to bring the Israelites and Philistines together in peace. The attempt to bring the two groups together, however, fails in the end. Samson proposes a riddle, based on his discovery of the honey in the lion's carcass: "Out of the eater came something to eat. Out of the strong came something sweet" (v. 14). The riddle in turn is the center of a wager of sixty garments. When the Philistines cannot solve the riddle, they threaten Samson's wife and her family. She then nags him for the length of the festival until he reveals the solution to the riddle. When she discovers the answer to the riddle and provides it to the thirty Philistines, they give Samson the answer just before their time is up ("before the sun went down," v. 18). Their response is formed as a question, "What is sweeter than honey? What is stronger than a lion?" (v. 18).

Samson gives a poetic response to his companions that is also filled with sexual (and chauvinistic) overtones: "If you had not plowed with my heifer, you would not have found out my riddle" (v. 18). Throughout the Samson story (and throughout much of Judges) women are treated as commodities, as those owned or controlled by men. So here Samson refers to his wife as "my heifer," and his charge that the companions have "plowed" with her may imply that they have used her sexually. Whoever is in control of the woman sexually has the advantage in the narrative. But ironically the women Samson tries to control end up controlling him (note that the wife at Timnah in 14:17 handles Samson, as Delilah does in 16:19). After being bested by the Philistines at Timnah, Samson goes into a rage, attributed again to the spirit of the Lord (v. 19), and kills thirty men at Ashkelon, one of the Philistines' major cities (see Josh. 13:3). Then Samson abandons his wife, an act tantamount to divorce. So her father gives her to Samson's best man. Samson

144

again attacks the Philistines, and the Philistines respond by killing Samson's wife and her father (Judg. 15:6).

Chapter 15 continues the story of Samson's wedding at Timnah with Samson returning to reclaim his wife whom he left earlier. This chapter continues themes in the previous chapter, particularly the picture of women as desirable property used by husbands and fathers (v. 3) and of Samson's hotheaded action. Verses 4–8 tell the first story of Samson's Herculean strength, and verse 6 confirms that he uses it to settle the personal vendetta against the Philistines. When the Philistines bind him and he breaks the ropes, the scene anticipates the Delilah story in which he will twice be bound and break free (16:7–12). But the story of Samson concludes with Samson bound by the Philistines, his strength drained when his hair is cut (16:18–22). His one final act is to kill the Philistines and himself when the Philistines gathered to sacrifice to their god Dagon (16:28–31). The narrator's conclusion simply states that "He had judged Israel twenty years" (16:31; cf. 15:20). Like the time of Jephthah before him (12:7), Samson's period as judge does not bring "rest" to the land, as had the time of previous faithful judges (Othniel, 3:11; Ehud, 3:30; Deborah, 5:31; Gideon, 8:28). Indeed, Samson's actions anticipate a time of severe unrest that comes next in the book and continues until the story of Judges ends.

The Levite's Concubine (Judges 19:1–30)

The story in Judges 19 recounts how a Levite's concubine was wantonly raped and killed during an attack on her family and the family that gives them refuge in the city of Gibeah. While the men of Gibeah are portrayed in the darkest way possible, the most sinister character in the story may be the Levite. After apparently abusing his concubine and thus causing her to leave him, he gets her back only to give her over to the vicious crowd. Later he lies about what happened and incites an intertribal war. The picture of the Levite is subtly drawn. It is thus consistent in style with the rest of Judges, which uses subtlety and irony to portray the condition of Israel when it does not follow its God. As already noted, the Levite's treatment of his concubine and the horrific crime committed against her are part of Judges' portrayal of Israel's downward spiral into violence. The increasing violence toward women symbolizes

145

the more general escalation of violence that leaves Israel completely torn apart by the end of the book (see Lapsley, *Whispering the Word*, 64).

The story begins appropriately with the note, "In those days, . . . there was no king in Israel" (19:1). Although the full summary formula is not present, it is clear that the Levite in the story "did what was right in his own eyes" (see 17:6; 18:1; 21:25). He did not act as though God was king and as though justice and righteousness were the utmost priorities. Indeed, it becomes clear by the end of the narrative that this fellow acts completely out of self-interest and with total disregard for his concubine or his fellow Israelites.

The story centers on the Levite's concubine and the fact that she has left him and returned to her father's house. A concubine is a wife of secondary status, sometimes obtained from an impoverished family as a slave and then designated by the master as his wife (Exod. 21:7–11). While the practice of taking a wife of this type is accepted in the Old Testament, the nature of the marriage seems noteworthy here in light of the role women play in Judges and the way the deterioration of the treatment of women seems emblematic of the larger deterioration of Israelite society. The relationship between the Levite and this wife is identified as different from the way the marriage relationship is otherwise labeled. The designations "man" (*ʾîš*) and "wife" (*ʾiššâ*) reveal a complementarity and, in intention at least, a mutuality in relationship (see Gen. 2:18–25 and the discussion in chap. 1 above). But the Levite treats the concubine in Judges 19 as someone whose interests and well-being are subordinate to his own.

The NRSV translation of verse 2, "his concubine became angry with him [the Levite]," follows two ancient manuscripts, one Latin and one Greek, that suggest the concubine had cause to leave her husband. The Hebrew of the verse, however, uses a verb (*zānâ*) that is usually translated "to prostitute/act the whore" (as NIV translates; see the same verb in Deut. 22:21; Hos. 1:2). This is probably due to the fact that Israelite law had no provisions for a woman to divorce her husband, and thus the concubine's leaving could only be characterized as unfaithfulness. Marriage contracts were male-centered. That the Levite sought to bring the concubine back and that he "spoke tenderly to her," however, might be construed as an indication that he had been abusive or had mistreated her (see the same language in Gen. 34:3, where Shechem tried to get Dinah to

146

marry him after he had raped her). More certainly, it indicates that she has been alienated from him and now he seeks to get her back (see the same language in Isa. 40:2).

Judges 19:4–9 presents an exaggerated display of hospitality as the concubine's father bids the Levite stay as his guest for five days. Hospitality was an important institution that offered protection for sojourners (Exod. 22:21; Lev 19:33–34; Deut. 16:14). It also served as a primary illustration of God's love for Israel, who had been a "stranger" in the land of Egypt (Deut. 10:18–19). The portrait of hospitality here also reveals the male-centered world in which the main benefits of hospitality are shared between men. The concubine is not even part of the conversation. As Jacqueline Lapsley suggests, however, the woman's absence highlights the fact that the Levite is interested only in himself. He seems ready to leave his father-in-law's house without reconciling with his concubine at all; it is only through the constant urging of the father-in-law that the Levite finally takes his concubine with him. The woman's absence from the conversation points further to the moral decay of Israel in general as it is seen in the reduced status of women by the end of Judges (Lapsley, *Whispering the Word*, 41–42).

Verses 10–21 continue the story's focus on hospitality, but now the account turns to the lack of hospitality in the city of Gibeah. The Levite departs his father-in-law's house in Bethlehem at a late hour, so it is necessary to find shelter for the night. He does not want to stop in Jerusalem because it is populated with Jebusites (thus the name Jebus for the city), so he continues on to Gibeah, a city that should welcome the travelers as fellow Israelites. The Levite and his company, however, wait in vain for someone to offer them shelter. Only a resident alien from the hill country of Ephraim (the area to which the Levite is traveling) takes them in.

The next scene (vv. 22–26) echoes the account of Sodom and Gomorrah in Genesis 19. As in the Genesis account, the men of Gibeah surround the house, pound on the door, and demand that the traveler (the Levite) be sent out "that we may have intercourse with him" (v. 22; see Gen. 19:5). "Have intercourse" translates a verb that literally means "to know" (*yādaʿ*), a term used to refer to sexual relations (see Gen. 4:1). The old man responds to the crowd by saying, "Since this man is my guest, do not do this vile thing" (Judg. 19:23). The characterization of their intent to have sex with the Levite as "a vile thing" is probably not a statement about

147

same-sex relations in general (though see Lev. 18:22). Rather, for the men of the city to have intercourse with him would be to treat him as an enemy. By this act they would "feminize" him, just as victorious armies often treated those they defeated as women (see Niditch, *Judges*, 193).

Perhaps the greatest horror in the story, however, regards the action of the Levite who is under attack. As in the Sodom and Gomorrah story (Gen. 19:8), the owner of the house offers his daughters to the crowd, along with the Levite's concubine (19:24). This in itself is an unthinkable injustice that the text itself does not treat (again, the issue of male-centeredness is at play). But the Levite goes further by putting his concubine out to the crowd. Specifically, verse 25 says the Levite "seized" his concubine and put her out. The term translated "seize" (*ḥāzaq*) appears in 2 Samuel 13:14 to denote the force a man exerts over a woman when raping her. Therefore, the text seems to indicate that the Levite is guilty not just of cowardice and lack of compassion, but of the same kind of violence that characterizes the rape itself. As we will observe below, this language appears again when the Levite cuts up the concubine's body (v. 29). His crime is emphasized further by the twofold notice that he stayed in the house until it was light (vv. 26, 27). Then, when he leaves the house and finds his concubine lying with her hands on the threshold, he shows no emotion or remorse. When later asked how the crime occurred, the Levite is disingenuous. He speaks as though he and his concubine were together through the ordeal and as though his life was threatened as well. Indeed, the Levite says, "The lords of Gibeah rose up against me, and surrounded the house at night. They intended to kill me, and they raped my concubine until she died" (20:5).

The scene in 19:27–30 reinforces the image of the Levite just described. The Levite finds his concubine at the door with her hands on the threshold. He commands her to get up. When she does not, he puts her on his donkey and leaves for home. The scene is remarkable in that it does not say whether the woman is dead or alive; the Levite does not express any concern over the matter. His silence is far removed from his "speaking tenderly" to the concubine when he sought to bring her back from her father's house. When he arrives home he takes a knife, cuts up her body, and sends the pieces "throughout all the territory of Israel" (v. 29).

148

The Levite's horrific actions again indict him, and they have significant symbolic importance. Three words in verse 29 are noteworthy in this regard. In order to cut his concubine in pieces, the Levite "grasped" her. The word here again is *ḥāzaq*, the same word that described the Levite taking the woman in order to put her out to the men of Gibeah (19:25). After cutting the concubine in pieces, the verse says he "sent" (*šālaḥ*) her "throughout all the territory of Israel." The word for "sent" was also used in verse 25 to communicate the actions of the mob; after raping the woman they "sent her" (NRSV "they let her go"). Hence the repetition of the word reminds the reader of the crime in Gibeah. As Peggy Kamuf suggests, the Levite "repeats the Benjaminites' crime in order to signify it" ("Author of a Crime," 197). Indeed, the language of seizing and sending connects the Levite's actions with the violent actions of the men of Gibeah and essentially identifies the Levite with them in his guilt over the state of Israel.

The third significant word in verse 29 is *hamma'ăkelet*, "the knife." The word appears only three other times in the Old Testament. One occurrence is Proverbs 30:14, but in this case the term is indefinite; the reference is simply to "knives" ("there are those whose teeth are swords, whose mouths are knives"). In Judges 19:29, however, the knife seems to be one that is known or already identified, even though the story has not mentioned a knife to this point. The only other text that has this word also includes the definite article, "the knife"; the passage is Genesis 22 (vv. 6 and 10). The possible connection between these two texts is intriguing because both involve the presence of a knife for the purpose of killing or cutting a human being into pieces. In Genesis 22 Abraham is willing to use the knife to sacrifice his son because of his extreme devotion to God. In Judges 19, however, the Levite uses the knife to dismember his concubine out of sheer self-interest.

The conclusion to Judges 19 seems to give a final judgment on the Levite's cowardly and violent action, but there is some confusion as to who is actually speaking the words. The NRSV follows the Greek version and places the last words of verse 30 in the mouth of the Levite: "Then he [the Levite] commanded the men whom he sent, saying, 'Thus you shall say to all the Israelites, "Has such a thing ever happened since the day the Israelites came up from the land of Egypt until this day? Consider it, and take counsel, and

149

speak out.""" In this reading of verse 30 "such a thing" refers to the rape of the concubine. The Masoretic Text, however, seems to read the words quite differently. It introduces the quote with the words, "all who saw [it] said." Thus the quote is placed in the mouth of those who received the pieces of the concubine's body, and "such a thing" seems to refer to the Levite's act of desecrating the body by cutting it into pieces (see Lapsley, *Whispering the Word*, 50). Those who "saw" the dismembered body do not know the story behind it, but they react to the sight with horror. In the Masoretic Text's reading, the final words ("Consider it, take counsel, and speak out") also take on different meaning. Instead of communicating the Levite's injunction to respond to the rape of the concubine (as in the Greek version), the last statement now speaks against the Levite. In fact, this final line seems to make most sense as the words of the narrator, who now gives a final judgment against the Levite, not against the residents of Gibeah.

Civil War and the Lying Levite (Judges 20–21)

As the book of Judges nears its end it is clear that the Israelites have moved far from the ideals of life in the land with which the book began. Judges started with an account of the Israelite tribes attempting to secure the territory God had given them, but it ends with the Israelites fighting one another. The Israelite tribes begin a civil war over the death of the Levite's concubine. Judges 20:1–2 emphasizes that "all" Israel came together to inquire about what happened to the woman. In reality not all the tribes are present, and the ones who gather at Mizpah will attempt to annihilate the one tribe (Benjamin) that is absent.

The Levite's testimony (20:4–7) is correct in labeling the rape of the concubine as a "vile outrage" (v. 6), but several features of his testimony are less than honest. He reports that the "lords of Gibeah" rose against him (20:5), but the account indicates the perpetrators were a perverse group in the city (19:22), not necessarily the city's leaders. The Levite also says the men of the city intended to kill him (20:5). Judges 19:22, however, only says they wanted to have intercourse with him. He also does not report that he "seized" his concubine and put her out to the crowd (19:25), which, as already noted, implicates the Levite in the rape as well as the men

150

of Gibeah. By distorting the story in these ways the Levite creates a conflict between the tribe of Benjamin and the other Israelite tribes that diverts attention from his own guilt.

This description of the action as a "vile outrage" may suggest that the rape of the Levite's concubine and his subsequent act of cutting her in pieces has symbolic dimensions that deserve attention. The word translated "vile" (*nĕbālâ*), which also appears in 19:23, typically refers to action that goes directly against divine intentions. Thus the man Nabal in 1 Samuel 25 is so named because he returns David's peaceful overtures with rebuke; in the story he turns aside the one God has chosen and therefore opposes God's plan for Israel. In Judges 19 and 20 the most shocking "vile" act is the Levite's dismemberment of the concubine (see Olson, "Book of Judges," 878). In light of the Levite's misleading testimony about what happened in Gibeah it is hard not to read his description of a vile act as an ironic indictment of his own action. The possible symbolism then might involve both the Levite and Israel. The woman's body might well represent Israel, cut into pieces because of the Levite's false testimony. It is also interesting that the Levite is not named but identified only by his tribe. Does he represent the religious establishment and its failure to lead Israel in the right way but instead leads the people into violence and bloodshed?

Those who hear the Levite's carefully edited story respond with what is perhaps an unknowing distortion of justice. The law of Moses stipulates that punishment of a crime should be proportional, "an eye for an eye" (Exod. 21:24). This means that more than "an eye for an eye, a tooth for a tooth," is a miscarriage of justice. The Israelite tribes, however, respond to the rape and death of the Levite's concubine by destroying the entire city of Gibeah (Judg. 20:37).

The book of Judges ends with the Israelite tribes attempting to reconcile with the tribe of Benjamin, but the effort at peace shows what a mess Israel has become. The tribe of Benjamin is cut off from the other tribes and threatened with extinction since no one will give their daughters as wives to the Benjaminites (21:7). The people weep over Benjamin's fate (21:2). In a society that is based on kinship and that assumes stable families and male heirs are necessary for survival, the absence of potential wives is indeed something to weep over. But the solutions the other tribes propose lead to more violence against women like the violence done to the

151

Levite's concubine. The final chapter portrays Israel's trafficking in women to benefit Benjamin (vv. 12, 14) and Benjamin's wife stealing to ensure a future for itself (vv. 20–23).

Although the text does not outwardly condemn these practices, the treatment of women in this chapter and in the final section of Judges (chaps. 19–21) is a clear sign of Israel's deterioration. At the beginning of the book women like Achsah are held in high honor, they take initiative, and they effect positive change (1:13–15). Deborah successfully liberates Israel from its foes (chaps. 4–5). But by the end of the book women are reduced to chattel, commodities traded, stolen, and abused. The final verse of the book ("there was no king in Israel"; 21:25) might be read rightly as an ironic statement about Israel's failure to recognize God's rule over God's people.

CHAPTER 6

Seeking Vengeance, Part I

Prophetic Speech and Action

In previous chapters I have emphasized that God engages in violence in order to counter and correct human violence. I have also
said that God acts destructively in order to restore or preserve the
order God intends; that means, then, that such activity is God's
exclusive prerogative. Human violence is rendered inappropriate.
In this way of thinking I have also noted a particular understanding of enemies: the enemies in many texts are primarily symbols of
larger forces of evil. Though they may have an historical identity,
that identity does not seem to be primary. The pharaoh of Exodus
represents the larger forces of evil, as evinced by the fact that he is
never named in the account. In a different but equally significant
symbolic portrayal, the Canaanites of the conquest story, who were
not a social or political entity at all at the time of the writing of the
account, represent temptations to impure worship and devotion to
strange gods.

Despite the frequent emblematic role of enemies in the Bible,
however, there are texts that clearly present enemies for whom
the historical identity is primary. Moreover, in some of these texts
God's people seek vengeance. Even if vengeance comes only
through speech—prophetic prediction of the enemies' destruction
or prayers that the enemies come to an end—it raises a question of
the violent intentions of that speech. In this chapter I address three
types of material that pose this problem: (1) narratives that present

153

the prophets Elijah and Elisha killing their enemies either directly or by supporting bloody rebellion; (2) prophetic indictments of foreign nations; and (3) predictions of and calls for final judgment against the ungodly.

In order to address this material we should consider three important points and perspectives:

1. In the passages treated here the enemies spoken or acted against are all characterized by their arrogance in relation to God and their cruel abuse of other people. The enemies exalt themselves, believing they act independent of God's control of the world. As the introduction noted, this stance in relation to God is the root of violence. Therefore when the people of God call for the destruction of such an enemy they are aligning themselves with God's order and against evil.

2. The first point is reinforced by the language often used to describe the enemy. The enemies and their victims are described in terms that name their status vis-à-vis God. The predominant biblical word for those who vaunt themselves to the place of God is "wicked"; those they abuse are often called "righteous." The latter word does not denote moral purity in an absolute sense. Rather, it is a relational term, suggesting their reliance on God's protection from "the wicked."

This language is most prominent in the Psalms, which will be treated in more detail in the next chapter. The prophets, however, also use these terms to refer to the enemies of Israel and Judah. Habakkuk uses the term "wicked" to describe the Babylonian army that has surrounded Judah, and the prophet in turn calls Judah "righteous" (Hab. 1:4b). This does not mean that Judah is blameless. It does indicate, however, that Judah is a victim of an enemy that vaunts itself into the place of God.

3. The most difficult question in this discussion regards the direct involvement of the people of God in violent conflict, with Elijah and Elisha being the key examples. Their actions are troubling because they are so tangible; according to the narratives, they kill people. We will observe some ambiguity in the texts about how these two prophets conduct themselves. Nevertheless, their violent rhetoric and action is most often directed against those who abuse their power, especially the royal circle and the false prophets in its employ. In those stories and elsewhere we shall observe such abuse manifested in (a) military might used to terrorize and oppress,

154

(b) economic injustice, and (c) slander and other verbal attacks. Each of these abuses is violence. The continuing question is how the people of God should address and confront it.

Practicing Vengeance: Elijah and Elisha

The prophet Elijah and his successor, Elisha, present a special problem. These two prophets take vengeance into their own hands, thus creating the problem of how the people of God and their leaders participate in God's justice.

Elijah's name means "Yah[weh] is my God," and this indeed characterizes him entirely. As Sylvester Burnham said long ago, "The consciousness that Jehovah was his God, that he stood before Jehovah, gave content to this character and form to his life" ("Mission and Work of Elijah," 180). But this singular devotion to the Lord leads Elijah and Elisha to kill many of those not devoted to the same God. In this way, these two are much like Phinehas. Indeed, the first-century CE Jewish text of Pseudo-Philo identifies Elijah closely with Phinehas (see *L.A.B.* 48:1), the fiery priest who stamped out the worship of other gods by killing the devotees of those gods (Num. 25:1–9). Hence the figures of Elijah and Elisha raise the problem of zealous religious commitment that prompts the devotee to violence.

The narratives in 1 Kings 17–2 Kings 13 present a wide range of actions by Elijah and Elisha characterized by the death of those who oppose them. The story of Elijah begins with the contest between Yahweh and Baal on Mount Carmel (1 Kgs. 18). After the Lord delivers fire from heaven to consume the sacrifice on the altar, which Baal could not match, Elijah orders, "Seize the prophets of Baal; do not let one of them escape." The text then reports, "They seized them; and Elijah brought them down to the Wadi Kishon, and killed them there" (18:40). As the story continues, Elijah participates in the overthrow and death of Ahab with his prophecy of Ahab's violent death, a death that comes in response to the king taking Naboth's vineyard: "Thus says the LORD: 'In the place where the dogs licked up the blood of Naboth, dogs will also lick up your blood'" (1 Kgs. 21:19). The prophet also predicts a similar fate for Ahab's wife Jezebel: "The dogs shall also eat Jezebel within the bounds of Jezreel" (21:23; see also v. 24). In Elijah's

155

last act, just before ascending to heaven, he called down fire from heaven on representatives from King Ahaziah, who succeeded Ahab (2 Kgs. 1). Elisha similarly foments violent rebellion against the ruling house in Israel by supporting the bloody revolt of Jehu. During this event Jezebel is thrown from her window and her body eaten by dogs, as Elijah had earlier predicted (2 Kgs. 9:30–37). Perhaps the most shocking act of Elisha, however, is 2:23–25. As Elisha walked toward Bethel, some boys taunted him by calling him "bald-head" (v. 23). So Elisha cursed them, and two she-bears came out of the woods and mauled forty-two of the boys.

The perspective of the storyteller is that these two prophets are battling an alien, evil force. People in the narratives are divided, therefore, by whether they stand with Elijah and Elisha or against them. The prophets of Baal are minions of Jezebel. Jezebel is a foreigner who brings this worship with her from Tyre when she marries Ahab. Therefore, the contest between Yahweh and Baal, represented by their respective prophets, is a contest to determine the real Lord of heaven and earth. Much is at stake for Israel's faith. Moreover, the story presents Jezebel as a murderous woman, the quintessential enemy of the Lord and his prophets. She threatens to take Elijah's life or die trying (1 Kgs. 19:2), which sends Elijah into hiding. She plots against Naboth, whose vineyard she desires. She has him killed and possesses the vineyard (21:1–16).

But the question naturally arises as to the necessity of Elijah's execution of the prophets of Baal. Phyllis Trible makes the provocative suggestion that the Elijah story only favors Elijah because it is told by an Israelite worshiper of Yahweh. Had someone favorable to Jezebel composed the narrative the author would have surely indicted Elijah for the same crimes as the queen. Trible says, "In a pro-Jezebel setting Elijah would be censured for murdering prophets, for imposing his theology on the kingdom, for inciting kings to do his bidding, and for stirring up trouble in the land" ("Exegesis for Storytellers," 17). Whether this is true or not, Elijah's killing of the prophets of Baal does raise questions about the measures the prophet took to preserve the Israelite faith.

Critique of Elijah and Elisha within the Bible

Despite the difficulties the stories of Elijah and Elisha pose, there are indications within some of the narratives themselves, and certainly in the larger biblical canon, that the behavior of these two prophets is not fully accepted. We examine now three such signs of disapproval, signs that those who wrote or compiled the stories were uncomfortable with the violent action of the men of God.

Obadiah as Counterexample

The violent nature of Elijah's actions stands out when Elijah is compared with Obadiah, whom Elijah meets in 1 Kings 18. After Elijah pronounced, "there shall be neither dew nor rain these years, except by my word" (17:1), and after three years of drought, Elijah went to meet Ahab with Obadiah, who was "in charge of the palace" (18:3). Verses 3b–4 then give a parenthetical commentary on Obadiah that indicates his supreme piety: "Now Obadiah revered the LORD greatly; when Jezebel was killing off the prophets of the LORD, Obadiah took a hundred prophets, hid them fifty to a cave, and provided them with bread and water." When Obadiah meets Elijah, Elijah asks Obadiah to announce him to Ahab. Obadiah thinks this will now put him in jeopardy because Elijah will be carried off by the spirit of God as he had been the past three years (v. 12). When Obadiah expresses his fear to Elijah, he does so largely by telling him of all the efforts he has made to keep alive the prophets of the Lord, a fact he assumes Elijah already knows (v. 13). These two devotees of Yahweh stand in marked contrast: Obadiah reveres the Lord, but serves the king and engages in no violent revolt; Elijah passionately defends the faith to the point that he must live in secret and eventually engage in war with Ahab and Jezebel.

The account and description of Obadiah is particularly important when 1 Kings 19 is considered. This chapter reports that Jezebel threatens Elijah, and Elijah flees to the wilderness. When he comes to Mount Horeb he twice complains, "I have been very zealous for the LORD, the God of hosts; for the Israelites have forsaken your covenant, thrown down your altars, and killed your prophets with the sword. I alone am left, and they are seeking my life to take it away" (vv. 10, 14). Elijah's answer seems at odds with Obadiah's earlier testimony that he in fact hid one hundred prophets of Yahweh in caves and fed them (18:13). It is possible that 18:3–16 is a later addition to the story and that originally the word of God to Elijah to present himself to Ahab (18:1–2) was followed immediately

157

by their meeting (v. 17). If that is how the passage developed, however, the question arises as to why an editor would introduce such tension in the story. Was the editor trying to question Elijah's violent act by presenting an alternative in the person of Obadiah? Whether or not this is the case, the story in its present form does present such a contrast.

Hosea's Denunciation of the "Blood of Jezreel"

If the story of Obadiah in 1 Kings 18 offers a critique of the destructive actions of Elijah, the criticism is quite subtle. The prophet Hosea, however, gives a direct rejection of the similar actions of Elisha. Although Hosea does not mention Elisha specifically, he pronounces judgment on Jehu's bloody coup that Elisha supported. God directs Hosea concerning the first child his wife Gomer bore: "Name him Jezreel, for in a little while I will punish the house of Jehu for the blood of Jezreel, and I will put an end to the kingdom of the house of Israel" (Hos. 1:4).

In 2 Kings 9 Elisha directs a member of the company of prophets to anoint Jehu king over Israel. In so doing he foments rebellion and essentially commits treason. The rest of chapter 9 and chapter 10 narrate a series of bloody acts that take place in Jezreel. First, Jehu pierces Joram's shoulders with an arrow and he dies on the plot of ground once owned by Naboth (9:25). Jehu identifies Naboth as "the Jezreelite." Then Jehu comes to Jezreel, to the home of Jezebel, and orders that she be thrown down from the window, and two eunuchs do just that (9:33). In chapter 10 Jehu massacres the descendants of Ahab and slaughters the worshipers of Baal. In these stories the emphasis on the location in Jezreel is obvious (Jehu sent "to the rulers of Jezreel"; 10:1).

From the perspective of the zealous Elisha, these killings amounted to a purging of the land of an oppressive king who worshiped strange gods. But Hosea suggests that God expects something different from the one who would be king. Indeed, he implies that God rejected Jehu's violent acts as unworthy of divine sanction. As Hans Walter Wolff rightly says, "A monarchy in Israel that bases its power upon bloodletting can expect only a 'No' from Yahweh" (*Hosea*, 18). Moreover, Hosea does more than reject Jehu's violence as inhumane or unjust. He characterizes it as an act of "whoredom," as unfaithfulness to the Lord that pollutes the land (1:2).

158

Jesus Rejects Violent Practices of Elijah: Luke 9:51–56

Although Jesus in many ways appears as the new Elijah, at least one New Testament text suggests Jesus rejected Elijah's treatment of enemies. Luke 9:51–56 briefly but powerfully describes how a Samaritan village rejected Jesus, and Jesus' disciples considered calling down fire from heaven, but Jesus "turned and rebuked them" (v. 55). Here Luke alludes to 2 Kings 1:9–12, in which Elijah called down fire from heaven upon his enemies. Jesus seems clearly to repudiate Elijah's actions.

The parallels between 2 Kings 1:9–12 and Luke 9:51–55 are unmistakable, particularly when one compares the Greek version of the 2 Kings story to Luke's account of Jesus and his disciples being turned away from the Samaritan village. When the disciples ask Jesus, "Lord, do you want us to command fire to come down from heaven and consume them?" they are citing the Greek version of 2 Kings 1:10 and 12 almost word for word. The expressions "call down fire" (*pyr katabēnai*) in Luke 9:54 is nearly the same as the expression "let fire come down" (*katabēsetai pyr*) in 2 Kings 1:10 and 12. The words "out of heaven and consume them" are identical in the two stories. Some ancient manuscripts make the link between Jesus and Elijah even more explicit. When Jesus' disciples ask, "Lord, do you want us to command fire to come down from heaven and consume them?" some manuscripts add, "as Elijah did" (v. 54). These manuscripts further add to verses 55 and 56 the words, "You do not know what spirit you are of, for the Son of Man has not come to destroy the lives of human beings but to save them" (see NRSV margin; Brodie, "Departure for Jerusalem"). Thus the story in Luke 9:51–56 must be read in some sense as a reaction to the account of Elijah calling down fire on his enemies.

By rejecting the violent reaction against the Samaritan village, Jesus in Luke 9 is in line with the *Testament of Abraham*, an apocryphal work that dates to the first century CE. In this document Abraham is taking a tour of the earth and observes numerous unrighteous acts. Each time he observes such acts he calls for disaster to strike the perpetrators. One such disaster is fire coming down from heaven, an act patterned after 2 Kings 1. But finally God speaks to the angel Michael and commands him to stop Abraham. Abraham has not sinned, God says, and therefore he does not have compassion for sinners. But, God declares, "I made the world

159

nd I do not wish to destroy any of them" (*Testament of Abraham*); see Allison, "Rejecting Violent Judgment," 464–66). Thus this document, like the passage in Luke 9, seems to reject Elijah's action as a response to enemies. God desires reconciliation and waits for repentance.

Can the Elijah/Elisha Stories Be Redeemed?

Considering Genre

If the Elijah and Elisha stories are to be read as integral parts of Scripture, as they traditionally have been, it may be helpful to consider the genre or literary type into which most of these stories fit. Consideration of genre is important because it requires some account of how these stories likely functioned when they were told. Who would have listened to such stories and why they would have listened are key questions.

Most of the stories in the Elijah/Elisha cycle must be categorized as legend. Their original purpose was to focus attention "on wonderful attributes and miraculous action of God and his prophet" (Long, *1 Kings*, 181). The category of legend may be defined more narrowly as *prophetic* legend since the stories seem intended to teach proper attitudes toward the prophet, who is often called "the man of God" (*ʾîš hāʾĕlōhîm*). The stories of Elijah and Elisha thus are a particular kind of story that features a particular type of person. The label "man of God" deserves some attention in this regard.

As David Petersen points out, the label "man of God" in these stories denotes a "holy man," a type of person who possessed the power of the holy and thus could be dangerous (*Prophetic Literature*, 6). The term "holy" here refers to that realm separate from the profane world that requires great care when approaching or engaging. For many modern people the distinction is virtually nonexistent. But for those in the biblical world the holy was real and threatening. Stories of the ominous presence of God on Mount Horeb (Exod. 19:16–25) and accounts of the ark of God killing those who touch it improperly (2 Sam. 6:6–11; see 1 Sam. 5) illustrate the power of the holy. As Erhard Gerstenberger puts it, holiness "is a sphere of power and purity unique to God" that is "energy-laden to the highest degree" (*Leviticus*, 282). The stories of Elijah and

160

Elisha portray these prophets as persons especially endowed wit'
the power of the holy.

With this understanding of the nature of Elijah and Elisha, the
legends about them that appear so troubling to modern people are
more understandable. Because these two are holy men in the sense
just described, the stories often have to do with their power over
life and death. This is evident in the story of Naaman, the Syrian
general who sought out Elisha for healing from leprosy. Naaman's
servant girl urges him to travel to Israel and find the prophet.
Instead, he first sends word to King Ahab that he is coming for
healing. Ahab replies, "Am I God, to give life or death?" (2 Kgs.
5:7). Elisha is the one sought for life and healing, not the king.

One point of the Elijah and Elisha stories is that those who
have contact with the holy man must approach him properly.
Hence the brief account of the boys who taunt Elisha illustrates
what happens to those who bother a holy man: they end up dead!
On the positive side, however, Elijah and Elisha use their power
as holy men to preserve the lives of poor widows (1 Kgs. 17:8–16;
2 Kgs. 4:1–7). Because they have power over life and death they
bring to life children who have died (1 Kgs. 17:17–24; 2 Kgs. 4:32–
36). The conclusion of the account of Elijah raising the widow's
son at Zarephath reports the woman affirms Elijah's identity, "Now
I know that you are a man of God" (1 Kgs. 17:24). Although this
understanding of Elijah and Elisha as bearers of the holy does not
remove the offense of accounts like 2 Kings 2:23–24 completely, it
does cast them in a different light. Such accounts were not likely
told to present model behavior; they do not inculcate any particular
action against enemies or against taunting boys. Rather, the stories
testify to the power of God, the holy otherness of God experienced
in people like Elijah and Elisha. If they have any lesson to teach, it
is to approach the holy—whether a place or a person—with great
care, humility, and respect.

Elijah and Elisha as Champions of the Poor

Jesus' rejection of Elijah's calling down fire from heaven is a repudiation of an act described in a story that is now, in the New Testament, read out of its original context. This is appropriate as a
general response to treatment of enemies. But it is important to
understand why the stories of Elijah and Elisha were preserved. In

161

their earliest writing, these stories were probably knit together in part to support Jehu's rebellion against the Omride dynasty (Ahab and Jezebel; see 2 Kgs. 9–10). This use of the stories must have made an important theological point: Omri and his son Ahab went outside the communities of Yahweh worshipers and gained support from the worshipers of Baal (1 Kgs. 16:31–34). Thus they compromised religious identity and values because it seemed politically expedient to do so. But many of the Elijah/Elisha stories seem to have another purpose, namely, to support the peasants—particularly widows—who had a subsistence living at the bottom of society during the Omride dynasty. For them, Elijah and Elisha were powerful figures who championed their cause and stood for justice.

The Place of Elijah and Elisha in Christian Faith

What place do characters like Elijah and Elisha have in the life and faith of Christians? Although some of the actions of these two figures are certainly troubling, they continue to have a central place for good reason. They are helpful figures for those who are on the edge of life, who are threatened by death, poverty, and oppression. To such persons in the ninth century BCE Elijah and Elisha offered the power of God that could sustain life, and that could also take life from corrupt but powerful rulers like Ahab and Jezebel. These two prophets essentially offered to the widows and other peasants of their day a protection similar to that associated with St. Jude, the saint of desperate causes. Jude's reputation grows out of the book that bears his name. He speaks of holding fast to faith in the one "who is able to keep you from falling" (Jude 24). But at the same time Jude also promises that those who threaten the faith and the faithful will "go the way of Cain" (Jude 11). Elijah and Elisha embody the promise that God will judge the earth and that God has power over the ungodly.

Perhaps Elijah and Elisha are not to be invoked in all times and seasons. Nevertheless, there are times and seasons when the ominous presence of such persons is needed. This is undoubtedly why a tradition developed concerning Elijah that he would come to the aid of a righteous sufferer who called on him. There is indeed a God who judges on earth, the psalmist says (Ps. 58:11[12 Heb.]). The tradition of Elijah and Elisha continues as testimony to that truth, a truth that God is present and will act for the righteous when

162

they are in dire straits. As the pseudepigraphical book the *Apocalypse of Elijah* declares, the prophet will return to battle those who oppose God (4.7).

Proclaiming Vengeance: Oracles against Foreign Nations

One of the clearest examples of the Bible speaking against and calling for the destruction of the powerful for their abuse of the weak is in the prophetic oracles against foreign nations. Each book of the Major Prophets speaks at length against foreign powers (Isa. 13–23; Jer. 46–51; Ezek. 25–32). In the Minor Prophets Habakkuk (2:5–19) and Zephaniah (2:4–15) contain such oracles. Amos 1–2 is dominated by this type of material, and the books of Nahum and Obadiah speak against foreign nations in their entirety.

The oracles against foreign nations proclaim God's impending punishment of nations around Israel and Judah. The historical circumstances that prompted these oracles in each case seem to be the suffering of God's chosen people at the hands of the ones to be punished. At least three features of these judgment passages may cause concern by the way they present God destroying Israel's enemies.

1. God often appears as a warrior who fights against these nations, and thus God appears as one directly engaged in fighting and killing. For example, Isaiah 13:4b declares, "The LORD of hosts is mustering an army for battle. They come from a distant land, from the end of the heavens, the LORD and the weapons of his indignation, to destroy the whole earth." We dealt with the notion of God as warrior in chapter 2, noting that this image is closely associated with the notion that God establishes justice in the earth. We will observe a similar theme in the case of the oracles against foreign nations. But other problems appear as well.

2. The oracles against the nations sometimes seem to operate on the assumption that God punishes the enemies of God's people simply because they are the enemies of Israel and Judah; the nations did not recognize the special place God's people play in the world. Ezekiel's oracle against Moab says this directly: "Thus says the Lord GOD: Because Moab said, 'The house of Judah is like all the other nations, therefore I will lay open the flank of Moab

163

from the towns on its frontier'" (Ezek. 25:8–9a). This may seem like crass favoritism, the worst of what many associate with the complex theological notion of election (see Kaminsky, "Did Election Imply Mistreatment?").

3. Finally, and related to the second point, the oracles against foreign nations have scattered through them promises that God's people will be restored; thus the oracles against the nations are essentially salvation oracles for Israel and Judah. For example, after an oracle against Babylon (Isa. 13), Isaiah 14:1 begins, "But the LORD will have compassion on Jacob and will again choose Israel, and will set them in their own land." The passage continues with the promise that the tables will turn, that "the house of Israel will possess the nations" (v. 2). This raises the question, are the oracles against foreign nations simply declarations that Israel and Judah will be empowered by God to do to the nations what the nations did to them?

Although the oracles against foreign nations do raise difficult questions, they have features that will not allow a narrow reading of them as proclamations of revenge on Israel's enemies. Several points are important in this regard. It should be noted, for example, that the overarching indictment of the nations is not that they defeated and devastated Israel and Judah, but that they acted arrogantly by assuming they had control over the world, control that belongs only to God. Indeed, these nations are often presented as instruments God intended to use to accomplish God's purpose. The nations assume, however, that they are autonomous and defeat other peoples by their own power. As Fretheim says, "God acts in Israel and in the world in and through agents," but "God's agents of judgment commonly exceed their mandate" ("I Was Only," 365).

This theme of the arrogance of the nations runs through most of the oracles in question here. Isaiah 13:11 declares in the oracle against Babylon, "I will punish the world for its evil, and the wicked for their iniquity; I will put an end to the pride of the arrogant, and lay low the insolence of tyrants" (see further 14:4b, "How the oppressor has ceased! How his insolence has ceased"). Jeremiah satirizes the overconfidence of Egypt by comparing the Egyptian army to the mighty Nile: "Who is this, rising like the Nile, like rivers whose waters surge? Egypt rises like the Nile, like rivers whose waters surge. It said, Let me rise, let me cover the earth, let me destroy cities and their inhabitants" (Jer. 46:7–8). Similarly, Ezekiel

indicts the prince of Tyre for thinking himself divine: "Because yo
heart is proud and you have said, 'I am a god; I sit in the seat of t
gods, in the heart of the seas,' yet you are but a mortal, and no gc
though you compare your mind with the mind of a god" (Ezek.
28:2).

On this indictment of the nations turns a crucial point about
violence: humans who assume the place of God inevitably act violently in order to exercise and maintain their control. Thus one general conviction behind the oracles against foreign nations is that
God acts against these nations to correct their violence, not to perpetrate more violence (see Fretheim, "I Was Only," 371).

Another important point about the oracles against foreign
nations is that they neither completely exclude Israel and Judah
from judgment nor do they universally condemn the foreign nations.
As the discussion below will show, Amos 1–2 uses the indictment
against foreign nations primarily as a foil for proclamation against
Israel and Judah. Moreover, all the oracles against the nations
except the books of Nahum and Obadiah (books that are, from start
to finish, proclamations of judgment against foreign nations) are set
in the larger context of God's judgment on Israel. Hence the oracles
against foreign nations are part of the larger message about God's
attempt to correct all peoples, to realign all humanity according to
the divine vision for the world.

Just as the oracles against foreign nations are part of the larger
picture of God's judgment, these passages also include the nations
in the larger picture of God's grace. Isaiah 13–23 illustrates the
point best. Isaiah's oracle against Assyria predictably declares "I will
break the Assyrian in my land, and on my mountains trample him
under foot" (14:25a). But 19:18–25 promises that Assyria, along
with Egypt, will be joined with Israel, all counted as the people of
God: "On that day Israel will be the third with Egypt and Assyria,
a blessing in the midst of the earth, whom the LORD of hosts has
blessed, saying, 'Blessed be Egypt my people, and Assyria the work
of my hands, and Israel my heritage'" (19:24–25).

Perhaps the most memorable claim, however, comes a few
verses earlier when God explains the reason the Egyptians suffered
judgment. Verse 22 declares, "The LORD will strike Egypt, *striking
and healing*, and they will return to the LORD, and he will listen to
their supplications and heal them." In other words, God punishes
Egypt in order to restore the Egyptians to the purpose God had for

165

them. God does not strike Egypt because Egypt is Israel's enemy and God favors Israel. Rather, God strikes Egypt because Egypt is God's creation just as Israel is. Particularly interesting is that the Hebrew word translated "strike" (*nāgap*) appears numerous times in the plague stories in Exodus (8:2 [7:27 Heb.]). This includes God's declaration to kill the firstborn of all Egyptian households in the final plague: "For the Lord will pass through to strike down the Egyptians" (12:23). Although the intended significance of this language shared between Isaiah's oracle and the Exodus narrative is not certain, it raises the interesting possibility that even in God's striking Egypt to rescue Israel from slavery God was also working to rescue Egypt from its own sinfulness. Isaiah declares that God's attack on Egypt was not so much divine violence and destruction aimed at a foreign enemy as it was God's attempt to restore Egypt to fellowship with its maker.

To be sure, this kind of inclusion of foreigners does not appear in all the oracles against the nations. Jeremiah 46–51 includes no such offer of grace to Israel's enemies. In that case, the oracles against foreign nations end with a promise that Babylon will be "leveled to the ground" (51:58a). Nevertheless, when one considers the larger context of these oracles, it is clear that they are part of a much more comprehensive message about God's sovereignty and justice that also includes God's compassion. Some particular examples will help fill out this picture.

Amos 1:3–2:3

The earliest example of a collection of oracles against foreign nations is in Amos 1:3–2:3. These oracles are interesting for two reasons. First, they share with similar oracles in Isaiah and Jeremiah the concern for misconduct in war. Amos is unique, however, in that he indicts the nations for their misconduct in general, not just for their mistreatment of Israel and Judah. Amos 2:1, for example, points to Moab's crime of burning "to lime the bones of the king of Edom." Amos seems to indict the nations in each case for violating recognized international standards that are based on what might be called natural law (see Barton, *Understanding Old Testament Ethics*, 77–129). Thus Amos shows awareness of rules of engagement that are widely accepted by ancient Near Eastern peoples. But more importantly, that Amos embraces such international

166

standards suggests that the prophet saw the conduct of war under certain guidelines as a crucial theological matter. Certain ethical standards in war were extended to the nations as a reflection of the fact that the Lord's sovereignty was also extended to them (see Mays, *Amos*, 27–28).

Second, the crimes of the nations in Amos 1–2 are not ultimately the focus of Amos's attention. Rather, Amos uses the issue of war crimes to raise another issue closer to home: the treatment of the poor. By setting the plight of the poor in the context of oracles against nations that waged war with excessive force and cruelty, Amos essentially raised the problem of economic injustice in Israel to the status of war crimes committed by Israel's neighbors. Thus we see in Amos 1–2 a dual concern for the violence of war and the violence of social inequity, with the accent on the latter.

Amos communicates this message by means of a repeated formula. Each oracle begins, "For three transgressions of . . . and for four, I will not revoke the punishment" (1:3, 6, 9, 11, 13; 2:1, 4, 6). The name of the nation and the specific crime changes each time, but from 1:3 through 2:3 the oracles focus on the horrors of war. Indeed, this section is a litany of cruel acts: Damascus "threshed Gilead with threshing sledges of iron" (1:3b); Edom "pursued his brother with the sword and cast off all pity" (1:11b); the Ammonites "ripped open pregnant women in Gilead" (1:13b). The nature of the indictment changes, however, in the oracles against Judah (2:4–5) and Israel (2:6–8). The oracle against Judah is very general and thus out of character with the rest. That in part has led scholars to conclude that 2:4–6 was added later to update the collection of Amos's oracles for an audience in Judah that inherited the prophecy when the northern kingdom fell in 721 BCE (note that the oracles against Tyre and Edom are very similar in form to the oracle against Judah and may also be secondary, but Tyre and Edom are specifically accused of war crimes, while Judah is not). The oracle against Israel, however, is quite specific:

> They sell the righteous for silver,
>> and the needy for a pair of sandals—
> they who trample the head of the poor into the dust of the earth,
>> and push the afflicted out of the way;
> father and son go in to the same girl,
>> so that my holy name is profaned;

167

> they lay themselves down beside every altar
>> on garments taken in pledge;
> and in the house of their God they drink
>> wine bought with fines they imposed.
>
> (2:6–8)

Here Amos raises what was for him the greatest problem, the failure of "justice" (*mišpāṭ*). Amos uses this term without explanation. Several times, however, he places it in parallel with the word "righteousness" (*ṣedeq* or *ṣĕdāqâ*). The combination of the two words indicates that justice was not defined primarily by whether things accorded with laws established by the king, but by whether social relationships fulfilled God's intentions for human society. Laws could be manipulated by people with power and wealth. When the prophets speak of justice they refer to a practice of law that "requires righteous people for whom the social well-being of others is a higher priority than gain" (Mays, "Justice," 14). In other words, justice was the opposite of violence.

A key problem that is reflected in Amos 2:6–8 was the acquisition of land as capital. Land was essential for each Israelite, both practically, to produce food and graze herds, and theologically, as a sign of having been rescued by God in Egypt. The land was a gift from God to people who had once been landless slaves to Pharaoh. In the land at harvest time each Israelite family was to bring the firstfruits of the ground to the place of worship and profess, "Today I declare to the LORD your God that I have come into the land that the LORD swore to our ancestors to give us" (Deut. 26:3). Land was key to the integrity of the covenantal promise; it was the sign of hope for people who had once lived without hope. There was no problem with acquiring more land per se, but as James Mays puts it, "If its acquisition and possession cost the economic freedom and welfare of others, they [the prophets] called it violence and oppression" ("Justice," 14). Hence Amos indicts Israel for the condition of the poor that resulted directly from their source of income and identity being taken away. Amos 2:6–8 refers to conditions of poverty and debt, and perhaps debt slavery (the reference to father and son going "in to the same girl" may indicate the abuse of a slave).

168

Although Amos turns from the atrocities of war to social inequities in his indictment of Israel, the rhetorical shape of this indictment communicates the violent nature of the actions Amos highlights.

The impact of the indictment against Israel comes in part from its placement in line with the indictments of Israel's neighbors and also from the form of the oracle against Israel, which is so close to the rest. Thus Israel in its economic injustice is lumped together with those who wage war with unspeakable cruelty, who gain territory by deception and breach of covenant, and who strike fear into their enemies by their violent acts.

Ezekiel's Oracles against Tyre

Ezekiel's oracles against Tyre rail against the Phoenician kingdom because of its oppressive trade practices. Like much in the book of Ezekiel, the oracles against Tyre contain some confusing features. These uncertainties, however, raise interesting possibilities about the meaning of the oracles as they proclaim against Tyre's violent economic acts. Ezekiel 28 addresses the ruler of Tyre as "prince" in verse 2 and as "king" in verse 11. It is possible that these two titles refer to the same person. The second, loftier epithet may be used to anticipate the great humiliation soon to come (vv. 16–19; so Greenberg, *Ezekiel 21–37*, 580). Regardless of the identity of the two figures, however, it is clear that the ruler of Tyre in both cases is guilty of soaring hubris, and his violent practice of commerce grows from his pretentious sense of autonomy. The prince of Tyre says, "I am a god; I sit in the seat of the gods, in the heart of the seas" (v. 2). Moreover, it is by the ruler's godlike wisdom that he increased wealth (v. 5). Also the king of Tyre appears pristine, like the first human in paradise, but Ezekiel declares, "Your heart was proud because of your beauty; you corrupted your wisdom for the sake of your splendor" (v. 17). So, whether the prince and king of Tyre represent the same figure or not, it is clear that the ruler was "filled with violence" expressed in economic practice and that violence grew from the ruler's denial of God's sovereignty.

The "abundance of trade" mentioned here seems to refer to the expansive commercial operations Tyre enjoyed on both land and by sea from 630 to 585 BCE. During that period the Assyrian Empire waned and Tyre flourished economically with the political freedom that resulted (see Fleming, *History of Tyre*, 39–40). Tyre was a port city that relied on its extensive shipping industry. But it also used trade over land to complement its trade by sea. This required a stable political situation in the region. As Nina Jidejian puts it, "the city depended upon peace for prosperity" (*Tyre through the Ages*, 42). Ezekiel suggests, however, that Tyre's prosperity was at the expense of others and therefore did not promote "peace" at all. Whether this is a fair criticism of Tyre's economic activity is hard to determine. Homer identified the traders of the Phoenician coast as "mariners renowned, greedy merchant men" (*Odyssey* 15.415). In the Old Testament Hosea 12:7 (8 Heb.) identifies the trader as one who has false balances and "loves to oppress." The word for "trader" is *kĕna'an*. Used as a personal name, it designates Canaan, the father of Sidon (Gen. 10:15). The characterization of the mariners along the Mediterranean coast as dishonest profiteers was known in the ancient world. Ezekiel's portrait of the ruler of Tyre may be drawn from such a tradition.

But the picture of the ruler of Tyre may also suggest that Ezekiel was trying to speak against the violent actions of traders closer to home. Christian tradition has identified the king of Tyre who was cast out of Eden to the ground (v. 17) as none other than Satan. Tertullian used this text to say that Satan was created good but then rebelled against the Creator (*Marc.* 2.10). This interpretation is interesting but it reads later Christian theology into Ezekiel (for an historical interpretation, see Pope, *El in the Ugaritic Texts*, 97–104). Nevertheless, it is interesting that this understanding of the king of Tyre as Satan identifies Satan's greatest expression of evil with the unrighteousness of trade (v. 18).

But the identity Ezekiel probably has in mind is indicated by the description of the king of Tyre as covered with precious stones (v. 13). The stones listed here are nearly identical to the gems on the breastplate of the high priest as described in Exodus 28:17–20 and 39:10–13 (though the order is different in Exodus). The allusions to the Israelite high priest could hardly have been missed by Ezekiel's audience (see Wilson, "Death of King of Tyre," 217). Other references to Zion and its temple also support this identity (the "stones of fire" in vv. 14 and 16 may represent the coals on the altar; the seal or signet in v. 12 may refer to the vestments of the high priest as in Exod. 28:11, 21, 36; 39:6, 14, 30; see Tuell, *Ezekiel*, 197–98, for a summary of the evidence). In other words, Ezekiel here seems to criticize Israel's high priest through a veiled portrait of the king of Tyre. Thus while Ezekiel rails away at Tyre for its violence in economic endeavors, he does so with an eye toward

170

Israel's priesthood, the members of which also seemed to be guilty of haughtiness expressed in greed and economic oppression.

Nahum: God's Wrath on Nineveh

The book of Nahum is a collection of oracles that proclaim God's destruction of Nineveh, the capital of Assyria. Made prominent by the Assyrian king Sennacherib (d. 701 BCE), Nineveh represented a major military power that threatened Judah and destroyed Israel in 722 BCE. Nahum's oracles against Nineveh raise two primary and interrelated problems: the prophet declares God will destroy the Assyrians, and there is no apparent offer of hope for them. The question of God's mercy arises: is there any hope for Nineveh, or has God just determined to wipe it out? The book also has no indictment of Israel or Judah; so there arises the question of God's fairness in meting out punishment. Does Nahum simply present God as vengeful and violent toward those who opposed Israel?

The opening section of the book places the judgment against Nineveh in the broad context of God's sovereignty that, in turn, makes that judgment more understandable. The book begins with a theological portrait of God and God's expectations for all people, whom God created. Although the title of the book identifies it as "an oracle concerning Nineveh" (1:1), Nahum 1:2–11 focuses on the nature of God. The first word that characterizes God is "jealous" (*qannôʾ*; v. 2a): "A jealous and avenging God is the LORD, the LORD is avenging and wrathful; the LORD takes vengeance on his adversaries and rages against his enemies" (1:2). This is the same word that describes God in the Second Commandment, the command against making idols (Exod. 20:5). God's jealously means God will not tolerate other gods (Exod. 20:3), but God will also not be taken lightly. "Jealous" has the connotation of "zealous." This God demands attention and devotion. It is significant, however, that in Nahum 1:2 God's jealousy defines God's relationship with all people, not just with Israel. God is the universal sovereign and expects all creatures to comply with the demand for justice and righteousness.

The second word that describes God in the opening of Nahum complements and defines the first. God is "avenging" (*nōqēm*). The English word "vengeance" often denotes an irrational and harsh

171

response to a wrong. The Hebrew term, however, should be understood in the context of justice meted out by a legitimate authority (see Ps. 94:1 and the discussion in chap. 7 below). God expects all who are under God's authority to heed God's demands. In this case, Nineveh has disregarded those demands and now will be punished. The expressions of God's wrath in Nahum 1:2 certainly imply harsh treatment for wrongdoing (see also v. 6). But this is due to its blatant disregard for the order of the world God established. Thus as J. J. M. Roberts says, "The rule of Yahweh will not allow the oppressors to go unpunished" (*Nahum, Habakkuk, and Zephaniah*, 49).

Following these strong statements about God's wrath, three statements in the rest of the section qualify the notion that God is an angry avenger.

1. Verse 3 puts God's anger in perspective with a reference to a frequently cited line in the Old Testament: "The LORD is slow to anger" (see Exod. 34:6). This is an extremely important claim. It assumes that the one who created heaven and earth is justified in being angry when creatures go their own way, but it proclaims that God acts with great patience toward such creatures.

2. Verse 7 makes another positive declaration about God's character that clarifies who God defends with divine wrath: "The LORD is good, a stronghold in a day of trouble; he protects those who take refuge in him." Although the context of the book of Nahum makes clear that God will defend Judah against Assyria, this statement indicates that the larger concern is for those who "take refuge" in the Lord. This language denotes those who stand humbly before God, those who trust in God's salvation rather than in their own might or wisdom. In the Psalms this is the dividing line between the righteous and the wicked (see Creach, *Yahweh as Refuge*, 79–80). So also here Judah is defended because it recognizes its helplessness; Nineveh will be defeated because it vaunted itself to the place of God.

3. Nahum also makes clear that the Assyrians are brutal in their dealings with other peoples and thus directly oppose the will of God. Verse 9 seems to present in a rhetorical question the main flaw of Nineveh: "Why do you plot against the LORD?" Assyria is presented clearly in the book as a powerful and oppressive nation that disregards God's intentions. Nahum 3:1 sums up Nineveh's blatant rejection of God's vision of peace: "Ah! City of bloodshed, utterly deceitful, full of booty—no end to the plunder." The verses

that follow describe further how Assyria conquered, plundered, and terrorized nations like Judah. The killing was so rampant that there were "piles of dead, heaps of corpses, dead bodies without end—they stumble over the bodies!" (v. 3). This sounds like hyperbole, but the Assyrians produced artwork depicting their military exploits that suggests it is accurate. A relief discovered in the palace of Tiglath-pileser III (745–727 BCE) shows their soldiers attacking a city with residents of the city impaled around its perimeter and bodies piled at the base of the wall, with more combatants falling from the ramparts above (see Keel, *Symbolism of the Biblical World*, 102, 394). As noted in chapter 4, the Assyrians also portray themselves cutting down fruit trees *after* the battle for the city is decided. In other words, these people performed great acts against humanity and creation and took pride in them. For this reason the book of Nahum ends by saying to Nineveh, "who has ever escaped your endless cruelty?" (3:19). Thus the message of Nahum is that God's actions against Nineveh are intended to stop violence and correct it, not perpetuate it. It is a grand claim that any empire that relies on violence will eventually meet the wrath of the Great Judge who "protects those who take refuge in him" (1:7).

Jonah: God's Mercy for Nineveh

In light of the Assyrians' arrogant domination of other nations and their many acts of cruelty, God's judgment on Nineveh is understandable. It might even be said that God's destruction of the Assyrian capital was necessary to maintain God's demand for justice. But that is not the last word on the matter even for the cruel Assyrians. The book of Jonah recognizes that God has pity on the people of Nineveh too, just as God has mercy on all nations. The main point of Jonah does not seem to be universalism in general, however, but God's compassion, which ultimately overrides retributive justice. If any city and its people might put this notion to the test it would be Nineveh.

The book of Jonah begins with God's call to Jonah to announce judgment to Nineveh: "Arise, go to Nineveh, that great city, and cry against it; for their wickedness has come up before me" (1:2). As noted above, Nineveh represented a foreign power that threatened Israel and Judah (see 2 Kgs. 17–19). Indeed, the Assyrians would destroy Israel in 721 BCE and render Judah a vassal. Such

173

experiences with the Assyrian military surely colored the picture of Nineveh for the Israelites. Nineveh's identity in Jonah, however, seems primarily related to the city's great size (Jonah 3:3) and population (4:11; note the description "great city" in 1:2; 3:3; and 4:11; see Gen. 10:11–12). That prominence is matched by the magnitude of its sins. God's statement to Jonah that the wickedness of the city "has come up before me" is reminiscent of God's words about Sodom (Gen. 18:21). Mention of the great wickedness is also similar to the description of human corruption that led to the flood (Gen. 6:5; see Simon, *Jonah*, 4). Thus the story begins with the anticipation that God will destroy Nineveh.

When Jonah hears God's call he famously flees toward Tarshish aboard a ship (Jonah 1:3). The book does not at this point give any motivation for this action. As the story develops, however, the possibility of the pagans recognizing God's reign and submitting to divine authority becomes a prominent feature of the tale. When the ship is threatened by a storm and the sailors learn that Jonah is fleeing from God, "who made the sea and dry land" (1:9), they pray to the Lord not to be destroyed (1:14). Moreover, when Jonah finally arrives in Nineveh after a ride in the fish's belly, the people of the city heed the prophet's words: "the people of Nineveh believed God; they proclaimed a fast, and put on sackcloth, from the greatest of them to the least of them" (3:5). The meaning of the story's sympathetic portrayal of the residents of Nineveh is not completely clear, but it is clear that the prophet Jonah is set over against the people of the city in terms of their level of attention to the power of God. Jonah certainly believes God is powerful enough to destroy Nineveh, as do the residents of the city. Jonah also knows of God's grace, but the Ninevites also hope that God's grace will outweigh God's desire to punish them for their sins, a sentiment Jonah does not share.

Jonah 3:10 states that God saw how the people of Nineveh turned from evil and "changed his mind about the calamity that he had said he would bring upon them." Then the final chapter reveals the reason Jonah fled toward Tarshish in the first place—he feared God would withhold punishment for the people of Nineveh. When Jonah reveals his feelings about the matter he quotes a description of Israel's God that appears in abbreviated form in Nahum 1:3: "I knew that you are a gracious God and merciful, slow to anger, and abounding in steadfast love, and ready to relent from punishing" (4:2).

174

This characterization of God appears first in Exodus 34:/ and echoes throughout the Old Testament (Num. 14:18; Neh. ʃ 31; Ps. 103:8; Jer. 32:18). In the Exodus text the Lord gives Moses this description of himself in response to the golden calf episode. God thus extends mercy to Israel. God also declares, however, that he "will by no means clear the guilty" (Exod. 34:7; see also Num. 14:18). Nevertheless, the accent is on God's mercy. Probably for that reason some occurrences of these words contain only the assurance of divine compassion. Jonah offers a nearly exact quotation from Joel 2:13 in which the prophet encourages Israel to repent since God is merciful.

Two points about Jonah's statement of God's compassion seem clear. First, God extends mercy because mercy is central to God's character. The story of Jonah declares that divine mercy is offered to all, to foreign nations as well as to Israel. Second, this feature of God's character, which should provide comfort, is the bane of Jonah's existence, as he says in not so many words (4:3; see the summary of this point in Simon, *Jonah*, 37–38). The book of Jonah has many dimensions, but these two points converge to form one major theological point: God punishes evil, indeed, but God has more compassion than wrath, and that compassion extends not only to Israel but also to the nations.

Final Judgment

As difficult as the problem of prophetic judgment in the Old Testament is, an even greater problem would seem to be the New Testament's presentation of final judgment. Indeed, some passages in the supposedly more loving Testament seem to speak of punishment that has no redemptive purpose. Moreover, some predictions of final judgment include portrayals of punishment in hell, and that punishment appears to be characterized by anguish and torment. Thus as Dale Allison says, "Even more odiously, hell—in its popular, ordinary acceptation—has depicted a transcendental violence that has issued in a transcendental paradox, a God who loves all yet insatiably tortures some" (*Resurrecting Jesus*, 94). This is made even more difficult by the fact that hell appears most often on the lips of Jesus. Although the teachings of Jesus are commonly assumed to present nonviolence and divine love, as opposed to the

175

Old Testament's portraits of God's wrath, the idea of hell in the New Testament is most prominent in his teachings. For example, Matthew 25:41 speaks of the place of punishment for humans as "the eternal fire prepared for the devil and his angels."

The Problem of Hell

Old Testament Background

The Old Testament has no conception of hell per se. It speaks only of Sheol, which, though not desirable, is simply a shadowy place separated from the land of the living (Ps. 16:10). The abode of the dead is also called "the grave," Abbadon (Ps. 88:11 [12 Heb.]), or "the Pit" (Job 33:24); and those who have died are referred to as those who have gone down to the dust (Ps. 22:29 [30 Heb.]). Sheol is not a place where the wicked are punished but more generally the abode of the dead (in some texts it seems to be the destination of those who have died prematurely or dishonorably; thus it is dreaded; see Job 33:12–28).

The general idea of judgment and punishment after death, however, appears clearly in two Old Testament passages. First, Daniel 12:2 states: "Many of those who sleep in the dust of the earth shall awake, some to everlasting life, and some to shame and everlasting contempt." The specific notion that some will be judged unworthy and will be sent away to be tormented "eternally" is a common Jewish belief in the first century CE. For example, the expression "eternal punishment" appears in the Aramaic Version (see *T. Reub.* 5:5; *T. Gad* 7:5). Related Hebrew expressions appear in the Dead Sea Scrolls numerous times (1QS 2:15; 5:13; 1QM 1:5; 9:5–6; 4Q510 1:7). Hence Jesus speaks within a tradition that is already well established.

The second Old Testament passage worth noting is Isaiah 66:24: "And they shall go out and look at the dead bodies of the people who have rebelled against me; for their worm shall not die, their fire shall not be quenched, and they shall be an abhorrence to all flesh." This conclusion to the book of Isaiah, a passage from the so-called Third Isaiah (dating to ca. 515 BCE), looks forward to the death of those who rebel against God. The description of the dead, however, is cast in terms of ongoing punishment. The book of Isaiah began with references to those who rebelled against God

176

(1:2, 28), but there the rebels were specifically the people of Judah who were to be defeated by the Assyrians. Now at the end of Isaiah there is a new heaven and new earth (66:22), and all who have opposed God meet their end in judgment. The image of worm and fire as agents of judgment becomes common after this passage. For example, Judith 16:17 declares,

> Woe to the nations that rise up against my people!
>   The Lord Almighty will take vengeance on them in the day of
>   judgment;
> he will send fire and worms into their flesh;
>   they shall weep in pain forever.

The question of whether to take these images literally, however, is not certain, and that question persists in the New Testament passages that include these images.

Isaiah 66:24 is crucial for understanding the New Testament idea of hell, for it seems to conceive of a place of punishment that directly precedes the New Testament idea of hell. The Isaiah passage seems to have in mind the Valley of Hinnom as the location of the dead bodies. It contrasts the state of those worshiping in the temple (66:22–23) with those who rebel against God (66:24). Hinnom is the name of a valley on the southwest side of Jerusalem, just outside the city walls (see Josh. 18:16). The Valley of Hinnom was the antithesis of Mount Zion, and anyone who left the temple on Zion and descended could have come quickly and naturally to a view of the dreaded place (see Whybray, *Isaiah 40–66*, 294). The contrast between the Temple Mount and the abode of the dead makes sense in ancient Near Eastern cosmology in which temples connected worshipers to the heavenly realm (as assumed in Gen. 11:1–9), while caves, valleys, and other low areas were often conceived as entrances to the underworld (Bailey, "Gehenna: Topography of Hell," 190).

The Greek term for the Valley of Hinnom and the main name for hell is *geenna,* often simply translated "Gehenna." It is commonly said that in the New Testament period this valley was essentially a garbage dump where the city's refuse was burned. This connection has often been assumed as the background for the concept of hell. As logical as this may seem, no records indicate that the valley was used as a garbage dump, and likewise no ancient sources

177

indicate a connection between Gehenna as a garbage dump and eternal punishment. A more likely connection may be the association of the valley with human sacrifice. In the Old Testament the valley was identified with child sacrifice and the worship of Molech, which would explain why the place became identified with the punishment of the wicked in the life to come (2 Kgs. 28:3; 33:6; Jer. 7:31–32; 19:29; 32:35; see Blenkinsopp, *Isaiah 56–66*). The practice of human sacrifice, in turn, perhaps fostered the notion that the valley was an entrance to the underworld.

New Testament Texts

Mark 9:42–48

The first reference to hell among the strands of Gospel material appears in Mark 9:42–48, in a cluster of admonitions Jesus gives to his disciples about falling into sin. Verse 42 warns against leading astray the "little ones," by declaring that one who does lead them astray would be better off with a millstone tied around the neck. The references to hell come in verses 43–47. The sayings in these verses are identical in form. Each one begins with a warning about sinfulness that includes a reference to a particular part of the body that leads to sin ("If your hand/foot/eye causes you to sin"). Then Jesus admonishes them to be rid of the body part that led them astray ("cut it off/tear it out"), because it is better to "enter life" maimed than to be thrown into hell with the body intact. After the final reference to being cast into hell, verse 48 adds a near quotation of Isaiah 66:24, "where their worm never dies, and the fire is never quenched."

There is some debate about whether this line is original to Mark. It does not appear in some of the best manuscripts and therefore was perhaps added by a scribe who was familiar with the line from Isaiah (see Allison, *Resurrecting Jesus*, 79). Assuming the line is original, however, the question arises as to the meaning and significance of the references to fire and worm. Do these terms refer to agents that feed on the flesh, or are they figurative statements about the punishment of the wicked? If the references to fire and worm are to be taken literally, do they suggest the bodies of the wicked will be destroyed so they cannot share in the afterlife? Or do they imply that fire and worm continually feed on the flesh without consuming it? The questions are impossible to answer.

178

This is striking since such questions are posed in some texts outside the Bible. For example, sinners suffering punishment after death in *1 Enoch* 63 ask for a break from their punishment. Some Jewish sources suggest those suffering in hell get the Sabbath off (see Babylonian Talmud *Sanhedrin* 65b; *Genesis Rabbah* 11:5). Such questions become a major focus of many writings after the biblical period. That Jesus does not explain these images seems to indicate that the nature of punishment in hell is not the main point of the sayings. Indeed, Jesus does no more than mention the fire and worm here with no elaboration or explanation.

Matthew 25:31–46

These verses report Jesus' teaching about the judgment of "the nations." The identification of the "nations" (*ethnē*) here may refer to non-Christians, as it clearly does three other times in Matthew (24:9, 14; 28:19). But it could also be the case that this expression refers here to all humanity (this is the opinion of Davies and Allison, *Matthew*, 3:422–23). Regardless of what group is being judged, it seems clear that the passage has in mind the final judgment after the resurrection.

Drawing from images and language in Daniel 7:14 ("one like a son of man . . ."), Jesus declares that the Son of Man will come as judge after the resurrection to separate people according to their deeds (Davies and Allison, *Matthew*, 3:420–21). The basis of separation of the "sheep from the goats" (v. 32) is whether those being judged showed compassion to others: the central question is, did they feed the hungry, welcome the stranger (v. 35), clothe the naked, and care for the sick and those in prison (v. 36)? The punishment for those who did not show such compassion is described in two expressions. In verse 41 it is "the eternal fire prepared for the devil and his angels," and in verse 46 it is simply called "eternal punishment."

As the translations of many of the passages above indicate, Jesus declared that the wicked would suffer "forever" or "eternally." For Origen the key to interpretation of texts like this one was the meaning of "eternal." The meaning may seem straightforward at first. As Origen points out, however, the term rendered "eternal" or "everlasting" in many texts clearly does not refer to a never-ending period of time. For example, Exodus 21:6 stipulates that a Hebrew slave who desires to serve his master after the prescribed six-year

179

period may choose to do so. If so, he allows his master to pierce his ear with an awl "and he shall serve him for life." The term rendered "for life" is *lĕʿōlām*. The Greek equivalent is *eis ton aiōna*. It might be rendered woodenly "into the ages." In this passage the term clearly refers to a period with a definite end (the death of the slave). Similarly, 1 Maccabees 14:21 includes this expression to say that Simon "should be their leader and high priest *eis ton aiōna*." This does not mean Simon was immortal. An example from the New Testament is Romans 16:25–26: "Now to God who is able to strengthen you according to my gospel and the proclamation of Jesus Christ, according to the revelation of the mystery that was kept for long ages [*chronois aiōniois*], but is now disclosed." The period referred to with the term *aiōniois* clearly has an end and, indeed, has already ended. Hence Origen reasoned that "eternal" actually refers to a fixed time that does end. Or it does not refer to a specific time as we do when using the term (see the discussion in Allison, *Resurrecting Jesus*, 91–92, and the fuller treatment in Ramelli and Konstan, *Terms for Eternity*).

Luke 16:19–31

In Luke 16:19–31 Jesus tells a story about the fate of a poor beggar named Lazarus and a rich man at whose gate Lazarus begs. The story contrasts the two characters in life and after death: the rich man is finely dressed and "feasted sumptuously every day" (v. 19), while Lazarus lay uncovered, with exposed sores, and longed for the crumbs that fell from the rich man's table (vv. 20–21); after death, however, the poor man was carried by angels to be comforted by the side of Abraham (vv. 22–23), while the rich man was in Hades, "being tormented" (vv. 23–24).

This story is important in part because of the details it gives about punishment of the wicked after death. In some ways the picture of suffering here is more clear and complete than in the two passages described above. The rich man is tormented by flames; he can see the place of reward and comfort (and those in the place of reward see him!), but it is not possible to cross over. But the story also differs from the other teachings of Jesus in some important details. The place of punishment is Hades, a general name for the abode of the dead that seems to draw from the Old Testament concept of Sheol (Fitzmyer, *Gospel According to Luke*, 2:1132).

180

It is also worth noting that Luke 16:19–31 is a story, not didactic speech. One important Greek manuscript (Codex Bezae) introduces the story as a parable ("and he uttered another parable"), but the majority of manuscripts simply present it as a story that begins in typical fashion: "There was a rich man. . . ." Regardless of the label, however, the nature of the passage as story raises the question of its intention and how literally we should take the details of the story.

The story is often touted as one that gives a clear picture of the punishment of the wicked in the afterlife. Despite the details of the account, however, their significance remains somewhat vague. What is the nature of the torment the rich man suffers? Is it physical or mental anguish or both? If the flames torment him as fire would harm a person physically, will his body be destroyed in the flames? These are questions the story does not address at all. Hence the nature of Luke 16:19–31 as story is significant. Jesus seems to tell the story to inculcate obedience to the law of Moses (vv. 29–31) and particularly its teaching on compassion for the poor (v. 25), but not to teach the exact nature of eternal punishment for those who did not obey. The question naturally arises, however, how much we can draw from such a story about the nature of punishment.

Expansive Pictures of the Suffering in Hell

The passages above raise at least three crucial questions about the New Testament's teaching about hell. First, and most generally, what is the nature of the punishment in hell? Christian tradition has sometimes presented hell as a place of torture. Does the New Testament really present God tormenting the wicked? A second question, closely related to the first, is whether the punishment described is physical or psychological. The distinction is important because if the punishment is physical, it means God has established a torture chamber for the disobedient. If the punishment is psychological, however, it can be understood more as the natural consequences of separation from God and God's blessings. The punishment is essentially separation from God, from the source of goodness. Finally, is the punishment of hell never ending? This question is crucial because it speaks to the reason God enters the realm of violence in the first place. We observed in numerous Old Testament texts

181

that God's punishment was for redemptive purposes, to restore the creation to its intended state (Gen. 6–9; Isa. 19:18–25). But if God punishes with no chance of repentance or restoration, where is the love that stands behind the wrath?

The passages above clearly assume the reality of hell, but they do not linger on that point or show any interest in how the punishment will take place or what form the torment will take (see the discussion of these points in Davies and Allison, *Matthew*, 3:432–33). Simply put, the concept of hell is not developed or expanded in the teachings of Jesus beyond the basic assumptions of punishment in the afterlife that existed in the Judaism of Jesus' day. It should also be noted that in Jesus' teachings there are no pronouncements about the nature of hell. It appears as secondary to another major concern, the nature of the righteous life. Thus the mention of hell and the threat of hell seem part of a larger call to faithfulness (for a summary discussion see Allison, *Resurrecting Jesus*, 80–81).

Nevertheless, Christian tradition has developed a concept of hell that includes many lurid details of suffering. As noted in the sketch of passages above, references to the suffering in hell are limited to veiled references to fire, weeping, and gnashing of teeth. There are no sadistic details in the Gospels. Later Christian writings, however, seem greatly concerned about such details (see, for example, Tertullian, *Shows* 30). One of the earliest known expansions of the biblical concept of hell is the *Apocalypse of Peter*, composed in Ethiopic in Egypt around 135 CE with a Greek fragment (the Akhmim fragment) that differs slightly in content. This document is dominated by lurid descriptions of corporeal punishment. The text is written from the perspective of Peter, who is taken in a vision to see the place the righteous occupy in the life hereafter. Then Peter sees opposite that place the place of punishment for the wicked. The descriptions of the place and its punishment are extended and gruesome. For example, in the Akhmim fragment verse 21 says, "And those who were punished there and the angels who punished had dark raiment, clothed according to the air of the place"(Schneemelecher, *New Testament Apocrypha*, vol. 2). The description then goes on to the horrid nature of the punishment: "And some there were hanging by their tongues: these were those who had blasphemed the way of righteousness; and under them was laid fire, blazing and tormenting them" (v. 22). Still more: "And there were also others there: women hanging by their hair over that boiling mire. These were they who adorned themselves for adultery. But those (men) who had united with them for the adulterous defilement <were hanging> by their feet <and> had their heads in the mire" (v. 24). The description in some verses of the text is enough to make any reader cringe: "And in another place were glowing pebbles, sharper than swords or any spit, and men and women, clad in filthy rags, rolled upon them in torment" (v. 30). One thing seems certain: the *Apocalypse of Peter* depicts hell as an eternal torture chamber. Torture will be a central feature of almost all subsequent descriptions of hell.

As views of hell expanded in early Christian tradition, the question of whether the suffering in hell is physical or psychological became quite important. The question has traditionally centered on the meaning of "worm" and "fire" in Mark 9:42. The main interpretations were put forward by Origen and Augustine. The reference to "their worm" seemed to both interpreters a figurative expression that spoke of the conscience. A crucial part of the sinner's punishment would be the anguish of knowing he or she had lived a disobedient life. On the matter of the fire, however, these two had very different views. Origen argued that the fire, like the worm, was figurative. This seemed to make sense especially since Isaiah 66:24 speaks of the two with identical language ("their worm"/"their fire"). Indeed, what would be the justification of interpreting these two signs of punishment as essentially different? But Augustine proposed that the fire should be interpreted literally (*City of God* 20.22). Fire refers to the source of physical anguish for those in hell. Augustine's view would win out and shape much of the Christian conception of hell thereafter (see Allison, *Resurrecting Jesus*, 92).

An interesting fact in the history of interpretation of the nature of hell is that some church leaders agreed with Origen that the fires of hell were not literal, but they continued to teach the traditional view nonetheless. They did this because they believed that the fear of hell was a deterrent to antisocial behavior. An example of this bifurcated teaching on eternal punishment was William of Auvergone, bishop of Paris and theologian at the University of Paris from 1228 to 1249. Auvergone had an academic position that was similar to Origen's. He thought the fires of hell were figurative and that hell was not eternal. The fires of hell must be psychological, he reasoned, because otherwise they would consume the body. Only the

183

soul could be punished and tormented indefinitely. But he thought such an idea would confuse the masses. Hell, he believed, was a significant tool to keep people morally straight. Therefore, in public he advocated a simple view of hell in order to keep people in line (Bernstein, "Esoteric Theology," 509–16).

This brief treatment of the concept of hell in the New Testament has shown that hell in most New Testament texts is rather amorphous. The nature of the place and the punishment that takes place there is largely undefined. It is only in later reflections that hell is portrayed in detail as an eternal torture chamber. This idea seems linked, however, with the conception of the role of imprisonment. The dominant idea throughout the Middle Ages was that prison was to inflict pain and suffering on criminals. As such, it was also thought to be a deterrent to crime. Hell was conceived simply as an extension of the prison system. It was a place where the wicked would be punished. It was also used by religious officials to keep the faithful in line. As attitudes toward prison changed in the Victorian era so attitudes toward hell changed as well. The notion of prison as a place of reform made it more difficult to embrace the picture of hell as a place of eternal punishment. Would a loving God sentence people to be tortured forever with no chance of redemption? The difficulty of answering such a question has made hell a very unpopular topic in many religious circles.

The "Lake of Fire" and the End of Evil

The problem of final judgment is closely linked to the punishment of the wicked in the New Testament's teaching about hell, of punishment for those who oppose or reject God. This concept, in turn, is often associated with the book of Revelation. It may come as a surprise, however, that the term "hell" (Greek *geenna*) does not appear in the book and that there are no direct, unambiguous statements about the eternal punishment of humans here. In Revelation eternal punishment is described as "the lake of fire" and it most clearly refers to a place where Satan and the forces of evil will be held and where death itself will meet its end.

184 The first two references to the lake of fire (Rev. 19:20; 20:10) speak of it as the destiny of the beast that symbolizes the forces opposed to God. The beast demands to be worshiped. He is supported by a false prophet who led people so to worship (Rev. 13),

and he is empowered by the devil to deceive humankind (12:18). According to 20:10 these three—the beast, the false prophet, and the devil—"will be tormented day and night forever and ever" in the lake of fire. Hence eternal punishment here focuses on the forces of evil.

The last two references to the lake of fire do include human beings (20:13–15; 21:8), but the nature and scope of their punishment, or if they are punished in the lake of fire, are somewhat unclear. Revelation 20:13–15 describes Death and Hades giving up their dead that they might be judged according to their deeds ("as recorded in the books," v. 12). Then verse 14 reports that "Death and Hades were thrown into the lake of fire." Verse 15 adds, "anyone whose name was not found written in the book of life was thrown into the lake of fire." But in this case the lake of fire is not described as a place of torment. Rather, it seems to represent a state of oblivion, of no longer existing. It is qualified and explained by the expression, "this is the second death" (v. 14). This expression appears four times in Revelation (2:11; 20:6, 14; 21:8), but nowhere else in the New Testament, nor does it have an equivalent in any Old Testament passage. "Second death" does appear, however, in the Targums (loose Aramaic translations) on Deuteronomy 33:6, 15; and Jeremiah 51:39, 57. In the Targum on these passages "second death" refers to a denial of a place in the afterlife. For example, Targum Onqelos on Deuteronomy 33:6 reads: "Let Reuben live in life eternal, and not die the second death; and let his children receive their inheritance according to their numbers."

Similarly, the Targum on Jeremiah 51:39 and 57 uses the expression "second death" to communicate the idea that Babylon will not continue in the age to come (the Masoretic Text refers to perpetual sleep or rest; see NRSV: "sleep a perpetual sleep and never wake"). If the use of these terms is any indication, "second death" in Revelation would seem to refer generally to the elimination of forces that oppose God, to the denial of their continuance in the age to come. Thus the lake of fire "which is the second death" marks the end of evil, which is a necessary precursor to God's completion and renewal of creation (presented in Rev. 21–22). The point is similar to the one Paul makes in 1 Corinthians 15:26: "The last enemy to be destroyed is death." The human beings who are included in Revelation 20:15 are therefore not tortured, but suffer the same fate as death itself. They will be no more because they cooperated with the forces of death. Conversely, those who were faithful (2:11) or who had been martyred for their faith (20:6) would "share in the first resurrection" (20:6) and not be touched by the second death.

At least two questions remain, however, about the meaning of "second death" in the book of Revelation. First, the identification of the second death with the end of Death and Hades may seem illogical if the first death is understood as physical death, which Death and Hades did not experience. For that reason, some propose that Death and Hades "stand for all the unrighteous dead" who are mentioned in 20:15 as those whose names are not written in the book of life (Aune, *Revelation 17–22*, 1103). But the association of Death and Hades with the second death seems no more illogical than the portrait of Jesus as a lion that appears as a slain lamb (5:5–6). Moreover, the end of Death and Hades at this point in the book makes sense as preparation for the portrait of new creation that comes in chapters 21–22.

The second remaining question concerns the dead who are mentioned in Revelation 21:8. According to 20:15 anyone whose name was not found in the book of life experienced this second death. As noted above, this seems to clear the way for the renewal of creation. But as Revelation 21 begins to describe the new creation, it includes another group that will be thrown into the lake of fire, the second death: "the cowardly, the faithless, the polluted, the murderers, the fornicators, the sorcerers, the idolaters, and all liars" (v. 8). Since 20:15 has already said the wicked were judged and cast into the lake of fire, this additional reference is confusing. Is 21:8 a recapitulation of 20:15? Or is this a new group judged and sentenced to the second death? Some think that this verse is part of a larger section (21:5–22:2) inserted later. But that still leaves the question of the logic of the final form of the passage. The lack of clarity on these questions perhaps means that the author or final editor of Revelation is simply not concerned with giving a systematic understanding of the final judgment as it relates to the wicked. Rather, he or she is content to say what is most important, namely, that all the forces of evil, including all humans who cooperate with evil, will come to an end. In saying this, the accent seems to be on the end of evil and death, not on the punishment of disobedient human beings.

186

Note in conclusion that the fate of the wicked in Revelation is somewhat unclear as opposed to the future of creation that God will restore and the fate of the righteous whom God will vindicate and reward. To be sure, Revelation states strongly that those who follow the beast will meet their end. But the lack of clarity on how the wicked will meet that end and what it will be like for them seems to indicate the greatest concern is for the righteous, who at present suffer persecution. Indeed, the purpose of Revelation's description of the end of the wicked seems to be for the encouragement of the righteous.

The sequence of 14:1–13 bears this out. The chapter begins with a vision of the Lamb with one hundred forty-four thousand faithful followers singing praise to God (vv. 1–5). Verses 6–7 call for all people to "fear God and give him glory" and then promise that "the hour of his judgment has come" (v. 7). The vision of that judgment follows: "Fallen, fallen is Babylon the great!" (v. 8) Concerning those who conspired with the forces of evil, another angel then says, "Those who worship the beast and its image, and receive a mark on their foreheads or on their hands, they will also drink the wine of God's wrath, poured unmixed into the cup of his anger, and they will be tormented with fire and sulfur in the presence of the holy angels and in the presence of the Lamb" (vv. 9–10). The purpose of this description of the end of wicked, however, appears in verse 12: "Here is a call for the endurance of the saints, those who keep the commandments of God and hold fast to the faith of Jesus." In other words, the vision of the end of the wicked is not for the righteous to enjoy or gloat; the righteous are still suffering injustice and they cannot so enjoy it. Rather, the vision gives assurance that the present injustice will one day end. Hence the vision gives essentially the same message as Jesus' statement that "the meek shall inherit the earth" (Matt. 5:5; see also the discussion of imprecatory psalms in chap. 7 above).

Is Judgment the Final Word?

The assignment of one's opponents to hell is common in the literature of the first century, so it should not be a surprise that the New Testament includes such judgment (see Allison, *Resurrecting Jesus*, 88; 4QPsa 3:12; 4:1–2; 1QpHab 10:9–13; 11:12–15). It seems important to recognize, however, that the Bible's last word literally is not about judgment, but about God's completion of the creation. Moreover, this order of material is significant because all the discussion of judgment that went before Revelation 21–22 was in preparation for this final, climatic portrait of God renewing the heavens and the earth.

It is also important to recognize that the New Testament contains some suggestions that the judgment portrayed should not be taken as a final pronouncement about the end of the wicked. Just as the Old Testament qualifies divine judgment with predictions of restoration, even for enemies of Israel, the New Testament contains some passages that leave the door at least ajar for such hope to enter. One such passage concerns the descent of Jesus into the abode of the dead. First Peter 3:19–20 declares that the crucified Christ "went and made a proclamation to the spirits in prison, who in former times did not obey, when God waited patiently in the days of Noah, during the building of the ark." Much is uncertain about the meaning of this passage: who are the "spirits in prison"; what was proclaimed to them; does this passage suggest a chance for repentance after death? But one possible interpretation is that the author is speaking of Jesus' descent into hell mentioned also in other passages (Acts 2:31; Eph. 4:7–10) and that the author of 1 Peter is declaring that Jesus preached the gospel to those who had died without repenting of their rebellion against God (see 1 Pet. 4:6; for a full discussion of this and other possible interpretations see P. Achtemeier, *1 Peter*, 244–45). The general notion that Jesus descended into the realm of the dead is mentioned in several passages, and it creates the possibility that there is an opportunity beyond the grave for responding to God's call to faithfulness.

In addition to 1 Peter 3:19, several other passages suggest that God will ultimately bring everything and everyone into God's fold. Acts 3:21 is perhaps most prominent in this regard. It is part of Peter's speech about the power of God through Christ to heal and restore (3:12–26). In verse 21 he speaks of "the time of universal restoration that God announced long ago through his holy prophets." The expression "universal restoration" (*apokatastaseōs pantōn*) is more accurately translated "the restoration of all things" (Patrides, "Salvation of Satan," 468). The meaning of "all things" is not completely clear. If taken literally, however, one might conclude with Origen that all creation would be restored to its pristine state. To Origen "all things" included even Satan, who was one of God's fallen creatures (*De Principiis* 1.6.1–4). Most interpreters since Origen have concluded that his interpretation of Peter's

188

speech "goes far beyond what Peter means here" (Fitzmyer, *Acts of the Apostles*, 289). Nevertheless, if taken at face value, "all things" would presumably include the forces of evil presently working against God, and there is nothing in the context of Peter's speech to rule out Origen's idea.

A related passage is 1 Corinthians 15:28. Here Paul argues much like the author of Revelation that God will defeat death, the final enemy (15:26). Then, when "all things are subjected to him," God will "be all in all" (v. 28). The context of this statement is the final resurrection that is made possible because of God's work in Christ. Paul argues that "as all die in Adam, so all will be made alive in Christ" (v. 22). As the argument continues Paul speaks of defeating enemies ("every ruler and every authority and power," v. 24), including death itself. This might be interpreted to mean that those who oppose God will be sent to eternal punishment, but that is not the easiest conclusion to draw. Indeed, the concluding note that God will be "all in all" (v. 28) more easily suggests that God will redeem all things and all people. At least it affirms that God will be sovereign in the end and that no power will exist that does not conform to God's will.

This line of reasoning may be traced to Clement of Alexandria (ca. 150–ca. 215) who first proposed that even Satan would be redeemed in the end. It was Origen, Clement's younger contemporary (ca. 185–ca. 254), however, who has received most of the credit for this idea (Patrides, "Salvation of Satan," 467–68). Origen's reasoning proceeded from the passages mentioned above, as noted, particularly the idea that God would destroy "the last enemy" (1 Cor. 15:28) and restore all things to their original state (Acts 3:21). Origen reasoned that God would not obliterate any portion of the creation. Therefore, "the destruction of the last enemy must be understood in this way, not that its substance which was made by God shall perish, but that the hostile purpose and will which proceeded not from God but from itself will come to an end" (*De Principiis* 3.6.5; cited in Patrides, "Salvation of Satan," 468). Augustine, among others, spoke against such views by attributing them to the "tender hearts" of Origen and his followers (*City of God* 21.17). Augustine's popularity among the Reformers then helped solidify his position in the Western church, and the idea that all would be redeemed was roundly rejected (Patrides, "Salvation of Satan," 471). Nevertheless, numerous theological luminaries such as Gregory of

189

Nyssa (330–395) and John Chrysostom (347–407) followed Origen, and the idea of universal redemption has remained an important minority position. Moreover, with the changing understanding of punishment, not as penal but as curative and restorative, the idea becomes more attractive. At the very least it should be said that Scripture and Christian tradition do not require the idea that God condemns persons to eternal torture.

Conclusions

In this chapter we have explored various examples of the people of God predicting God's punishment of the wicked, of them calling on God to bring vengeance on an enemy, or of the faithful taking vengeance into their own hands. In each case the plea to God or the action was considered appropriate because the enemy had far superior power and was arrogant and oppressive. Nevertheless, God's punishment of the enemies is not the full picture and does not give the last word. Accounts of and calls for God to punish foreign nations, recalcitrant kings, or others who oppose God's authority are tempered by declarations of God's mercy and the hope of including these powers in the kingdom of God.

This perspective may be found in the prophetic material that predicts the downfall of the nations. It would be possible to conclude from a selective reading of such passages that the Bible presents God completely *for* Israel and completely *against* foreign nations at odds with Israel. There are significant examples, however, that require us to consider this idea more carefully. Isaiah 19:16–25 presents a vision of Egypt being healed and ultimately included in the community that worships the Lord. The passage also includes Assyria in this vision; thus the prophet declares God will say, "Blessed be Egypt my people, and Assyria the work of my hands, and Israel my heritage" (v. 25). The reference to Egypt as blessed is related in content at least to Genesis 12:3, which states that all people find their blessing in relation to Abraham and his descendants (see Wildberger, *Isaiah 13–27*, 280). What is clear is that it is God's will that ultimately Egypt and Assyria should be blessed and not cursed, welcomed and included, not destroyed.

190

The ending of Isaiah is surprising in that the prophetic books typically end with a prediction of restoration that follows judgment.

Rabbinic tradition therefore held that true prophecy followed this pattern. For that reason, the rabbis argued that in the synagogue Isaiah 66:23 should be read again after verse 24. Verse 23 looks forward to all God's creatures worshiping their maker: "From new moon to new moon, and from Sabbath to Sabbath, all flesh shall come to worship before me, says the LORD." The final word, the rabbis thought, should be about worship, not judgment. Although this rabbinic "correction" is later than the book of Isaiah, it is consistent nevertheless with the larger picture the canon gives. The final word is about restoration and renewal, not punishment.

CHAPTER 7

Seeking Vengeance, Part II

Praying against the Enemy

Praying Vengeance

Another set of texts that shows the people of God acting against enemies are the psalms that call on God to bring vengeance. In these so-called imprecatory psalms human involvement is limited to speech. But texts like these are troubling because they seem to ask God to act in ways inconsistent with God's intentions to bring good to humankind. Indeed, as I emphasized in the first chapter of this book, God's main effort in creating and sustaining the world was and is to bless those God created (Gen. 1:26–28). A careful reading of Scripture reveals that God blesses and curses. Psalm 37:22 speaks of those whom God blesses as well as those whom God curses. Deuteronomy 28 spends as much time describing the curses God will place on disobedient Israel as the blessings that will result from obedience. Nevertheless, most contemporary religious faith assumes rightly that the accent in divine/human relations is on blessing (see Miller, *They Cried to the Lord*, 281).

Perhaps the most troubling aspect of the psalms that call for vengeance is that they are cast largely as prayers. Such psalms raise in the first place the question of how one understands the God to whom prayer is made. But prayer not only expresses and assumes certain beliefs about God; it also reveals the shape and intentions of the human heart. Furthermore, given their status as Scripture, the

193

imprecatory psalms implicitly present themselves as models of how to speak to God and how to relate to others.

Many contemporary Christians immediately recognize that the psalms of vengeance seem to run counter to Jesus' instructions to love and pray for one's enemies (Matt. 5:43–48) and to contradict his model prayer, which calls on God to "forgive us our debts as we forgive our debtors" (Matt. 6:12). The apostle Paul echoes Jesus' teachings and holds up his practice as an example when he says, "Bless those who curse you" (Rom. 12:14), and further, "Do not avenge yourselves" (Rom. 12:19). Therefore, the psalms that curse the enemy and call on God to bring vengeance seem to be rejected as legitimate modes of prayer for the church.

Despite these common impressions of the imprecatory psalms, however, the church historically has neither used these psalms as prayers against personal enemies nor rejected them as sub-Christian. Indeed, there is a tradition, going back at least to Augustine, of reading the imprecatory psalms as the prayers of Jesus.

That raises the question of what place these texts have in Christian worship and devotion today. How can Christians embrace such passages while also holding to the teachings of Jesus and Paul concerning the nature of Christian prayer and the treatment of one's enemies? I will attempt to answer these questions by working out three premises. First, the psalms that pray for vengeance are actually praying for God to address violence done to the poor and lowly; therefore, imprecation is not extraneous to the Psalms or to the Bible; rather, it is a central part of the Bible's testimony to the faith of God's people. Second, imprecation has its proper setting in the struggle for justice to be done for the powerless; this means then that the imprecatory psalms can only be prayed rightly by and on behalf of the powerless. Third, these psalms are important resources for the church to speak out against violence, particularly the more subtle forms of violence done through economic injustice and the misuse of words. In other words, the imprecatory psalms are protests against violence, not approvals of violence. Therefore, they are necessary for a robust life of faith and prayer. This reading of the imprecatory psalms should not surprise us since the New Testament expresses the same concern for the problem of evil. Paul says directly in 1 Corinthians 16:22, "let anyone be accursed who does not love God." Jesus also testifies to his opposition to evil by

194

his exorcisms (Mark 1:21–28). A few brief points may help fill out this perspective on the imprecatory psalms.

1. As prayers for an end to evil the psalms of vengeance are not personal or petty; they are essentially prayers for God's will to be done "on earth as it is in heaven" (Matt. 6:10).

2. The imprecatory psalms are theologically necessary in that they give a crucial perspective on the meaning of victimization and suffering. These psalms assume that God will not ultimately tolerate the abuse of the lowly. Persecution is not viewed as something that brings God's favor, but as something God is working to bring to an end. Indeed, as René Girard says, psalms like this one "subvert the whole mythology of persecution" (*Scapegoat*, 108). This faith in God who desires and works for the end of the righteous' suffering in turn allows Christians to read the imprecatory psalms alongside Jesus' command to love their enemies, not in opposition to it. To love enemies and pray for those who persecute the righteous is possible because of the belief that God alone has the prerogative to mete out justice; conversely, to pray for God to avenge the wrongs perpetrated by the wicked is to believe that there is a larger system of justice that, if the righteous trust in it, gives them space to love their enemies. The psalms of vengeance express one pole of this theological tension (see Zenger, *God of Vengeance?*, 63–86).

3. Despite their ardent opposition to victimization, however, the imprecatory psalms do not propose violent means of preventing victimization. To the contrary, these psalms are prayers to God. Those who pray the psalms do not ask God to empower them to attack their enemies. Rather, they call on God as judge of the universe to deal with the enemies. Thus the psalms of vengeance counter violence in two ways. First, they speak against those who are violent and call into question their actions. But, second, they turn vengeance over to God. The psalmist does not claim vengeance for himself or herself.

Imprecation and the Plight of the Righteous

The Psalter's concern for violence done to the weak by the powerful is directed more than any other part of Scripture at the problem   195 of the suffering of those the Psalms call "righteous" (*ṣaddîq*; plural *ṣaddîqîm*). Although this language appears throughout the Bible, it appears in its greatest concentration in the Psalms. Indeed, much suggests that the entire book of Psalms is about the plight of the righteous, who are continually plagued by those the Psalter calls "wicked." The imprecatory psalms are the prayers of the righteous as they plead for God to deliver them from the clutches of the wicked.

The righteous are those who depend on God and, as a result, participate in God's desire to create a community of justice and equity. In other words, the righteous grant God-given rights to others. But most important for the psalms being discussed here, the designation "righteous" also applies to those who have had their rights taken away (E. Achtemeier, "Righteousness in the Old Testament," 83). Therefore, the righteous are often described as helpless and afflicted. They are called "poor" (*ānî*) 23 times in the Psalter; they are also "powerless" and "oppressed" (*dal*, 5 times; cf. Exod. 23:3) and "needy" (*ʾebyôn*, 23 times; cf. Amos 4:1). God has compassion on such persons because they are victims, and God works to bring them salvation, to restore shalom. It is not that the victim status alone renders one righteous, but that in the Psalms the "poor" signify a spiritual "poverty" that leads to reliance on God and God's rule (each of these terms can indicate a particular social or economic status, as Deut. 15:4, 7, 11 indicate). In other words, the experience of being a victim is closely tied to faith in and dependence on God.

Conversely, violence is closely connected to and is a key part of the character of those the Psalms call "wicked" (*rĕšaʿîm*). The wicked are characterized primarily by their attitude of independence from God, their air of self-sufficiency, and their confidence in their own security. The Psalter opens with a psalm that presents the wicked over against the righteous, thus anticipating the concern for these two groups that will be expressed in psalms that follow (see Creach, *Destiny of the Righteous*, 56–57). Psalm 1 gives a general contrast between the two groups: the righteous rely on God and recognize God's sovereignty, while the wicked do not. This psalm does not mention violence explicitly, but in the psalms that follow violence clearly appears as a result of the attitude the wicked have toward God. For example, Psalm 10 contains a litany of descriptions of how the wicked oppress the righteous:

196

In arrogance the wicked persecute the poor.
(v. 2a)

They sit in ambush in the villages; in hiding places they murder
the innocent.
(v. 8a)

They seize the poor and drag them off in their net.
(v. 9b)

They stoop, they crouch, and the helpless fall by their might.
(v. 10)

These descriptions of the destructive and life-threatening
activity of the wicked are clearly linked to the arrogance of the
wicked and disregard for God. For example, verse 3 states that "the
wicked boast of the desires of their hearts," and they "renounce the
LORD." The following verse presents even more blatant denial of
God's sovereignty: "In the pride of their countenance the wicked
say, 'God will not seek it out'; all their thoughts are, 'There is no
God'" (v. 4). As the psalm comes to an end the wicked are quoted as
saying to God, "You will not call us to account" (v. 13). The wicked
believe they are out of God's reach or concern. Therefore, they act
as though they can simply take what they want to the detriment of
the poor and needy.

The Violence of Words

Some of the descriptions of the violent actions of the wicked refer
to physical assault. But such violence also includes disruptive and
damaging language, language used falsely or maliciously. Indeed,
the righteous' direct complaint about violence and often their complaint about the activity of the wicked in general is a complaint about
the misuse of words. That is, the term *ḥāmās* ("violence") appears
in complaints that the wicked are coming against the psalmist with
false accusations, malicious words. In Psalm 27:12 the psalmist asks
God not to deliver him or her to "false witnesses." But the phrase
might better be rendered "violent witnesses." The descriptive term
here is *ḥāmās*, "violence" (thus, "witness of violence"). A similar
expression appears in 35:11.

In order to understand the role of imprecation in the Psalms
it is important to recognize that many curses on the enemy arise

197

within a judicial setting in which the one who prays has been falsely accused of a crime. In such texts the speaker often protests innocence or claims essentially to be righteous (see Ps. 7:3–5 [4–6 Heb.]). This claim may seem strange to those who have been taught to think that "all have sinned" as the primary understanding of human relationship with God (see Miller, *They Cried to the Lord*, 109). The claims of innocence in texts like these, however, are case-specific. The speaker does not claim to be guiltless in the abstract (see 143:2, which states the larger perspective). Nevertheless, the profession is often quite bold and must be understood in the context of justice.

The Old Testament starting point for considering the violence of words is the Ninth Commandment: "You shall not bear false witness against your neighbor" (Exod. 20:16; cf. Deut. 5:20). This commandment follows instructions against murder and violating relationships and property that belong exclusively to the neighbor. At first glance, therefore, the commandment against giving false testimony may seem less serious than the ones that precede it, and it may seem to have little to do with violence. But as Patrick Miller appropriately says, this rule is "a guard against the capacity of words and speaking to endanger one's neighbor in various ways, or indeed, to bring about violation of the commandments that precede this one" (*Ten Commandments*, 343). Furthermore, the general command against speaking false words has a trajectory that points directly to issues of violence.

The destructiveness and violent nature of false words becomes clearer in statutes that expound on the Ninth Commandment. Exodus 23:1 says, "You shall not spread a false report. You shall not join hands with the wicked to act as a malicious witness." The expression "malicious witness" here, as in Psalm 35:11, literally reads "violent witness" (see also Deut. 19:16). The use of the word *ḥāmās* to describe such witnesses indicates how destructive words could—and can—be.

The Psalms also express concern over speech that is used more generally for destructive purposes. The use of speech as a violent tool in some psalms helps delineate between the righteous and the wicked. For instance, Psalms 15 and 24 present the righteous as those who uphold the community with the positive use of words, while the wicked use words destructively: the righteous "do not slander with their tongue" (15:3) and "do not swear deceitfully"

(24:4). But the wicked are said to threaten the righteous with their speech. The wicked have "lying lips" (31:18 [19 Heb.]); "they make their tongue sharp as a snake's, and under their lips is the venom of vipers" (140:3 [4 Heb.]); they are always "plotting destruction" with a tongue "like a sharp razor" (52:2 [4 Heb.]).

The deadly potential of words is often not recognized until a community is dramatically disrupted or an individual is damaged by them. Lloyd Rediger has written a book on how this happens within churches and particularly how it happens too often to pastors. The book, appropriately titled *Clergy Killers*, describes the phenomenon of pastors being attacked and forced from office even though they have not done anything to warrant such removal. Most of the examples he gives involve the use of rumor and false reports. Rediger gives a typical case: "A member of the board, Tim Johnson said, 'A lot of people are complaining to me about Pastor Enright. They're saying he doesn't call enough; he can't be reached when they want to talk to him; and he's not friendly enough.'" As Rediger describes Pastor Enright's case it is clear that he is the victim of more than gossip. He is under attack, attack that comes in the form of words. The attacker continues to spread rumors of the congregations' dissatisfaction with the pastor, and he begins to suggest the pastor may be guilty of sexual misconduct or misappropriation of funds. As Rediger reports, none of the allegations against the pastor are true, but the words against him have a violent effect nonetheless:

> The pastor was absent from the next meeting. After six months of this harassment, he was in the hospital. The board voted to send a delegation to the bishop and at a following delegation reported that the bishop recommended removal of the pastor. By that time, the pastor was scheduled for bypass surgery. And it was rumored that his wife had become addicted to tranquilizers.
>
> (*Clergy Killers*, 5–6)

A case like this illustrates in dramatic fashion how damaging false words can be. Indeed, they can be deadly.

Violence and the Marketplace

The Psalms also depict economic activity as a venue in which violence is done. The wicked are often depicted acting violently in the marketplace. Psalm 15:5 includes in its outline of requirements for entry into the house of God not lending money at interest (Deut. 23:19–20 [18–19 Heb.]). Acting faithfully in matters of lending and trade is an essential feature of righteousness, a reflection of one's dependence on God. To appreciate the extent to which the wicked are indicted in this matter, however, we must remember that in ancient Israel's tribal culture the family gave access to the economy. Therefore, the economically deprived are identified not only as "poor and needy" (Ps. 37:14), but also, and especially, as widow, orphan, and stranger. These terms describe those who lost their place, or never had a place, in the basic patriarchal unit, the "household of the father" (*bêt ʾāb*; see Meyers, "Family in Early Israel," 36–38). Such individuals existed on the edge of life and were to have extended to them compassion and generosity (Deut. 24:17–22).

In opposition to this divine mandate, however, the Psalms declare that the wicked "kill the widow and the stranger, they murder the orphan" (Ps. 94:6; 109:16). That is, they take advantage of the most vulnerable members of society for their own advancement. Psalm 10 deals almost entirely with this aspect of the wicked. "Greedy for gain" (v. 3), the wicked "stealthily watch for the helpless; they lurk in secret like a lion in its covert; they lurk that they may seize the poor" (vv. 8b–9a). Later the psalm identifies the "helpless" specifically as the widow and orphan, as it calls God to rescue those oppressed by the wicked (vv. 14, 18). Hence the wicked oppose the very foundational tenets of Israel's system of justice and compassion. Their behavior is "antisocial" on the largest scale possible in that they attempt to undercut that which makes for a healthy society to prosper themselves.

The terms used to describe the righteous, along with some of the descriptions of their plight before the wicked, seem to locate these vulnerable members of society in the failed system of justice that the eighth-century prophets criticize so severely. Although the exact causes of the crisis are debated, it is clear that this period saw the development of a sharp difference between rich and poor. The wealthy in turn used laws of credit to confiscate the land of those indebted to them. In some cases they also enslaved the landless in order to allow them to pay off their debts.

This information does not remove the difficulty of imprecation in the psalms, but it does cast the request for vengeance in an

200

important light. As liberation theologians have often pointed out, the dominant (and oppressive) group always finds it easier to speak kindly of those who oppose them because those who oppose them pose no threat to them. The weak and vulnerable, however, sometimes have their very lives at stake as a result of injustice. Moreover, the language of reconciliation without any call to justice simply reinforces the dominant forces of the world while simultaneously keeping those who suffer in their place, all under the rubric of imitating Christ.

Psalms That Call for Vengeance

Psalm 109

Psalm 109 "contains the most vehement of the imprecations in the Psalter" (Mays, *Psalms*, 348). Indeed, the psalm contains wishes—indeed, prayers!—for an opponent to be killed, his wife left a widow and his children orphans (vv. 8–10), and his possessions ravaged by creditors (v. 11). It is hard to imagine language much more suggestive of violence than this psalm presents.

The circumstances of the one who prays the psalm are relatively clear. This is not always the case since many of the complaint psalms use language and imagery that make it nearly impossible to determine the circumstances of the supplicant. When the psalmist appeals to God to deal with an enemy, it is difficult to determine exactly how and why the psalmist is being threatened. Psalm 109, however, presents a clear situation about which the psalmist prays: the psalmist is being falsely accused or slandered. Although verse 3 contains language related to war, this seems clearly to be metaphorical ("they have fought me" appears in parallel to "words of aggression"). The problem, from start to finish, is that the psalmist is the victim of false accusation. Hence the psalmist's complaint is that the wicked are violently attacking with words. The petition to God, in turn, is a plea to stop the abusive treatment.

The psalm develops this complaint in three main sections. Verses 1–5 plead to God for help ("do not be silent"; v. 1b) because of the verbal assaults and accusations. References to aggression through words abound in this opening portion of the psalm, making clear that the problem is public defamation. The psalmist complains

201

that the opponents come at him with a "deceitful mouth" (v. 2a), "lying tongue" (v. 2b), and "words of aggression" (v. 3a).

The most objectionable language of the psalm appears in the second part, verses 6–19, but the role of this section is debated. The question is whether this section is the speech of the psalmist against opponents or if the psalmist is quoting what the opponents have said about him. The second option is attractive because the speech is against an individual and therefore it could be the accusation against the psalmist. For example, verse 6 states, "Appoint a wicked man *against him*; let an accuser stand on *his right*." The psalmist is attacked by a group (v. 3, "*they* beset me with words of hate"), so the singular references in verses 6–19 would make sense in the mouth of the psalmist's opponents. The NRSV adopts this position and clarifies it by adding "They say" at the beginning of verse 6.

This understanding of the section would also seem to lessen the offensiveness of the language since it would represent the words of the wicked, not of the psalmist. Despite the attractiveness of this position, however, it may not be correct. There is no break in the speech between verses 5 and 6. The words "they say" do not appear in Hebrew (see NIV for a translation that shows this continuity between vv. 5 and 6). Furthermore, verses 16–19 characterize the opponents of the psalmist better than the psalmist. Verse 16 is typical of the Psalter's description of the wicked: "For he did not remember to show kindness, but pursued the poor and needy and the brokenhearted to their death" (see 10:9). The charge that the person in question loves to curse (vv. 17–19) sounds much like the description of the wicked in 10:7 ("their mouths are filled with cursing and deceit and oppression"). Given the psalmist's opponents' deceitful and violent words, this section would make sense as the psalmist's speech against them. As McCann says, in verse 6 "the psalmist asks for redress, suggesting in effect that the accusers get a dose of their own medicine" ("Book of Psalms," 1125). Verses 8–19 essentially represent the sentence for the psalmist's enemies who have tried to destroy him with their words.

The final main section of Psalm 109 (vv. 20–29) returns to prayer and petition. The first verse of this section declares that the opponents deserve what is described in verses 6–19. But the last portion of the psalm puts this prayer in perspective. The psalm ends not with hatred for the enemy, but with trust in God. Verses 28–29 capture what the psalmist is essentially asking throughout the psalm, that is, for the accusers to be proven wrong, to be rebuffed publically. In a culture in which public opinion about honor and shame are paramount issues, the psalmist finally desires his own innocence to be known, when their lies have been exposed. Despite the extensive petitions of verses 6–19, the overall shape of the prayer suggests that those who use the psalm are not to dwell on the prospect of their opponents' suffering. Instead, the psalmist holds out the hope that God "stands at the right hand of the needy, to save them from those who would condemn them to death" (v. 31).

This final line captures the essence of the psalm: the opponents are out for blood; they are merciless in their attacks on the psalmist; but the psalmist trusts in the protection of God, the only hope available for one powerless in the hands of the wicked. Hence a careful reading of Psalm 109 indicates that the psalm is not ultimately a wish or call for violence. Rather, the psalm responds to a violent, verbal attack. In the end the psalmist turns the need for justice over to God: "help me, O LORD my God! Save me according to your steadfast love" (v. 26). Most importantly, the psalmist trusts that God is the polar opposite of the enemies: "They may curse, but you will bless; when they attack they will be put to shame, but your servant will rejoice" (v. 28).

The psalm ends with another statement of trust that casts new light on the difficult words of verses 6–19: "For he stands at the right hand of the needy, to save them from those who would condemn them to death" (v. 31). Recognizing the seriousness of the charges against the psalmist and the helplessness of the psalmist to rebuff the accusers, verses 6–19 become more understandable. What at first may sound like a yearning for vengeance, on further examination is closer to a legal claim submitted to God, who judges rightly (Brueggemann, "Psalm 109," 154). Indeed, the psalm is ultimately the prayer of one of the righteous who looks to God as the true arbiter of justice, the one who is praised for acting with equity and steadfast love (vv. 21, 26).

Psalm 137

Psalm 137 is often cited as the most difficult and troubling psalm in the Psalter and indeed as one of the most problematic passages in the Bible. The problem is really the final verse (v. 9), which extols those who repay Babylon for its destruction of Jerusalem. The difficulty of the verse is magnified by the focus on Babylon's children, presumably innocent victims of the psalmist's rage: "Happy shall they be who take your little ones and dash them against a stone!" Hence some have suggested that the conclusion to the psalm be rejected. The words spoken against Babylon and its children seem to contradict Jesus' commands to his disciples like the one in Luke 9:54–55 not to call down fire from heaven on their opponents (see Deissler, *Psalmen*, 3:185–86).

The church often ignores the most difficult parts of Psalm 137 while readily embracing verses 1–6. The psalm is included in the Revised Lectionary (Year C, Proper 22, Sunday between October 2 and 8), but verse 9 and the larger section in which it appears (vv. 7–9) are seldom read as part of the Scripture lesson. Furthermore, a common practice is to offer the psalm in a musical version that excludes the last three verses (see Bower, *Handbook*, 255). Indeed, hymns based on Psalm 137 typically include only the mourning for Zion that occurs when "by the rivers of Babylon—there we sat down and there we wept" (v. 1), and the torment of the captors with their taunt, "Sing us one of the songs of Zion" (v. 3; see, for example, "By the Babylonian Rivers," *Presbyterian Hymnal*, 246).

This illustrates, however, that Christians seem to accept the love of and lament over Jerusalem with great sympathy, but they insist there be no expression of anger over the devastation of the Holy City. Or perhaps those who reject verses 8–9 would like a response to Jerusalem's fall that is more thoughtful and forgiving. That perspective, however, misses the impact the final two verses are intended to make. As Erich Zenger says, "The elimination of verses 8–9 would not only destroy the literary structure of the psalm, but would deprive it of an essential key to a correct and theologically acceptable (!) understanding of its perspective on violence" (*God of Vengeance?*, 48).

Psalm 137 divides naturally into two parts. Verses 1–6 express the grief of those who held Jerusalem as their "highest joy" (v. 6d). The first three verses recall the circumstances that produced such grief: as verse 1 indicates, the problem is that those who speak the psalm "remembered Zion" (v. 1c). The central subject of the psalm, indeed, may be expressed in the word "remember." In verses 1–6 the issue is that the memory of Zion produces intense pain and grief, and yet Zion cannot be forgotten.

Zion was the place of God's presence, the place Israel gathered to worship and to celebrate God's goodness and justice, but it is now a memory. The memory is brought on by separation. Indeed, the mourners sat and wept over Zion while in Babylon (v. 1a-b). To make matters worse, the victorious Babylonians taunted the lovers of Zion by saying, "Sing us one of the songs of Zion" (v. 3c). To this the mourners offer the reflection in verse 4, "How could we sing a song of Zion in a foreign land?"

The problem implied in these verses is the loss of what Zion signified for the captives in Babylon. The expression "songs of Zion" likely refers to psalms such as 46, 48, 84, 87, 122, 127, and 132. These psalms typically speak of God enthroned on Zion as king and protector of the city and its people. The taunt of the captors, therefore, includes ridicule of Israel's belief in the power of its God. But the belief that the Lord reigns in Zion is more than just a political conception of where Israel stands among the nations. Israel's belief in God's rule on Zion is a faith that God maintained the order of the world. Included in that order was protection for the poor and helpless (132:15). From an Israelite perspective, Babylon represented just the opposite: coercive imperial power, military might, and oppressive force. Israel's experience with Babylon in the late seventh and early sixth centuries BCE shaped this impression. Babylon pressed Judah into vassal status, and when Judah rebelled, Babylon took measures to punish the small kingdom, culminating in Babylon's destruction of Jerusalem in 587 BCE. The role of Edom in the devastation is not completely clear. One plausible theory, however, is that Edom refused to participate in a rebellion against Babylon and thus left Judah to fend for itself (Jer. 40:11 places some Judeans in Edom, perhaps indicating that Edom has made itself safe from Babylonian attack).

Because of the trauma of Babylonian attack the destruction of Jerusalem at the hands of Babylon seemed to signal the onset of chaos. In Psalm 137:5 and 6 those who mourn over Jerusalem struggle to maintain hope that chaos has not conquered forever.

With this understanding of what Israel lost when it lost Jerusalem (vv. 1–6), the second part of Psalm 137 (vv. 7–9) is not only understandable—it becomes essential to the theology of the psalm as well. Verses 7–9 address God concerning those who destroyed Jerusalem, and they address the oppressive forces as well. Verse 7 is spoken to God concerning the Edomites who cheered on the Babylonians and thus participated in the destruction of Jerusalem. Verse 7 uses again the word "remember," but now it is God who is called not to forget. Specifically, the psalmist calls on God to "remember against Edom." The problem with Edom is that, as Israel's "brother" (see Gen. 25:19–28), this neighbor state is heir to the promises to Israel and should understand the importance of Jerusalem for the stability of the world. Verses 8–9 then speak to Babylon directly. Babylon is called "devastator" (v. 8a).

Then the psalm concludes with two beatitudes: "Happy shall they be who pay you back what you have done to us! Happy shall they be who take your little ones and dash them against the rock!" (vv. 8b–9). Two points are important to put verses 7–9 in their proper theological context. First, it is important to recognize that verses 8b–9 do not contain a petition or request of God. Although commentators sometimes refer to these verses as a curse, the only curse Psalm 137 contains is the self-curse in verses 5–6. Rather, verses 8b–9 contain two statements of confidence that God will return to Babylon what it deserves (see Goldingay, *Psalms*, 3:608–9). This is the nature of statements introduced by the Hebrew term *ʾašrê* ("happy," "fortunate," "blessed"), the word that begins verses 8b ("Happy shall they be who pay you back") and 9 ("Happy shall they be who takes your little ones . . ."). The word, often translated "happy" (NRSV) or "blessed" (NIV), really means something like "privileged." Or as *The Message* puts it, "how well God must like you." That is, the word does not pronounce a blessing; it simply denotes what the speaker believes to be the state of affairs, at least the state that will surely come.

The second point is that the Edomites and the Babylonians are spoken against because they fail to recognize the reign of God and hence are doomed to failure. Isaiah and Jeremiah declared Babylon's fall in similar terms (Isa. 47:1; Jer. 50:42). The indictment against these two nations is essentially that the Babylonians imagined themselves to be in control of the world and the historical processes. Although Psalm 137 does not say this directly, many other Old Testament texts do. For example, Habakkuk 1 indicates that although God used Babylon to punish Israel, Babylon did not recognize God's control, but thought instead it accomplished its defeat by its own abilities. Therefore, God would put Babylon in its place as well.

The type of arrogance and the sense of autonomy Babylon displayed is how the Psalms characterize the wicked (*rĕšāʿîm*). As already noted, the wicked are not personal enemies and the evil they perpetrate is not petty; rather, they are the enemies of God. The main sign that they are against God is that they oppress the poor and powerless, those called "righteous" (*ṣaddîqîm*) in the Psalter. For that reason the Psalms rightly set God's righteousness over against wickedness, and God opposes the wicked directly: "For you are not a God who delights in wickedness; evil will not sojourn with you" (Ps. 5:4 [5 Heb.). Therefore, when the psalmist asks God to act against the Edomites or especially the Babylonians, the plea is to protect the poor and to reestablish justice. Indeed, the language and tone of 137:7–9 are really legal. It asks for the perpetrators of crime (Edom and Babylon) to be repaid according to the severity of that crime (Zenger, *God of Vengeance?*, 49–50). Hence the psalmist shows a limit in his request for vengeance, however harsh the request may seem. Most importantly, the legal overtones of verses 7–9 clarify that the psalmist is not asking for Israel to take on the place in the world order previously occupied by Babylon. Israel is not praying to be empowered as the devastator of Babylon. Rather, the prayer is for God to act as judge over Babylon and to set the world aright, to allow God's control to reappear.

The identity of those who speak the words of verses 8–9 is important. They are not terrorists or vigilantes asking for power to retaliate. They are in fact powerless to bring about any change in their circumstances. All they can do—or all they choose to do—is plead with God to "remember against Edom," and they speak (rhetorically) against Babylon. In other words, verses 7–9 are the prayer of the powerless. That means then that the prayer to God in these verses is offered instead of acts of violence. It places the request for justice where it belongs, in the hands of God.

But the beatitude that concludes the psalm must be clarified further. The reference to "dashing your little ones against a stone" describes in the harshest language possible a reality of warfare. Children of a conquered people were often killed in order to cut off the future of those people. This is particularly important regarding the children of the rulers of a conquered land. When the Babylonians destroyed Jerusalem in 587 BCE they killed the two sons of King Zedekiah to prevent a resurgence of the Davidic empire (2 Kgs. 25:7). The final line of Psalm 137 may well have been influenced by the experience of seeing Jerusalem's children dashed against the rocks.

Despite the reality of children being killed in warfare, however, the church has not traditionally read the end of Psalm 137 along these lines. Instead, verse 9 has been read in such a way that the "little ones" were figures of evil thoughts and desires. Augustine understood the Babylonian little ones to be "evil desires at their birth" (Augustine, *Expositions on Psalms*, 632). For Augustine Babylon represented those forces that hindered the child of Jerusalem from reaching her true home. Therefore, he embraced 137:9 almost as an imperative to rid the soul of evil. He said, "when lust is little, by no means let it gain the strength of evil habit; when it is little, dash it. But thou fearest, lest though dashed it die not; 'Dash it against the Rock; and that Rock is Christ'" (1 Cor. 10:4; *Expositions on Psalms*, 632; see further Kriegshauser, *Praying the Psalms in Christ*, 286).

Augustine's interpretation of Psalm 137:9 may seem far removed from the historical situation behind the psalm, and it may seem to have nothing in common with the angry words of the psalmist. But this figurative reading has more to commend it than is sometimes thought. Babylon's destruction of Jerusalem produced such ire precisely because it disrupted the purpose of God that was administered from Mount Zion (Isa. 2:2–4). The psalmist's intense memory of Zion (Ps. 137:1–6) was not due to personal or sentimental associations alone; rather, the psalmist remembered Zion as the place of worship, the place Israel celebrated God's reign (note that the references to hand and tongue suggest the worship leadership of Levites who played and sang in the temple; see 1 Chron. 15:16). Therefore, the psalmist's wish for the Babylonian "little ones" to be dashed may rightly be taken as a wish for the source of evil to be quenched. This disturbing end to Psalm 137 may be understood under the psalm's overarching concern to remember. In verses 1–6 the psalmist declares it is impossible not to remember Zion. Though Zion is now in ruins, the psalmist pledges never to forget. To forget Zion would be to forget God's order and purpose for the world. The raw emotion at the end of the psalm may be attributed in part to this love for Zion. As John Bright said of this psalmist, "It would not be too much to say that he hated because he loved so" (*Authority of Old Testament*, 237). But the psalmist also speaks against those who destroyed Jerusalem because they represent and cooperate with the forces of evil. The psalmist calls for God to "remember against" those who destroyed Zion. These forces are cast as enemies of Israel and enemies of God. They represent evil that runs rampant in the world. In such a circumstance, for the victim of evil, "to forget is to submit to evil" (McCann, "Book of Psalms," 1228).

The raw emotion behind this verse should not be denied; the brutal imagery may have come from real experiences of the death of children during the Babylonian destruction of Jerusalem. But it is possible to interpret 137:9 symbolically without losing entirely the connection to historical Babylon and the event of the Babylonian exile. As Zenger suggests, given the larger issues of justice that lie behind the psalm, the Babylonian little ones must be taken on another more important level as the children of the Babylonian royal house who are poised to continue the brutality experienced in 587 BCE (Zenger, *God of Vengeance?*, 50). So Zenger proposes a helpful paraphrase/alternative rendering of verses 8–9:

> O daughter Babylon, you devastator!
> Happy the one who brings you to judgment
>   because of what you have done to us!
> Happy the one who seizes you
>   and puts an end to your rule forever!
>   (*God of Vengeance?* 91)

One final point must be made about the final verse of Psalm 137. The beatitude that seems ready to reward baby killers is cast as speech to Babylon, but it is in reality spoken to God. This obvious point is how the discussion of these psalms began, with the problem of these words as prayer. But in the end the character of 137:9 as prayer may be what makes it acceptable and understandable. As a prayer this line is an act of faith. It assumes that God hears and acts. It also assumes that God knows how to deal with the likes of Babylon, but the psalmist can do nothing directly to respond to the injustices of Babylon. This identity of the psalmist, in turn, may provide an important guideline for anyone who would allow this psalm to shape his or her prayer. Indeed, the psalm may be embraced fully—and prayed—only by those who are unarmed.

Another clue to how Psalm 137 should be applied is the brutal honesty with which verse 9 makes its point. The honesty makes

209

the prayer authentic in that the one who prays does not need to worry about appearances before God. This honesty runs the risk of being misunderstood by outside observers or by dangerous insiders—those who are not defenseless (thus the potential for Ps. 137 to be misused as encouraging violence). But if one truly reads *with* the psalmist, one must admit that similar feelings of anger and vengeance are within all people. The question then becomes, what is to be done with such anger? Psalm 137 provides the answer: submit that sign of human frailty to God in prayer (see McCann, "Book of Psalms," 1230). Such an act of prayer, though rough in its particular expression in this psalm, has two important effects that lead away from violence. (1) It frees the one who prays from violence. (2) It also has potential to lead to forgiveness and reconciliation. As McCann says, the one who prays this honestly to God "begins a journey that transforms grief and anger into compassion" ("Book of Psalms," 1230).

Psalm 139

Although the theological problem in Psalm 137:7–9 is often presented as the greatest such problem in the Psalter, the concluding verses of Psalm 139 seem to contradict Jesus' teaching more directly. When the psalmist says, "I hate those who hate you, O LORD," the expressions of hatred seem on the surface at least to directly oppose Jesus' instructions to "bless those who curse you, pray for those who abuse you" (Luke 6:28; cf. Matt. 5:44).

Psalm 139:19–24 is like the conclusion of Psalm 137 in that it seems to contrast sharply in tone and content with the previous section of the psalms, a section beloved and well known. In fact, 139:19–24 is so different in tone and content from verses 1–18 that some scholars have concluded that this final section was not originally intended to go with the first part. In 139:1–18 the word "know" appears five times (vv. 1, 2, 4, 6, 14). The psalmist is perfectly, intimately, and graciously known by God. It is impossible to escape God's presence, the psalmist declares (139:7–12). Even in Sheol God is there (contrast Job 17:12–16). The nearness of God is closely linked to God's acts of creating and re-creating. Just as God's spirit (*rûaḥ*) hovered over the chaotic waters in Genesis 1:2, so God's spirit is present always with the psalmist to bring order,

210

purpose, and beauty (vv. 7–12). Thus the psalmist reflects on how God formed him or her in the womb (v. 13) and made purposeful all the days of life (v. 16).

Although the testimony of the psalmist being known by God in verses 1–18 may seem incongruous with the prayer against enemies in verses 19–24, it is connected quite strongly by the double appearance of the word "know" in verse 23: "Search me, O God, and know my heart; test me and know my thoughts." Indeed, the prayer for God to destroy the wicked may be read as the conclusion to which verses 1–18 logically lead. The prayer for God to "test" and "know" the psalmist's heart may have its origin in the psalmist's defense against false charges and may have been originally a request for hearing in the presence of temple personnel. Regardless of the original setting, however, the psalm in its present form is a prayer for God to deal with the wicked, those who personify evil as they oppose the will of God. The prayer is based on the psalmist's confidence in God's justice and order on the one hand and the problem of evil, represented by the wicked, on the other hand. The psalmist here wants it to be known that he or she stands with God and God's purpose, which means she or he stands naturally against the wicked.

The language of hate in Psalm 139 must be read in this larger context of the psalmist aligning with God's intentions in creation. It is telling that the psalmist does not say, "I hate those who hate me." Rather, the psalmist says, "Do I not hate those who hate *you*, O Lord? And do I not loathe those who rise up against *you*?" (v. 21). In other words, the wicked are not personal enemies or merely persons who have a grudge against the psalmist. As with the wicked in Psalm 137, they are the very enemies of God, perpetrators of evil (v. 20). Regarding this stance against the wicked, therefore, two points are important about the psalmist's "hate" of them. First, it should be recognized that the term "hate," like the opposite word, "love," is a term that is often used to describe covenant making, or not making (Jenni, "אהב *'hb* to love," 52). It communicates absolute loyalty to a covenant partner. For example, the love between David and Jonathan is described in the context of the covenant they enter with each other (1 Sam. 20:12–17). In Deuteronomy the covenant into which Moses leads Israel is marked by Israel's love for and obedience to God (Deut. 29–30, especially 30:6; see Moran, "Love of God in Deuteronomy"). So by saying, "I hate those who hate you," the psalmist refuses to engage in and formally support those who act against God's intentions.

Second, the declaration of hatred for the enemies of God is part of the psalmist's profession of being known by God and dependent on God. That the psalmist is "with" God (v. 18) is demonstrated significantly by the fact that the psalmist does not align with evil. The intention of 139:19–24 is captured by a portion of Psalm 141, two psalms later. The psalmist prays to be kept from evil and to be kept with the righteous, even though such an alliance is costly: "Let the righteous strike me; let the faithful correct me. Never let the oil of the wicked anoint my head, for my prayer is continually against their wicked deeds" (141:5).

So Psalm 139 is a testimony to being known by God and being shaped and governed by God's will rather than the activities of those the Psalms call wicked. The wicked, of course, are perpetrators of violence. They go against God's intentions for peace and reconciliation. So the psalmist's opposition to the wicked is another way of expressing concern for God's good order that is shalom. Moreover, this way of speaking is not intended to promote violence. Rather, it is a refusal to ally with those who *are* violent.

Vengeance and Christian Identity

This investigation of the imprecatory psalms from various angles indicates one clear point that has echoes throughout Scripture: vengeance belongs to God alone (Deut. 32:25; Ps. 94:1; Isa. 63:4; Rom. 12:19; Heb. 10:30). Vengeance is not the rite or responsibility of humans. When humans take vengeance into their own hands it inevitably crosses into violence. As Walter Brueggemann rightly says, "to keep some vengeance for self and to withhold it from God is to mistrust God, as though we could do it better than God" (*Praying the Psalms*, 72). Such a conclusion is liberating in one sense. It places retaliation outside the bounds of acceptable human behavior and thus frees human beings to work at reconciliation and forgiveness.

212   This exclusive association of God with vengeance, however, may also be troubling. A God who is concerned with vengeance may not seem like a God to be loved and sought after. But a closer

consideration of the matter shows that the Psalms' close affiliation of God with vengeance is theologically and ethically essential. It is so, first of all, because divine vengeance is the other side of divine compassion. If Scripture declared only that God shows compassion but did not also declare that God is involved in vengeance, it would then portray God as inept in expressing compassion in concrete ways. Simply put, when God promises Israel or the righteous that his steadfast love to them is certain, God shows that steadfast love by punishing those who oppress them. This is how God "rightwises" human life (Brueggemann, *Praying the Psalms*, 73).

This association of God with vengeance is essential also because it has to do with God defending a moral order in the world. It may be helpful to consider further the word "vengeance" that sometimes appears in translations of these psalms (e.g., Ps. 94:1). Zenger points out that this English word, which is generally associated with retaliation and anger, may not express the Hebrew word adequately. Rather, *nĕqāmôt* signals something like justice or fairness. Thus in 94:1 the psalmist calls on the "God of *nĕqāmôt*" to "shine forth." The word translated "shine forth" (*hôpîa'*) in Psalm 50 is directly related to God judging righteousness (vv. 2–6). In Psalm 80 God shines forth to save God's people who have been ravaged by their neighbors (vv. 2, 7, 19). Thus the prayer in Psalm 94 is for the sovereign God to bring fairness and equity to the world (Zenger, *God of Vengeance?*, 70–71). Indeed, 94:2 continues, "Rise up, O judge of the earth. Return to the proud what they deserve." The petition is not for irrationality or vengeance in the sense often used, but for equity that only God can bring.

God's vengeance nevertheless should not be understood as God's dispassionate objectivity. To the contrary, "*God has taken sides in history* and acts effectively on behalf of 'his' special partners" (Brueggemann, *Praying the Psalms*, 74). God rises up as judge with a preference for certain people and groups to whom God offers special care. In the Old Testament Israel is the object of God's compassion. But Israel never possesses God's compassion exclusively, and Israel never controls God's vengeance. Israel is the special object of God's care only because and to the extent that Israel is righteous, faithful, and obedient. When people display these characteristics and they are also oppressed, then God's vengeance works in their favor. In other words, God's actions are actually on behalf of the "poor and needy," of which Israel is the primary

213

example (but see again Kaminsky, *Yet I Loved Jacob*, 153–57 for discussion of Israel's unconditional election).

The identification of God's vengeance with the poor is expressed strongly in the New Testament. The hymnic expression in Luke 1:51–53 depicts a radical reversal of fortunes in which God raises up the poor, needy, and hungry while God puts down the rich, proud, and well fed. Also in Luke, Jesus' inaugural appearance in the synagogue has him reading from Isaiah 61:1–2, which includes anticipation of "the day of vengeance of our God" on behalf of the afflicted. Thus, as already noted, this dimension of prayer in the Psalms is not opposed by the teachings of Jesus. Rather, it is a cry for aspects of what Jesus calls the kingdom of God. To pray the imprecatory psalms is to lay claim to the promise that the meek will inherit the earth (Matt. 5:5).

Vengeance and Christian Prayer

What place then do the prayers of vengeance have in Christian prayer? I have suggested that they are important to Christian prayer because they plead for the end of evil. Hence the imprecatory psalms are closely related in theological outlook to the Lord's Prayer and its petition for God's will to be done on earth as in heaven. These psalms may be read and prayed also in a more literal way if the context of such reading and praying is considered carefully.

The answer to this question is perhaps captured best by Brueggemann's characterization of Christian use of the Psalms "in Jewish territory" (*Praying the Psalms*, 43). Brueggemann describes the Psalms in terms of Jewishness first of all because the Psalms grew out of situations of suffering like those the Jews have experienced throughout their history. Hence the "Jews are a paradigm of the deepest longings and yearnings of all of humanity" (ibid., 47). The first and perhaps most essential feature of praying the imprecatory psalms is to enter such prayer from the perspective of that deep longing of humankind. People who enjoy privilege and power must be cautious, therefore, when using these psalms lest they simply use them as yet another means of securing the privilege they already enjoy. For such persons the psalms of vengeance should evoke self-criticism, generosity, mercy—and when warranted, repentance.

Conclusions

In this chapter we have explored various examples of the people of God calling on God to bring vengeance on an enemy or taking vengeance into their own hands. In each case the plea to God was considered appropriate because the enemy had far superior power and was arrogant and oppressive. Nevertheless, God's punishment of the enemies is not the full picture and does not give the last word. Accounts of and calls for God to punish foreign nations or recalcitrant kings are tempered by declarations of God's mercy and the hope of including these powers in the kingdom of God.

An appropriate summary of the theological convictions this chapter has attempted to present comes in rabbinic reflection on Psalm 104:35. The Babylonian Talmud tells a story that illustrates the truth well. As the story goes, a certain rabbi prayed for the death of a violent person who had attacked him (*Berakot* 10a). The rabbi prayed the words of Psalm 104:35, "Let sinners be consumed from the earth, and let the wicked be no more." But the rabbi's wife corrected her husband. She pointed out that the verse does not actually say, "Let *sinners* [*ḥōṭĕʾîm*] cease." Instead, it reads, "Let *sins* [*ḥaṭṭāʾîm*] cease." Therefore, she argued, the psalm is a prayer for the end of evil, not an end for a particular wicked person.

The rabbi's wife was reading what appears in the Masoretic Text (the main Hebrew tradition). Her husband, however, was apparently reading the verse as attested in a manuscript from Qumran that does say "let sinners cease" (NRSV follows the Qumran manuscript as well). His wife argued further that the verse's concluding comment, "let the wicked be no more," means that when sins cease there will be no one who is wicked (Jacobs, "Praying for Downfall," 297).

This story offers a very important perspective on this matter: the righteous are not to entreat God to punish individuals (Jacobs, "Praying for Downfall," 299). Rather, the righteous are to pray for the end of evil and its many expressions—injustice, malice, slander—so the reign of God might be evident in the world.

The same perspective may be found in the prophetic material that predicts the downfall of the nations. It would be possible to conclude from a selective reading of such passages that the Bible presents God completely *for* Israel and completely *against* foreign nations at odds with Israel. There are significant examples, however, that require this idea to be considered more carefully. Isaiah 19:16–25 presents a vision of Egypt being healed and ultimately included in the community that worships the Lord. The passage also includes Assyria in this vision, thus the prophet declares that God will say, "Blessed be Egypt my people, and Assyria the work of my hands, and Israel my heritage" (v. 25). The reference to Egypt as blessed is related in content at least to Genesis 12:3, which states that all people find their blessing in relation to Abraham and his descendants (see Wildberger, *Isaiah 13–27*, 280). What is clear is that ultimately Egypt and Assyria are blessed and not cursed, welcomed and included and not destroyed.

CHAPTER 8

Jesus, Nonviolence, and the Old Testament

In the previous seven chapters I have dealt largely with the problem of violence in the Old Testament, attempting to show that the Old Testament presents violence as human rebellion against God's intentions. Hence, according to the Old Testament, violence is an affront to the very authority of God. Nevertheless, particular sections of the Old Testament seem to allow or even promote violent resistance under some circumstances. The conquest of Canaan (which includes placing the Canaanites under the ban), the warring of the judges, and the violence of certain prophets persist as problems. These portions of the Old Testament give clues to reading them as a grand testimony against violence. But such a reading requires careful attention to many subtle details, and the subtlety necessary to make the argument is what gives some skeptics reason to question whether such a reading of the Old Testament is true to the message of the text.

In this final chapter we turn attention to an aspect of the problem that has been looming over the entire book: how the New Testament perspective on violence relates to the perspective of the Old Testament.

The life and teachings of Jesus have been conceived rightly as marking a significant turning point on the issue of violence. Jesus taught his disciples to pray for their enemies and not to retaliate against them. He modeled this instruction in his own life, even to

217

the point of death. In so doing and teaching, Jesus presented the ultimate truth about violence: it is an affront to God's sovereignty, and any rule by violence is a rule that cannot stand the truth. Jürgen Moltmann expresses the idea this way: "What is now ended is not only evil, but the law which repays evil by evil—not merely the act of violence, but also its restriction through violent resistance" (*Way of Jesus Christ*, 128–29). Moltmann continues, "The vicious circle of violence and counter-violence is broken. Non-resistance to evil shows up the absurdity of evil. Evil's strength is violence" (129).

But this radical, new value of nonviolence Jesus presented raises two crucial questions. First, when Jesus instructed his disciples, "Do not resist one who is evil" (Matt. 5:39), did he in effect rule out all physical combat, even for self-defense? It is not possible to answer this question with certainty since it is impossible to know the unspoken thoughts of Jesus. But regardless of how the answer is framed, it seems clear that the New Testament intends to show that Jesus' teachings as well as his life unmask reliance on coercion for the lie it is.

This, in turn, raises a second question about the meaning of the Bible as a whole: Is it possible to read the Old and New Testaments as equally authoritative? Are the discussions presented on the Old Testament (chaps. 1–7) really sufficient to hold the Old Testament together with the New? If so, what understanding of violence emerges from the Bible as a whole?

The "Problem" of Jesus' Teachings

The difficulty in reconciling the two Testaments arises largely from the teachings of Jesus that seem to contradict certain parts of the Old Testament. The primary "problem" passages appear in the Sermon on the Mount in Matthew 5–7. Much of the material appears also in Luke 6:17–49, but the fuller version in Matthew provides a larger context in which to address the question of how Jesus' teachings relate to the Old Testament.

Matthew 5 opens with Jesus addressing "the crowds" on a mountain, reminiscent of Moses on Sinai receiving the law and bringing it down to the people (see Allison, *New Moses*, 97). As Jesus begins, he clearly speaks to and concerning those who are

218

powerless, those who suffer, and those who are victims of injustice: "the poor in spirit" (5:3), "those who mourn" (5:4), "the meek" (5:5), and "those who are persecuted for righteousness' sake" (5:10). The first section of the Sermon ends with an emphasis on this identity of the audience: "Blessed are you when people revile you and persecute you and utter all kinds of evil against you falsely on my account. Rejoice and be glad, for your reward is great in heaven, for in the same way they persecuted the prophets who were before you" (5:11–12).

Although Jesus does not say explicitly in the opening verses of the Sermon "do not retaliate against your oppressors," this becomes the main point soon thereafter. Matthew 5:21–48 begins and ends with emphatic injunctions to nonviolence. For example, in 5:21–22 Jesus says,

> You have heard that it was said to those of ancient times, "You shall not murder"; and "whoever murders shall be liable to judgment." But I say to you that if you are angry with a brother or sister, you will be liable to judgment; and if you insult a brother or sister, you will be liable to the council; and if you say, "You fool," you will be liable to the hell of fire.

This emphasis on a nonviolent response to adversaries appears again at the end of the section in two related teachings:

> You have heard that it was said, "An eye for an eye and a tooth for a tooth." But I say to you, Do not resist an evildoer. But if anyone strikes you on the right cheek, turn the other also; and if anyone wants to sue you and take your coat, give your cloak as well; and if anyone forces you to go one mile, go also the second mile. Give to everyone who begs from you, and do not refuse anyone who wants to borrow from you.
>
> (vv. 38–42)

> You have heard that it was said, "You shall love your neighbor and hate your enemy." But I say to you, Love your enemies and pray for those who persecute you, so that you may be children of your Father in heaven; for he makes his sun rise on the evil and on the good, and sends rain on the righteous and on the unrighteous. For if you love those who love you, what reward do you have? Do not even the tax collectors do the same? And if you greet only

219

> your brothers and sisters, what more are you doing than others?
> Do not even the Gentiles do the same? Be perfect, therefore, as
> your heavenly Father is perfect.
>
> (vv. 43–48)

A distinctive feature of this section of the Sermon is the formula Jesus uses to begin each instruction: "You have heard it said
. . . but I say to you." Here Jesus presents himself as an authority
who overturns or nuances other teachings or beliefs.

This raises a crucial question regarding the intention of Jesus'
teachings about nonviolence. Since some of the authorities Jesus
cites are Old Testament texts, some interpreters have concluded
that Jesus in the Sermon on the Mount is repudiating the Old Testament and presenting a new way of understanding and living. For
example, in Matthew 5:21–22 Jesus cites the Sixth Commandment
(Exod. 20:13; Deut. 5:17) and presents his teaching as a higher standard. In Matthew 5:38 he cites the well-known *lex talionis* ("an eye
for an eye, a tooth for a tooth"), which appears in Exodus 21:23–25;
Leviticus 24:19–20; and Deuteronomy 19:21 (in slightly different
forms in each passage). This law was intended to limit retribution
so punishment was meted out in accordance with the severity of
the crime (see Gerstenberger, *Leviticus*, 366–69). But Jesus again
presents a new and greater standard by which the one offended
does not retaliate at all.

Did Jesus Prohibit All Coercive Action?

The divide between the Old Testament and the New Testament on
the matter of violence becomes harder to resolve if Jesus' instructions concerning violence are read as absolute statements. That
is, the Old Testament will more likely be read as inferior to the
New Testament if Jesus' teachings about violence are understood
as blanket prohibitions against any form of physical coercion. Or
the Old Testament might be read as more realistic, as a true portrait of how life really works. Either way, the point remains that
the teachings of Jesus are often understood as presenting a much
higher moral standard than the Old Testament.

220   There is considerable debate about whether this interpretation
is correct. Jesus' audience was largely made up of powerless tenant
farmers and peasants. They were victims of Rome and its occupying

force as well as victims of the wealthy members of their own people who were either part of the religious elite or who had become partners with Rome (tax collectors, for example). So did Jesus instruct his listeners not to retaliate because retaliation against Roman officials or Roman soldiers would essentially be suicide? Or did Jesus tell his followers to turn the other cheek because it was for them the most effective political strategy? If the answer to either of these questions is yes, then perhaps Jesus was not trying to command nonviolence in all times and circumstances. Perhaps he left open the possibility of defending the abused with physical force or of responding with force to an unjust system (see Wink's discussion in *Jesus and Nonviolence*, 82–87).

The possibility that Jesus' teachings left open the use of war or police action to check abuses is important to consider in part because the Bible speaks unmistakably of a "sterner side of God's nature" as well as the love of God seen in Jesus' teachings (MacGregor, *New Testament Basis of Pacifism*, 70). The New Testament, as well as the Old Testament, speaks of the wrath of God, and Jesus refers to this stern side of God in response to those who would harm the innocent and helpless: "If any of you put a stumbling block before one of these little ones who believe in me, it would be better for you if a great millstone were fastened around your neck and you were drowned in the depth of the sea" (Matt. 18:6). Accenting passages like this, many in the church have developed a theology that includes legitimate uses of war and other coercive action in order to protect those who cannot protect themselves (see Simpson, *War, Peace, and God*, 80–81). Thus human action in war may be understood as just under certain circumstances, and "just war" is understood as human participation in God's corrective and punitive work (see further the discussion of Ps. 82 below). But does this idea really fit within the teachings of Jesus?

This question is impossible to answer with certainty. Since Jesus did not leave commentary on his teachings, we cannot know exactly how he intended his words to be applied, and this has created great difficulty for the question of how the two Testaments relate to each other. It seems clear, however, that none of the teachings of Jesus directly promotes or even offers support for the use of force, even against a brutal aggressor. Indeed, Jesus' declaration of God's punishment of the wicked is a far cry from support of war or other forms of aggression. Furthermore, there is much in his instruction

221

to disciples that would seem to preclude such use of force. It seems useful therefore to begin by considering nonviolence as Jesus' absolute standard for his followers.

Richard Hays for one argues very forcefully that Jesus intended his instructions on nonviolence as absolute and that the New Testament as a whole was shaped around those instructions. His conclusions are particularly important for thinking about how the two Testaments should be read together—or against each other—on the issue of violence (*Moral Vision*, 336–40).

Hays assumes that Matthew 5:21–48 constitutes Jesus' absolute insistence not to retaliate, to turn the other cheek. But Hays does not rely on his presuppositions. He bolsters his view by pointing out that other New Testament passages seem to interpret this way and that the New Testament seems to have three other dimensions that support the idea that Jesus taught his disciples pacifism.

In addition to the instruction in Matthew 5:21–48, Jesus' teachings on violence appear in the writings of the apostle Paul in the form of a more general principle: "Bless those who persecute you; bless and do not curse them" (Rom. 12:14). Here Paul seems to know the instructions of Jesus, and he extrapolates from them a maxim for the church. Hence it seems that Paul understands Jesus' teachings about nonviolence to apply to all Christians in all churches.

In addition to the New Testament record of a specific rule and a general principle regarding nonviolence, Hays notes that nonviolence is embodied in a paradigm, that is, Jesus' own death. Jesus refused to defend himself and suffered death as a result. Jesus embodies his teaching by refusing to call on his disciples to rescue him with violent action. In fact, he rebukes them when they begin such action on his behalf (Luke 22:49–51; John 18:11). According to some manuscripts, Jesus at his crucifixion even prayed for his tormentors, "Father, forgive them; for they do not know what they are doing" (Luke 23:34). Thus he exemplified his instructions in his own life.

Finally, Hays observes that a cosmic dimension to the New Testament's opposition to violence also supports the notion that Jesus prohibited violence altogether. This is seen particularly in the declaration that "our struggle is not against enemies of blood and flesh, but against the rulers, against the authorities, against cosmic powers of this present darkness, against the spiritual forces of evil in the heavenly places" (Eph. 6:12). In other words, God ultimately deals with violence, and humans are not to take it into their own hands (*Moral Vision*, 339–40). This dimension of the instruction rests on the belief that God will eventually judge the world and God will bring proper reward to those who live nonviolently. Indeed, concerning Jesus' command to turn the other cheek, Hays notes that the command makes sense "if and only if it really is true that the meek will inherit the earth" (ibid., 338). In other words, the command of Jesus to nonviolence is set in a theological context in which God is trusted as judge of the cosmos and in which all authority has been given to the risen Christ (ibid.). Hence the proper Christian response to aggression is trust in God rather than retaliation. First Peter 2:23 says directly that this was Jesus' assumption: "When he was abused, he did not return abuse; when he suffered, he did not threaten; but he entrusted himself to the one who judges justly." Just as Jesus did not retaliate, the Christian is not to retaliate because she or he believes that God will one day make all things right. The Christian does not respond in violence because to do so would be to take what is rightfully God's. Only God can really establish justice, and so that work is left to God. God will indeed establish justice on earth, as it already is established in heaven (ibid., 338–39).

Many interpreters throughout the history of the church have concluded that some circumstances warrant retaliation with force. For example, given the prevalence of evil in the world, it may seem necessary to protect the innocent from their oppressors. The Holocaust and genocides in Rwanda and Sudan are but a few examples in recent memory that might warrant physical force (see Allison, *Sermon on the Mount*, 95–97). Nevertheless, the teachings of Jesus at least require us to examine such responses closely. What seems quite clear is that for the church the cross is meant to shape an identity of service and suffering that precludes violence in most if not all cases.

The Cross and Early Christian Identity

The cross provides an orientation to human life and the rest of creation that is essential for reading Scripture's rough edges, particularly reading texts that seem to promote violence. In a book on the cross as the crucial identifying mark of Christianity today, Douglas John Hall observes that the cross represents God's suffering with

223

the world, and God's suffering is crucial for Christian identity (*Cross in Our Context*, 7). Without it, Hall rightly argues, the church in the West will inevitably identify with imperial goals of the larger society, and "its actions and ethical claims will be ambiguous" (ibid., 4). This accent on the cross in Christian theology follows carefully the same emphasis in the New Testament and, as I shall suggest below, in the Old Testament as well.

The cross places an accent on love rather than power. There is, to be sure, a power that God displays that must be acknowledged. But particularly for North American Christians the problem typically is that our identity with this dimension of God's character is overplayed. As a result, we are too willing to see God's justice being expressed through our show of power.

The cross of Christ in the New Testament is the greatest illustration of the truth of the incarnation. That is, as Paul Tillich says, it helps us see that God "made Himself small for us in Christ" (Tillich, *Shaking of the Foundations*, 143). In turn, the Christian community is called to take on the identity of love—smallness for the sake of others—rather than power. This is most apparent in Philippians 2 in which Paul instructs the Christians at Philippi to "do nothing from selfish ambition or conceit, but in humility regard others as better than yourselves. Let each of you look not to your own interests, but to the interests of others" (Phil. 2:3–4). Paul then grounds this injunction to humility and self-giving in the work of God in Christ in a hymn about the incarnation. Jesus is the one who "though he was in the form of God, did not regard equality with God as something to be exploited, but he emptied himself, taking the form of a slave, being born in human likeness" (2:6–7). In this grand hymn the cross then becomes the centerpiece, the focal point of the incarnation: "he humbled himself and became obedient to the point of death—even death on a cross" (2:8). The model here supports the notion that the church was commanded to practice nonviolence after the example of Jesus.

François Bovon has argued that many early Christians were quite self-conscious about identifying with the cross as the antithesis of violence ("Child and Beast"). He points out that the New Testament presents evil with images of beasts, either wild animals or chaos monsters (Rev. 12; the Old Testament uses the same symbols; see Ps. 22:16, 21 [17, 22 Heb.]; Isa. 51:9). By contrast, Christians are presented as children, helpless and dependent. This is particularly

224

apparent in Luke and Acts. The evangelist Luke reports that Jesus used the infant as the image of the one to whom God would reveal true wisdom. In Luke 10:21 Jesus says, "I thank you, Father, Lord of heaven and earth, because you have hidden these things from the wise and the intelligent and have revealed them to infants; yes, Father, for such was your gracious will." The term for "infant," *nēpios*, refers literally to one who cannot speak, thus the child who does not yet have her own voice (Bovon, "Child and Beast," 382). Again, when Jesus wanted to tell his disciples about true greatness, he placed a child in their midst and said, "Whoever welcomes this child in my name welcomes me" (Luke 9:46–48). In this case Jesus uses a term that means "little boy" or "little girl" (*pais*). These are children old enough to play games, but not much more. They are completely dependent on their parents. Such children would have been the least powerful and least considered persons in their world. But Jesus introduces a reversal of values and thus identifies himself with those who are completely dependent on others. Luke 18:15 uses a third term that refers to a newborn (*brephos*): "People were bringing even infants to him that he might touch them." When the disciples tried to keep them away, Jesus responded: "Let the little children [*paidia*] come to me, and do not stop them; for it is to such as these that the kingdom of God belongs" (v. 16).

Thus according to Luke, Jesus uses the whole range of childhood to speak about what it means to be his followers. Bovon argues that Jesus uses these images to counteract the tendency to violence and retribution. Children were an apt object lesson because "children have no articulate voice, no reasonable argument, because their freedom is circumscribed by boundaries of dependence, because their fragility is evident, because children can dream and play while the adults calculate and conduct wars" ("Child and Beast," 385). Hence the child became "a cherished metaphor for another civilization, for another world, for the presence of God" (ibid.). The image of the child came to be for Christians an image of new life and reconciliation, of the powerlessness of the people of God, who were accepted by God and protected by God alone. These "children of God," however, also accepted Jesus as a child. He was powerless before his enemies. By not retaliating and by not calling for vengeance, Jesus thus overcame evil and violence (ibid., 392).

So one point is clear: Jesus and the early church presented a way of responding to enemies and oppressive forces that was markedly

225

different from the Zealots (for the use of this term and the variety of resistance groups in the first century CE see the summary of Rhoads, "Zealots"). Indeed, Jesus did not at any point indicate that armed revolution was an acceptable way of expressing devotion to God. That rather clear stance on violence raises again the question of how the New Testament relates to the Old Testament.

Is the Old Testament an Inferior Witness?

Whether or not Hays is right that Jesus taught pacificism as a "one-size-fits-all" response to aggression, he certainly articulates an impressive ethical imperative to nonviolence based on the New Testament's various dimensions of instruction on the matter. But this raises a serious theological problem: the New Testament's vision seems at odds with certain parts of the Old Testament.

Hays identifies 1 Samuel 15:7–35 as perhaps the most diffi-cult case. As I observed in chapter 3, this passage reports how the prophet Samuel commanded King Saul to defeat the Amalekites and "utterly destroy" them. Hays points out that many have tried to redeem this story by treating it as a figurative account that empha-sizes the importance of rooting out evil and vices. But, he states flatly, this "can hardly pass muster as exegesis" (*Moral Vision*, 336). Hays concludes, therefore, that the New Testament is superior to the Old Testament or at least superior to some particular Old Tes-tament texts: "If irreconcilable tensions exist between the moral vision of the New Testament and that of particular Old Testament texts, the New Testament vision trumps the Old Testament" (ibid.). He observes that similar situations exist with the Old Testament's requirement of circumcision and dietary laws—the New Testament overturns such requirements. Hence there is a pattern that vali-dates the notion that Jesus' teachings constitute a new dispensation.

This position has some advantages. It rightly recognizes the unique authority of Jesus and his teaching within the canon and within Christian theology. It also purports to solve the problem of difficult Old Testament texts once and for all; they simply fall beneath the New Testament's authority.

226   Despite the apparent advantages to this position, however, it carries some very significant disadvantages. One of the most obvious problems with this view is that it seems not to consider adequately

Jesus' own statement about the Old Testament that appears immediately before his commands to love enemies and turn the other
cheek: "Do not think that I have come to abolish the law or the
prophets; I have come not to abolish but to fulfill" (Matt. 5:17; see
also vv. 18–20). Note that in the Jewish canon the Law contains the
instruction of Moses to "blot out the remembrance of Amalek from
under heaven" (Deut. 25:19). The section known as the Prophets
likewise includes the book of Samuel and the judgment against Saul
for not destroying Amalek when he had the chance. Thus Dale Allison rightly says,

> To do justice to Matthew, the reader must take seriously 5:17–20,
> verses which plainly say that the Law and the Prophets are still in
> force. The declaration stands as the preface to the imperatives in
> 5:21–48, about which there has been so much debate and confu-
> sion. We have here not a vestigial sentiment of an obsolete Jewish
> Christianity but a hermeneutical key.
>
> (*Sermon on the Mount*, 8)

In other words, the notion that Matthew 5:21–48 contradicts the
Old Testament in reality contradicts the Sermon on the Mount
itself. This at least requires some serious consideration that perhaps there are ways of reading Old Testament texts about warfare
and enemies that are consistent with Jesus' teachings. It seems that
Matthew at least thought this to be the case.

It is also interesting to note that Jesus' command to love enemies does not present any Old Testament text that it overturns.
Indeed, when Jesus says "You have heard that it was said, 'You shall
love your neighbor and hate your enemy,'" the last portion of what
the audience is understood to have "heard" is of unknown origin.
While the former ("love your neighbor") is a quote from Leviticus
19:18, the latter is probably a piece of popular wisdom. If it is based
on a passage like Psalm 139:21 ("Do I not hate those who hate you,
O LORD?"), it is a paraphrase that makes the verse nearly unrecog-
nizable and removes the verse from its context (see further chap. 7
above on the imprecatory psalms).

As Allison also points out, Jesus' teachings about not retaliating against an enemy are anticipated by numerous Old Testament
texts (*Sermon on the Mount*, 100). Exodus 23:4–5 says, "When you
come upon your enemy's ox or donkey going astray, you shall bring
it back. When you see the donkey of one who hates you lying under

227

its burden and you would hold back from setting it free, you must help to set it free." First Samuel 24 and 26 emphasize that David spared Saul's life, even though Saul sought to kill him. In Psalm 35:13–15 the psalmist says he mourned and prayed for those who did evil to him.

Hays's distinction between the Old Testament and the New Testament is a common one. It does not seem necessary, however. For example, Hays seems to assume that the New Testament presents a radically different understanding of how to approach the problem of enemies: "The evangelists are unanimous in portraying Jesus as a Messiah who subverts all prior expectations by assuming the vocation of suffering rather than conquering Israel's enemies" (*Moral Vision*, 329). Hays is right, of course, that many around Jesus expected the Messiah to deliver Israel from its enemies and they "tried to take him [Jesus] by force to make him king" (John 6:15). But such expectations were already subverted by parts of the Old Testament. The Servant poems in Isaiah 40–55 portray the servant as one who suffers, and at least one of these poems identifies the servant explicitly as Israel (49:5). Hence they are not a conquering power or even a people on behalf of whom God will conquer enemies, at least at the present time. They serve rather as a "light to the nations" (49:6).

The New Testament's understanding of the Messiah as one who suffers is anticipated more fully perhaps by the Old Testament presentation of David. Although David is the king of Israel and is portrayed in many Old Testament narratives as a mighty warrior, the most enduring picture of him is as one who suffers at the hands of enemies. This is certainly the image of David in the Psalms. The identity of the Psalms with David comes largely through thirteen psalms that present in their titles events in David's life as the context in which he prayed the words of those psalms (Pss. 3, 7, 18, 34, 51, 52, 54, 56, 57, 59, 60, 63, 142). In almost every case David is presented as one who suffers, who pleads to God for mercy, and who expresses confidence that God will deliver him. The sixty-one additional appearances of David's name in the simple ascription "of David" are then read in light of the longer titles. As James Mays says, David's name here and elsewhere in the Psalms "does not so much claim the psalms as the voice of a king as it identifies him, in the psalms that are claimed for David, with the lowly" (*Lord Reigns*, 123).

228

In Acts 2 Peter appeals to the suffering of David in the Psalms and to God's vindication of him to explain the suffering and resurrection of Jesus (Acts 2:25–36; see Moessner, "Two Lords"). In other words, the early church did not see Jesus here overturning expectations of what it meant for Jesus to fill the role of a "son of David." Rather, they saw David as one who preceded Jesus in suffering and whose life and destiny formed a pattern Jesus would follow (see Creach, *Destiny of the Righteous*, 10–11; for a justification of the portrait of David in the Psalms as precedent for the New Testament's picture of Jesus' suffering see Jipp, "Luke's Scriptural Suffering Messiah").

These examples raise serious doubts about the notion that the Old Testament is inferior to the New Testament on the subject of violence. It is perhaps more accurate to say that Jesus' instructions concerning violence should be understood as indications of what constitutes "scripture's true governing center," not about the validity of the Old Testament (see Seitz, *Word without End*, 4). If this is the case then, for example, Jesus' parable of the Good Samaritan (Luke 10:25–37) is not to be read as a repudiation of a narrow Old Testament idea of who is one's neighbor that allows one to ignore or even attack a "nonneighbor." Rather, it teaches a lesson firmly grounded in the Old Testament's identity of the neighbor that included foreigners living in Israel's midst. Indeed, Leviticus 19:18 expresses the particular law addressed in the story of the Good Samaritan when it says, "you shall love your neighbor as yourself." Later in the same chapter, the same language of love and inclusion is extended to foreigners: "The alien who resides with you shall be to you the citizen among you; *you shall the love the alien as yourself*, for you were aliens in the land of Egypt" (v. 34; cf. Exod. 23:9). In other words, Jesus did not offer a corrective to Old Testament ideas of hating those outside one's kinship group. Rather, Jesus identified those more inclusive portions of the Old Testament understanding of who the neighbor is as the normative one. Therefore, it is most accurate to say that Jesus presents for Christians a normative *interpretation* of the Old Testament, not a repudiation of it.

The idea that some passages in the Old Testament should be read in light of other passages is inevitable if the Old Testament is read as Scripture. In fact, this type of decision about a true governing center is necessary to read the New Testament as Scripture as well. For example, after Hays examines Jesus' statements about nonviolence in the Sermon on the Mount and their relationship to other New Testament texts, he declares that the rest of the corpus shows "how impressively univocal is the testimony of the New Testament writers on this point" (*Moral Vision*, 329). Nevertheless, Hays must proceed to explain parts of the New Testament in light of Jesus' teachings on violence and the teachings of Paul and others. For example, the book of Revelation appears at first glance to portray God acting violently. At one point Jesus even appears as a warrior. Indeed, Revelation 19:11 declares, "in righteousness he judges and makes war." Verse 13 says, "He is clothed in a robe dipped in blood," and verse 15 states, "From his mouth comes a sharp sword with which to strike down the nations." But Hays sees no contradiction between this picture and Jesus' rejection of violence in the Sermon on the Mount. He says that Revelation "seeks to inculcate in its readers precisely the same character qualities that we have seen extolled through the rest of the New Testament canon: faithful endurance in suffering, trust in God's eschatological vindication of his people, and a response to adversity modeled on the paradigm of the 'Lamb who was slaughtered'" (*Moral Vision*, 332; see further his chap. 8).

Hays's interpretation of Revelation is convincing. But it is significant that he does not begin his treatment of nonviolence with Revelation. Rather, Revelation is read in light of Jesus' teachings in Matthew 5:38–48 and in light of Jesus' response to his persecutors. Revelation has features that allow it to be read as consistent with these other texts, but those features are subtle. They might not be as clear if the gospel portrait of Jesus was not available. The same might be said of Luke's inclusion of soldiers among Jesus' followers (Luke 3:14; Acts 10). When such figures come to John the Baptist, Jesus, or the apostles, they are never told to cease being soldiers. Hays declares, however, that this serves "to dramatize the power of the Word of God to reach even the unlikeliest people" (*Moral Vision*, 335). Read in isolation, one might assume that the New Testament references to soldiers gave tacit approval to their profession, insisting only that they not take advantage of the citizens of the country they occupied.

The point is that Old Testament passages that seem to promote violence should be read like the New Testament's references to soldiers and like the book of Revelation. Instead of rejecting such passages as an inferior witness, the interpreter should find features

230

of those passages that allow them to be read in concert with Jesus' teachings on nonviolence. Such a reading of the Old Testament would make the interpretation of the Old Testament consistent with that of the New.

A Call to Nonviolence in the Old Testament?

The question then is, can the whole Bible be construed as a call to nonviolence? To answer the question, the issue of the true governing center of the Old Testament is paramount, and in addressing this issue as it relates to the matter of violence, Hays's approach to the New Testament may prove helpful. As noted above, he lists four dimensions of the New Testament's teaching on violence (a specific rule; a general principle; a paradigm, seen primarily in Jesus' life; and a symbolic understanding of enemies). Hays's description moves from the most concrete to more elusive and figurative dimensions of the New Testament. Hays works from the particular and specific (a rule that appears in Jesus' teaching) and from that draws out more systematic, overarching aspects of the New Testament's teachings on violence. One problem with comparing the New Testament to the Old Testament on the matter of violence (and perhaps on other issues as well) is that the Old Testament does not have a set of specific teachings on nonviolence and nonretaliation that are as clear as Jesus' Sermon on the Mount and Paul's teachings that derive from it. Indeed, the problem is often thought to be that the Old Testament contains texts that seem to say exactly the opposite. Such texts are then thought to have "irreconcilable tensions" with the New Testament. As already discussed, however, the Old Testament does have symbolic and paradigmatic dimensions that are quite consistent with the New Testament's teachings on violence. Furthermore, there is good reason to think that the more problematic texts on the matter of violence should be interpreted in light of the larger theological understanding of violence.

Such an evaluation of the Old Testament must begin then with the broad, paradigmatic theological tenets that dominate it in its present form. This notion of God as judge and provider of justice is more than just a passing claim in the Old Testament. Perhaps the most fundamental claim about God in the Old Testament is that expressed by the Hebrew sentence, *Yhwh mālak* ("the Lord

231

reigns!"; for the origin and meaning of this metaphor see Mays, *Lord Reigns*). An essential part of that claim is that God is judge of the world and works to ensure justice. Psalm 82 gives one of the clearest pictures of God fulfilling this role:

> God has taken his place in the divine council;
> in the midst of the gods he holds judgment:
> "How long will you judge unjustly
> and show partiality to the wicked?
> Give justice to the weak and the orphan;
> maintain the right of the lowly and the destitute.
> Rescue the weak and the needy;
> deliver them from the hand of the wicked."
> They have neither knowledge nor understanding,
> they walk around in darkness;
> all the foundations of the earth are shaken.
> I say, "You are gods,
> children of the Most High, all of you;
> nevertheless, you shall die like mortals,
> and fall like any prince."
> Rise up, O God, judge the earth;
> for all the nations belong to you!

The picture of God here is extremely important. John Dominic Crossan, a New Testament scholar, goes so far as to identify this psalm as "the single most important text in the entire Christian Bible" (*Birth of Christianity*, 575). While that claim cannot be substantiated, Crossan does here point to a central truth of Scripture: the New Testament vision of the kingdom of God rests on the conviction that God will ultimately right the wrongs in the world.

Psalm 82 has long held an important place in discussions of the nature of God in relation to violence. Luther held that the "gods" (v. 1b) to whom God speaks in the psalm refers to earthly princes, government officials with the capacity to defend the poor (Simpson, *War, Peace, and God*, 82–83). The psalm more naturally suggests, however, that the gods are members of the divine court. A similar image appears in Deuteronomy 32:8, in which God "fixed the boundaries of the peoples according to the number of the gods" (note NRSV here follows a manuscript from Qumran; the Masoretic Text has "sons of Israel" instead of "gods"; the Qumran reading, which is supported also by the Greek and Aramaic versions, was likely seen as unorthodox by a scribe who changed it; it is consistent with the picture of Ps. 82, however). Hence Psalm 82 suggests that the responsibility for establishing justice is God's. Any notion that earthly officials are carrying out a divine mandate should be viewed with caution, however necessary such officials may be to an ordered society. This is essentially the point Hays makes about how Jesus' followers are able to eschew revenge and retaliation. They trust in God to take care of the movement of history. As Psalm 82 emphasizes, "all the nations belong to" God (v. 8).

This paradigm—of God's exclusive prerogative in the matter of establishing justice—appears extensively in Isaiah 1–39. This portion of the book is arranged in large part to draw attention to two kings, Ahaz (Isa. 7–8) and Hezekiah (Isa. 36–39). The contrast between them is drawn precisely on the matter of their trust in the Lord to provide security for Judah. When Isaiah first meets Ahaz he is going out to inspect the security of Jerusalem's water source as he anticipates being attacked by Pekah (king of Israel) and Rezin (king of Syria; 7:1–9). The action seems reasonable and indeed responsible for a king. But Isaiah charges him, "If you do not stand firm in faith, you shall not stand at all" (7:9b). Isaiah insists Ahaz needs only to trust God. Ahaz opts for more practical response, refusing to ask for a sign of God's promised protection on grounds that he will not test God (7:12). But Isaiah declares Ahaz's response to be unfaithful.

At the other end of this portion of the book of Isaiah stands Hezekiah (Isa. 36–39). When faced with the impossible scenario of fighting back against Sennacherib of Assyria, Hezekiah trusts God and God delivers him and Jerusalem out of Sennacherib's hand (37:36–38). Unlike Ahaz, when Hezekiah is faced with the Assyrian threat, he responds with piety and complete trust. He "tore his clothes, covered himself with sackcloth, and went into the house of the LORD" (37:1). Then he sought Isaiah and asked for intercession (37:2–4). Finally, Hezekiah prayed and recognized God as universal sovereign (37:14–20). God defended Hezekiah precisely because "you have prayed to me concerning King Sennacherib of Assyria" (37:21).

Thus it is widely recognized that the final form of Isaiah 1–39 is intended to contrast these two kings, the one who showed exemplary faith by *not* relying on military resources and the other who failed to trust in God and instead sought refuge in the ability of his army (see Seitz, *Zion's Final Destiny*, 195–96).

233

The paradigmatic relationship of trust in God and not in military prowess continues in the identity of the servant in Isaiah 40–55. The identity of this figure is hotly debated. But there is little doubt that in the present form of Isaiah 40–55 and in Jewish interpretation the servant is Israel, the people of God. Isaiah 49:3 makes that identity explicit as do numerous other references to a servant outside the four Servant poems (43:10; 44:1–2).

If the Old Testament has paradigmatic dimensions that promote or at least support nonviolence, it has many specific texts that seem to do just the opposite. The conquest of Canaan and the wars of David are prime examples. But it would be a mistake to conclude that such accounts were read finally as grandiose claims about Israel's military capacity. Indeed, they may not have been written with that intention originally. But certainly the end of the process of writing and editing was dominated by assumptions diametrically opposed to assumptions David and Solomon likely had. As noted already, in the end David was a suffering servant (see Ps. 89:50 [51 Heb.]), a "covenant to the peoples" (Isa. 55:3), not a self-aggrandizing monarch with power illusions. Solomon becomes the wise king who judges the peoples with equity and thus anticipates the Messiah (see the superscriptions in Ps. 72 and in Proverbs). He is no longer the wealthy king who enacted forced labor. Therefore, there is good reason to believe that the governing center of the Old Testament on the issue of violence and military might is in the call to depend on God, to leave vengeance to God, and to call on God as judge of the earth.

To illustrate how the Davidic tradition gave way to notions of trust in God it may be helpful to consider how Jerusalem, David's capital, and Mount Zion, that most sacred portion of the city in which the temple was built, are depicted in the Psalms. Zion is presented as a place of security because God dwells there; sometimes Zion seems impregnable. For example, Psalm 48:1–3 (2–4 Heb.) states it this way:

> Great is the LORD and greatly to be praised
>   in the city of our God.
> His holy mountain, beautiful in elevation,
>   is the joy of all the earth,
> Mount Zion, in the far north,
>   the city of the great King.

Within its citadels
God has shown himself a sure defense.

Because God rules in Zion as king, God also protects Zion and makes it secure. It is a city "God establishes forever" (v. 8 [9 Heb.]); therefore, it is impermeable to enemy attack as long as the Lord dwells there. The psalmist portrays Zion's security by describing the assembly of foreign kings (v. 4 [5 Heb.]) who, "as soon as they saw it, they were astounded; they were in panic, they took to flight" (v. 5 [6 Heb.]).

Modern scholars have often dismissed the theological significance of Zion for many of the same reasons they have discounted the monarchy. Zion has been understood largely as the locus of the monarchy's power and thus as a seat of royal power and part of the ideology of the Judean monarchy. Indeed, some have taken the Psalms' theological portrait of Zion as little more than the propaganda of kings who were attempting to secure support for their reign. There is undoubtedly some truth in the idea that this city was controlled and its image shaped by and for the political benefit of Davidic kings. The enduring portrait of Zion in the Psalms, however, suggests that Zion's importance outstripped any manipulation of the place by human kings. The Psalms present Zion as a place controlled by God alone. God reigns on Zion and, consequently, Zion is a place where God's justice is known. Because of this identity as God's city, Zion is a place where the righteous are at home, but the wicked cannot enter. For the righteous it is a place of order and justice. Outside the gates of Zion they may be persecuted and oppressed, but inside they find shelter in God's presence. For that reason, the righteous long to be in Zion, to be "planted" there where they will be near God. In sum, Zion in the Psalms is a place where the destiny of the righteous becomes clear, where hope is manifest by an experience of God's reign (see Creach, *Destiny of the Righteous*, 111–23).

There is nowhere an explanation for why God chose this particular place. Scholars speculate that David made Jerusalem his capital, and the traditions of God's presence on Zion, the prominent hilltop on which the temple would be built, grew from an ideology meant to support the Davidic monarchy (Roberts, "Davidic Origin"). That may be an accurate assessment of the origins of this theology, but the Psalms themselves say nothing of the sort. They

235

emphasize merely that God desired this place. Psalm 132:13–14 expresses the idea best: "For the LORD has chosen Zion; he has desired it for his habitation; 'This is my resting place forever; here I will reside, for I have desired it.'"

The claim that the Lord chose Zion as a dwelling place has two implications that are important for the discussion of why the righteous might seek Zion as a place of safety. First, Zion is important because it gives access to God's presence, known fully only in God's heavenly temple (see Isa. 6, which describes a vision of the heavenly throne while in the earthly temple). Zion is not secure in and of itself. There are some texts that seem to imply as much, that Zion is impermeable to any attack or threat simply because of its own qualities (Ps. 125:1; Hayes, "Tradition of Zion's Inviolability"). But God's choice is noted time and again as the reason for the centrality of Zion. Other parts of the Old Testament communicate the same message, albeit in different terminology. The Priestly tradition speaks of God's "glory" that rests on this place, but that God can remove at any time (Ezek. 10). Similarly the Deuteronomist refers to Jerusalem as the place God chooses his "name" to dwell (Deut. 12:5). The "name" dwelt originally at Shiloh, but God changed the location because of the corruption of the original site (Jer. 26:6). In other words, Zion is important because God reveals God's self there. Thus the remarkable statement appears in Psalm 48:14 (15 Heb.) after a verbal tour of Zion: "this is God."

A second implication has to do with political claims of human rulers. As the Psalter describes Zion's unique place in God's economy, the notion that God chose Zion sets straight the nature of Zion and the place of those human political leaders who exercised authority over it. This point is important because it denies that the location has any stability apart from God; it is also important because it speaks against any claim by human rulers to have established Zion or rendered it secure. It was God's choice of Zion that established it as the central place on earth, not that any human ruler chose or founded it.

This second point is extremely important because it presents a theological counterclaim to what could be understood as David's establishment of Zion. It is historically probable that David captured Jerusalem, made it his capital, and refortified the city, as 2 Samuel 5:6–12 indicates. In these practical historical terms Zion was appropriately known as "the city of David." Moreover,

236

as J. J. M. Roberts argues, the traditions about Zion probably took present form when David made Zion his capital ("Davidic Origin"). Nevertheless, from the Psalms' point of view, it is God, not David, who chose and established Zion. Therefore, it is God, not David or a Davidic ruler, who made it secure.

Psalm 78 illustrates this point well. Psalm 78:67–70 presents God's choice of David and Zion in an order that is theologically significant:

> He rejected the tent of Joseph,
>> he did not choose the tribe of Ephraim;
> but he chose the tribe of Judah,
>> Mount Zion, which he loves.
> He built his sanctuary like the high heavens,
>> like the earth, which he has founded forever.
> He chose his servant David,
>> and took him from the sheepfolds.

Psalm 78 disregards the historical priority of David's reign in favor of a larger poetic and theological point. Verse 69 reports the building of the temple without reference to Solomon, David's son who constructed the sacred building. Instead it states that God "built the sanctuary." But perhaps more importantly, it suggests that God constructed the temple before David began to rule in Zion. In other words, in Psalm 78's presentation of these matters, God's choice of Zion, and even the reality of the temple, which came after David, predates and takes precedence over David's rule on Zion. As Jon Levenson observes, this sequence of events does not arise from an historical tradition different from that in Samuel and Kings. Rather, it appears "because to the psalmist, the essential meaning of the Temple lies in its foundation in primal times, *in illo tempore*, in other words, in its protological character" (*Sinai and Zion*, 106).

Whatever the origins and development of the Zion tradition, in the present form of psalms about Zion the human king is conspicuously absent as far as his power and influence go. Zion is God's dwelling place, and it is made secure because God is present. The heart of the message of these psalms may be summed up in a famous line from Psalm 46: "Be still, and know that I am God!" (v. 10a [11a Heb.]). As noted earlier, the beginning of this verse might better be translated, "Let go." The expression refers to humans giving up their efforts to control the world or correct the world. With this message the Davidic-Zionist tradition takes its place alongside the book of Isaiah (discussed above) as a grand testimony to the sovereignty of God and as a call to human beings to allow God to control the world. An essential part of this message is the claim that God "makes wars cease to the end of the earth; he breaks the bow, and shatters the spear; he burns the shields with fire" (Ps. 46:9 [10 Heb.]). Far from empowering any human being to engage in war, this tradition thus denies humans the right to fight. The battle is left to God, and God is working to bring war to an end.

Conclusion:
Both Testaments Reject Reliance on Force

In this chapter I have attempted to show that both Old and New Testaments have features that urge nonviolence, that call human coercion into question. The tension between the Testaments is real, however, and must be acknowledged. It is real precisely because Jesus did more than rehearse the Old. He introduced new demands on his followers. As Matthew makes clear, the new teachings of Jesus are consistent with the teachings in the Old Testament and are intended to fulfill them (Matt. 5:17–20). Matthew is also clear, however, in saying that Jesus pointed to a fresh interpretation of the Old. As Davies and Allison rightly put it, Jesus was attempting to "enable his followers to obtain righteousness greater than that exhibited by the custodians of the past" (*Matthew*, 1:565). In so doing, Jesus (and the early church) put the issue of violence at the center of the Scripture.

Perhaps the point that Jesus highlighted in so many ways is that the illusion of power through violence is the key for Christians who seek a way to read the Bible's testimony on violence altogether. The issue is not so much that the Old Testament contains instructions and stories that have values that Jesus then rejected. Indeed, as I attempted to show in chapters 1–7, much in the Old Testament is remarkably consistent with the teachings of Jesus on this matter. The issue rather is that Jesus' special focus on the concern for violence calls for similar attention to the matter throughout the canon. Hence when Christians read and interpret the Old Testament they are not directed by their tradition to place first the concern for the land, the temple, or torah, as important as each of those concerns

238

remains. Rather, they read the whole with the idea that the life and teachings of Jesus are the goal to which all leads. And if that is so, the main question becomes, what is the nature and shape of the kingdom of God? To that question both Testaments proclaim, "the LORD reigns!"—a proclamation that has definite ethical and political ramifications. For if the Lord truly reigns, it means no human being has the right to coercive power. The reality of this world is that many people act as though they do. Stanley Hauerwas is right when he says, "A leadership that cannot stand the force of truth must always rely on armies" ("Story-Formed Community," 195). When we allow Jesus to reveal this point to us, we are then called to wrestle constantly with the fact that we regularly participate in structures that deny the truth of both Testaments' claim that "the LORD is king."

BIBLIOGRAPHY

For Further Study

Bright, John. *The Authority of the Old Testament*. Nashville: Abingdon Press, 1967.

Brueggemann, Walter. *Revelation and Violence*. Milwaukee: Marquette University Press, 1986.

———. "Voice as Counter to Violence." *Calvin Theological Journal* 36, no. 1 (2001): 22–33.

Collins, John J. *Does the Bible Justify Violence?* Facets. Minneapolis: Fortress Press, 2004.

Creach, Jerome F. D. *Joshua*. Interpretation: A Bible Commentary for Teaching and Preaching. Louisville: Westminster John Knox Press, 2003.

Davis, Ellen F. "Critical Traditioning: Seeking an Inner Biblical Hermeneutic." *Anglican Theological Review* 82, no. 4 (2000): 733–51.

Earl, Douglas. *Reading Joshua as Christian Scripture*. Winona Lake, IN: Eisenbrauns, 2010.

Fretheim, Terence. *God and World in the Old Testament: A Relational Theology of Creation*. Nashville: Abingdon Press, 2005.

———. "'I Was Only a Little Angry': Divine Violence in the Prophets." *Interpretation* 58, no. 4 (2004): 365–75.

———. "The Plagues as Ecological Signs of Historical Disaster." *Journal of Biblical Literature* 110, no. 3 (1991): 385–96.

———. *The Suffering of God: An Old Testament Perspective*. Overtures to Biblical Theology. Philadelphia: Fortress Press, 1984.

Good, Robert M. "The Just War in Ancient Israel." *Journal of Biblical Literature* 104, no. 3 (1985): 385–400.

Hays, Richard B. *The Moral Vision of the New Testament: Community, Cross, New Creation. A Contemporary Introduction to New Testament Ethics*. San Francisco: HarperSanFrancisco, 1996.

Heim, S. Mark. *Saved from Sacrifice: A Theology of the Cross*. Grand Rapids: Eerdmans, 2006.

Kaminsky, Joel. *Yet I Loved Jacob: Reclaiming the Biblical Concept of Election*. Nashville: Abingdon Press, 2007.

Middleton, J. Richard. *The Liberating Image: The Imago Dei in Genesis 1*. Grand Rapids: Brazos Press, 2005.

Miller, Patrick D., Jr. *The Divine Warrior in Early Israel*. Harvard Semitic Monograph 5. Cambridge, MA: Harvard University Press, 1973.

———. *The God You Have: Politics and the First Commandment*. Facets. Minneapolis: Fortress Press, 2004.

———. *The Ten Commandments*. Interpretation: Resources for the Use of Scripture in the Church. Louisville: Westminster John Knox Press, 2009.

Origen. *Homilies on Joshua*. Translated by Barbara J. Bruce. Edited by Cynthia White. Fathers of the Church 105. Washington, DC: Catholic University of America Press, 2002.

Williams, James G. *The Bible, Violence, and the Sacred: Liberation from the Myth of Sanctioned Violence*. San Francisco: HarperSanFrancisco, 1992.

Yoder, John Howard. *The Politics of Jesus: Behold the Man! Our Victorious Lamb*. Grand Rapids: Eerdmans, 1994.

———. *The War of the Lamb: The Ethics of Nonviolence and Peacemaking*. Edited by Glenn Stassen, Mark Thiessen Nation, and Matt Hamsher. Grand Rapids: Brazos Press, 2009.

Zenger, Erich. *A God of Vengeance? Understanding the Psalms of Divine Wrath*. Translated by Linda M. Maloney. Louisville: Westminster John Knox Press, 1994.

Works Cited

Achtemeier, Elizabeth. *Preaching Hard Texts of the Old Testament*. Peabody, MA: Hendrickson, 1998.

———. "Righteousness in the Old Testament." Pages 80–85 in vol. 4 of *The Interpreter's Dictionary of the Bible*. Edited by George A. Buttrick. 4 vols. Nashville: Abingdon Press, 1962.

Achtemeier, Paul J. *1 Peter: A Commentary on First Peter*. Hermeneia—A Critical and Historical Commentary on the Bible. Minneapolis: Fortress Press, 1996.

Ackerman, Susan. "The Queen Mother and the Cult in Ancient Israel." *Journal of Biblical Literature* 112, no. 3 (1993): 385–401.

————. *Warrior, Dancer, Seductress, Queen: Women in Judges and Biblical Israel*. New Haven, CT: Yale University Press, 1998.

Allison, Dale C., Jr. *The New Moses: A Matthean Typology*. Minneapolis: Fortress Press, 1993.

————. "Rejecting Violent Judgment: Luke 9:52–56 and Its Relatives." *Journal of Biblical Literature* 121, no. 3 (2002): 459–78.

————. *Resurrecting Jesus: The Earliest Christian Tradition and Its Interpreters*. New York: T&T Clark, 2005.

————. *The Sermon on the Mount: Inspiring the Moral Imagination*. Companions to the New Testament. New York: Crossroad, 1999.

————. *Testament of Abraham*. New York: de Gruyter, 2003.

Augustine. *City of God*. Translated by Marcus Dods. Pages 1–511 in vol. 2 of *Nicene and Post-Nicene Fathers*. Edited by Philip Schaff. Reprint, New York: Cosimo Classics, 2007.

————. *Christian Doctrine*. Translated by J. F. Shaw. Pages 515–97 in vol. 2 of *Nicene and Post-Nicene Fathers*. Edited by Philip Schaff. Reprint, New York: Cosimo Classics, 2007.

————. *Expositions on the Book of Psalms*. Vol. 8 of *Nicene and Post-Nicene Fathers*. Edited by Philip Schaff. Reprint, Grand Rapids: Eerdmans, 1956.

Aune, David E. *Revelation 17–22*. Word Biblical Commentary 52C. Nashville: Nelson, 1998.

Bailey, Lloyd R. "Gehenna: The Topography of Hell." *Biblical Archaeologist* 49, no. 3 (1986): 187–91.

Bainton, Roland. *Christian Attitudes Toward War and Peace: A Historical Survey and Critical Re-evaluation*. Nashville: Abingdon Press, 1960.

Barker, Margaret. *Creation: A Biblical Vision for the Environment*. New York: T&T Clark, 2010.

Barr, James. *The Garden of Eden and the Hope of Immortality*. Minneapolis: Fortress Press, 1992.

Barth, Karl. *Church Dogmatics*. Vol. 3, *The Doctrine of Creation*. Part 4. Translated by A. T. Mackay et al. Edited by G. W. Bromiley and T. F. Torrance. Edinburgh: T&T Clark, 1961.

Bartlett, David L. *The Shape of Scriptural Authority*. Philadelphia: Fortress Press, 1983.

Barton, John. *Understanding Old Testament Ethics: Approaches and Explorations*. Louisville: Westminster John Knox Press, 2003.

243

————. *Holy Writings, Sacred Text: The Canon in Early Christianity*. Louisville: Westminster John Knox Press, 1997.

Bax, Douglas S. "From Constantine to Calvin: The Doctrine of the Just War." Pages 147–71 in *Theology & Violence: The South African Debate*. Edited by Charles Villa-Vicencio. Grand Rapids: Eerdmans, 1987.

Berkhof, Hendrikus. *Christian Faith: An Introduction to the Study of the Faith*. Translated by Sierd Woudstra. Rev. ed. Grand Rapids: Eerdmans, 1985.

Bernstein, Alan E. "Esoteric Theology: William of Auvergone on the Fires of Hell and Pergatory." *Speculum* 57, no. 3 (1982): 509–31.

Blenkinsopp, Joseph. "Abraham as Paradigm in the Priestly History in Genesis." *Journal of Biblical Literature* 128, no. 2 (2009): 225–41.

————. *Isaiah 56–66: A New Translation with Introduction and Commentary*. Anchor Bible 19B. New York: Doubleday, 2003.

Bonhoeffer, Dietrich. *Psalms: Prayer Book of the Bible*. Translated by J. H. Burtness. Minneapolis: Augsburg, 1970.

Bovon, François. "The Child and the Beast: Fighting Violence in Ancient Christianity." *Harvard Theological Review* 92, no. 4 (1999): 369–92.

Bower, Peter C., ed. *Handbook for the Revised Common Lectionary*. Louisville: Westminster John Knox Press, 1996.

Boyd, Gregory. *God at War: The Bible and Spiritual Conflict*. Downers Grove, IL: InterVarsity Press, 1997.

Boyle, Marjorie O'Rourke, "'In the Heart of the Sea': Fathoming the Exodus." *Journal of Near Eastern Studies* 63, no. 1 (2004): 17–27.

Brenner, Athalya. "Some Reflections on Violence against Women and the Image of the Hebrew God: The Prophetic Books Revisited." Pages 69–81 in *On the Cutting Edge: The Study of Women in Biblical Worlds: Essays in Honor or Elisabeth Schüssler Fiorenza*. Edited by Jane Schaberg, Alice Bach, and Esther Fuchs. New York: Continuum, 2004.

————. "'On the Rivers of Babylon' (Psalm 137), or Between Victim and Perpetrator." Pages 76–91 in *Sanctified Aggression: Legacies of Biblical and Post Biblical Vocabularies of Violence*. Edited by Jonneke Bekkenkamp and Yvonne Sherwood.

Journal for the Study of the Old Testament Supplement Series 400. London: T&T Clark, 2003.

Brettler, Marc Z. "The Book of Judges: Literature as Politics." *Journal of Biblical Literature* 108, no. 3 (1989): 395–418.

Bright, John. *A History of Israel*. 3rd ed. Philadelphia: Westminster Press, 1981.

———. *The Authority of the Old Testament*. Nashville: Abingdon Press, 1967.

Brodie, Thomas L. "The Departure for Jerusalem (Luke 9,51–56) as a Rhetorical Imitation of Elijah's Departure for the Jordan (1 Kings 1,1–2,6)." *Biblica* 70, no. 1 (1989): 96–109.

Brown, Cheryl Anne. *No Longer Be Silent: First Century Jewish Portraits of Biblical Women*. Louisville: Westminster John Knox Press, 1992.

Brown, William P. *The Ethos of the Cosmos: The Genesis of Moral Imagination in the Bible*. Grand Rapids: Eerdmans, 1999.

———. *Seeing the Psalms: A Theology of Metaphor*. Louisville: Westminster John Knox Press, 2002.

Bruckner, James K. *Implied Law in the Abraham Narrative: A Literary and Theological Analysis*. Journal for the Study of the Old Testament Supplement Series 335. Sheffield: Sheffield Academic Press, 2001.

Brueggemann, Walter. "The Book of Exodus." Pages 675–981 in vol. 1 of *The New Interpreter's Bible*. Edited by Leander E. Keck. Nashville: Abingdon Press, 1994.

———. *Genesis*. Interpretation: A Bible Commentary for Teaching and Preaching. Louisville: Westminster John Knox Press, 1982.

———. *Isaiah 40–66*. Westminster Bible Companion. Louisville: Westminster John Knox Press, 1998.

———. "Kerygma of the Priestly Writers." Pages 101–13 in *The Vitality of Old Testament Traditions,* by Walter Brueggemann and Hans Walter Wolff. 2nd ed. Atlanta: John Knox Press, 1982. Reprinted from *Zeitschrift für die alttestamentliche Wissenschaft* 84, no. 4 (1972): 397–414.

———. *Praying the Psalms*. Winona, MN: Saint Mary's Press, 1982.

———. *The Message of the Psalms*. Minneapolis: Augsburg Publishing House, 1984.

———. "Psalm 109: Three Times 'Steadfast Love.'" *Word and World* 5, no. 2 (1985): 144–54.

———. *Revelation and Violence*. Milwaukee: Marquette University Press, 1986.

———. *Theology of the Old Testament: Testimony, Dispute, Advocacy*. Minneapolis: Fortress Press, 1997.

———. "Voice as Counter to Violence." *Calvin Theological Journal* 36, no. 1 (2001): 22–33.

Burnham, Sylvester. "The Mission and Work of Elijah." *Biblical World* 24, no. 3 (1904): 180–87.

Caird, G. B. *The Revelation of Saint John*. Black's New Testament Commentary. 1966. Reprint, Peabody, MA: Hendrickson, 1993.

Calvin, John. *Commentaries on the First Book of Moses Called Genesis*. 2 vols. Translated by John King. Reprint, Grand Rapids: Eerdmans, 1948.

Carrol, Noël. "Horror and Humor." *Journal of Aesthetics and Art Criticism* 57, no. 2 (1999): 145–60.

Charles, R. H. *The Apocrypha and Pseudepigrapha of the Old Testament*. Oxford: Clarendon Press, 1913.

Childs, Brevard S. *The Book of Exodus*. Old Testament Library. Philadelphia: Westminster Press, 1974.

Christensen, Duane L. *Transformations of the War Oracle in Old Testament Prophecy: Studies in the Oracles Against the Nations*. Harvard Dissertations in Religion 3. Missoula, MT: Scholars Press, 1975.

Clifford, Richard J. "Psalm 89: A Lament over the Davidic Ruler's Continued Failure." *Harvard Theological Review* 73, no. 1 (1980): 35–47.

Clines, David J. A. *The Esther Scroll: The Story of the Story*. Journal for the Study of the Old Testament Supplement Series 30. Sheffield: JSOT Press, 1984.

Collins, John J. *Does the Bible Justify Violence?* Facets. Minneapolis: Fortress Press, 2004.

———. "The Zeal of Phinehas: The Bible and the Legitimation of Violence." *Journal of Biblical Literature* 122, no. 1 (2003): 3–21.

Craig, Kenneth M., Jr. *Reading Esther: A Case for the Literary Canivalesque*. Louisville: Westminster John Knox Press, 1995.

Craigie, Peter C. *The Problem of War in the Old Testament*. Grand Rapids: Eerdmans, 1978.

Creach, Jerome F. D. *The Destiny of the Righteous in the Psalms*. St. Louis: Chalice Press, 2008.

————. *Joshua.* Interpretation: A Bible Commentary for Teaching and Preaching. Louisville: Westminster John Knox Press, 2003.

————. *Yahweh as Refuge and the Editing of the Hebrew Psalter.* Journal for the Study of the Old Testament Supplement Series 217. Sheffield: Sheffield Academic Press, 1996.

Cross, Frank Moore. *Canaanite Myth and Hebrew Epic: Essays in the History of the Religion of Israel.* Cambridge, MA: Harvard University Press, 1973.

Crossan, John Dominic. *The Birth of Christianity: Discovering What Happened in the Years Immediately after the Execution of Jesus.* San Francisco: HarperSanFrancisco, 1998.

Dahood, Mitchell. *Psalms III: 101–150.* Anchor Bible 17A. Garden City, NY: Doubleday, 1970.

Davies, Eryl. "The Morally Dubious Passages of the Hebrew Bible: An Examination of Some Proposed Solutions." *Currents in Biblical Research* 3, no. 2 (2005): 197–228.

Davies, W. D., and Dale C. Allison. *A Critical and Exegetical Commentary on the Gospel according to Saint Matthew.* 3 vols. International Critical Commentary. 1988–1997. Reprint, London: T&T Clark, 2004.

Davis, Ellen F. "Critical Traditioning: Seeking an Inner Biblical Hermeneutic." *Anglican Theological Review* 82, no. 4 (2000): 733–51.

————. *Getting Involved with God: Rediscovering the Old Testament.* Boston: Cowley, 2001.

————. *Scripture, Culture, and Agriculture: An Agrarian Reading of the Bible.* New York: Cambridge University Press, 2009.

————. "Teaching the Bible Confessionally in the Church." Pages 9–26 in *The Art of Reading Scripture.* Edited by Ellen F. Davis and Richard B. Hays. Grand Rapids: Eerdmans, 2003.

Deissler, Alfons. *Die Psalmen.* 3 vols. 7th ed. Reprint, Düsseldorf: Patmos, 2002.

Dobbs-Allsopp, F. W. *Lamentations.* Interpretation: A Bible Commentary for Teaching and Preaching. Louisville: Westminster John Knox Press, 2002.

Earl, Douglas. *Reading Joshua as Christian Scripture.* Winona Lake, IN: Eisenbrauns, 2010.

Feldman, Louis H. *"Remember Amalek!" Vengeance, Zealotry, and Group Destruction in the Bible According to Philo, Pseudo-Philo, and Josephus.* Cincinnati: Hebrew Union College Press, 2004.

247

Finkelstein, Israel, and Neil Asher Silberman. *The Bible Unearthed: Archaeology's New Vision of Ancient Israel and the Origins of Its Sacred Texts*. New York: Simon & Schuster, 2002.

Fishbane, Michael. *Biblical Interpretation in Ancient Israel*. Oxford: Oxford University Press, 1985.

Fitzmyer, Joseph A. *The Acts of the Apostles: A New Translation with Introduction and Commentary*. Anchor Bible 31. New York: Doubleday, 1998.

———. *The Gospel According to Luke: Introduction, Translation, and Notes*. 2 vols. Anchor Bible 28–28A. Garden City, NY: Doubleday, 1981–1985.

Fleming, Wallace. *The History of Tyre*. Columbia University Oriental Studies 10. New York: Columbia University Press, 1915.

Fretheim, Terence E. "The Book of Genesis." Pages 319–674 in vol. 1 of *The New Interpreter's Bible*. Edited by Leander E. Keck. Nashville: Abingdon Press, 1994.

———. *Exodus*. Interpretation: A Bible Commentary for Teaching and Preaching. Louisville: John Knox Press, 1991.

———. *God and World in the Old Testament: A Relational Theology of Creation*. Nashville: Abingdon Press, 2005.

———. "'I Was Only a Little Angry': Divine Violence in the Prophets." *Interpretation* 58, no. 4 (2004): 365–75.

———. "The Plagues as Ecological Signs of Historical Disaster." *Journal of Biblical Literature* 110, no. 3 (1991): 385–96.

———. *The Suffering of God: An Old Testament Perspective*. Overtures to Biblical Theology. Minneapolis: Fortress Press, 1984.

Friedman, Richard Elliott. *The Bible with Sources Revealed*. New York: HarperOne, 2003.

Frymer-Kensky, Tikva S. *Studies in Bible and Feminist Criticism*. Philadelphia: Jewish Publication Society, 2006.

Gerstenberger, Erhard. "Der Klagende Mensch: Anmerkungen zu den Klagegattungen in Israel." Pages 64–72 in *Probleme biblischer Theologie. Gerhard von Rad zum 70. Geburtstag*. Edited by Hans Walter Wolff. Munich: Kaiser Verlag, 1971.

———. *Leviticus: A Commentary*. Translated by Douglas W. Stott. Old Testament Library. Louisville: Westminster John Knox Press, 1993.

248 ———. *Psalms, Part 1; with an Introduction to Cultic Poetry*. Forms of the Old Testament Literature 13. Grand Rapids: Eerdmans, 1988.

Ginzberg, Louis. *The Legends of the Jews*. 7 vols. Philadelphia: Jewish Publication Society, 1909–1938.

Girard, René. *The Scapegoat*. Translated by Yvonne Freccero. Baltimore: Johns Hopkins University Press, 1986.

———. *Things Hidden Since the Foundation of the World*. Translated by Stephen Bann and Michael Metteer. Stanford, CA: Stanford University Press, 1978.

Glatzer, Nahum, ed. *The Passover Haggadah: With English Translation and Commentary*. Rev. ed. New York: Schocken, 1969.

Goldingay, John. *Psalms*. Vol. 3, *Psalms 90–150*. Baker Commentary on the Old Testament Wisdom and Psalms. Grand Rapids: Baker Academic, 2006.

Good, Robert M. "The Just War in Ancient Israel." *Journal of Biblical Literature* 104, no. 3 (1985): 385–400.

Greenberg, Moshe. *Ezekiel 21–37: A New Translation with Introduction and Commentary*. Anchor Bible 22A. New York: Doubleday, 1997.

Guillermoprieto, Alma. "Troubled Spirits." *National Geographic*, 217, no. 5 (2010): 54–73.

Gunkel, Hermann. *Creation and Chaos in the Primeval Era and the Eschaton: A Religio-Historical Study of Genesis 1 and Revelation 12*. Translated by K. William Whitney Jr. Grand Rapids: Eerdmans, 2006.

Gunn, David M. *The Fate of King Saul: An Interpretation of a Biblical Story*. Journal for the Study of the Old Testament Supplement Series 14. Sheffield: JSOT Press, 1980.

Hall, Douglas John. *The Cross in Our Context: Jesus and the Suffering World*. Minneapolis: Fortress Press, 2003.

Halpern, Baruch. "The Resourceful Israelite Historian: The Song of Deborah and Israelite Historiography." *Harvard Theological Review* 76, no. 4 (1983): 379–401.

Hanson, Paul D. *Isaiah 40–66*. Interpretation: A Bible Commentary for Teaching and Preaching. Louisville: John Knox Press, 1995.

Hasel, Michael G. *Military Practice and Polemic: Israel's Laws of Warfare in Near Eastern Practice*. Berrien Springs, MI: Andrews University Press, 2005.

Hauerwas, Stanley. "A Story-Formed Community." Pages 171–99 in *The Hauerwas Reader*. Edited by John Berkman and Michael Cartwright. Durham, NC: Duke University Press, 2001.

Hauser, Alan. "Linguistic and Thematic Links between Genesis 4:1–16 and Genesis 2–3." *Journal of the Evangelical Theological Society* 23, no. 4 (1980): 297–305.

Havrelock, Rachel. "The Two Maps of Israel's Land." *Journal of Biblical Literature*, 126, no. 4 (2007): 649–67.

Hayes, John H. "The Tradition of Zion's Inviolability." *Journal of Biblical Literature* 82, no. 4 (1963): 419–26.

Hays, Richard B. *The Moral Vision of the New Testament: Community, Cross, New Creation. A Contemporary Introduction to New Testament Ethics*. San Francisco: HarperSanFrancisco, 1996.

Head, Peter M. "The Foreign God and the Sudden Christ: Theology and Christology in Marcion's Gospel Redaction." *Tyndale Bulletin* 44, no. 2 (1993): 307–21.

Hendel, Ronald. "The Exodus in Biblical Memory." *Journal of Biblical Literature* 120, no. 4 (2001): 601–22.

Henry, Matthew. *Concise Commentary on the Bible*. Grand Rapids: Christian Classics Ethereal Library, 2010.

Heschel, Abraham J. *The Prophets*. New York: Harper, 1963.

———. *The Sabbath: Its Meaning for Modern Man*. New York: H. Wolff, 1951.

Hirsch, Samson Raphael. *The Pentateuch: Translation and Commentary*. Vol. 2, *Exodus*. 2nd ed. Translated by Isaac Levy. New York: Judaica Press, 1956.

Hitchens, Christopher. *God Is Not Great: How Religion Poisons Everything*. New York: Hachette, 2007.

Hoffman, Yair. "The Deuteronomistic Concept of the Herem." *Zeitschrift für die alttestamentliche Wissenschaft* 111, no. 2 (1999): 196–210.

Homer. *The Odyssey*. Translated by A. T. Murray. 2 vols. Loeb Classical Library. 1919. Reprint, Cambridge, MA: Harvard University Press, 1994.

Huber, Wolfgang. *Violence: The Unrelenting Assault on Human Dignity*. Translated by Ruth C. L. Gritsch. Minneapolis: Fortress Press, 1996.

Hunter, Alastair G. "(De)Nominating Amalek: Racist Stereotyping in the Bible and the Justification of Discrimination." Pages 92–108 in *Sanctified Aggression: Legacies of Biblical and Post-Biblical Vocabularies of Violence*. Edited by Jonneke Bekkenkamp and Yvonne Sherwood. London: T&T Clark, 2003.

Jacobs, Louis. "Praying for the Downfall of the Wicked." *Modern Judaism* 2, no. 3 (1982): 297–310.

Jacobsen, Thorkild. *The Treasures of Darkness: A History of Mesopotamian Religion.* New Haven, CT: Yale University Press, 1976.

Jastrow, Marcus. *A Dictionary of the Targumim, the Talmud Babli and Yerushalm, and the Midrashic Literature with an Index of Scriptural Quotations.* New York: Choreb, 1926.

Jenni, Ernst. "אהב *'hb* to love." Pages 45–54 in vol. 1 of *Theological Lexicon of the Old Testament.* Edited by Ernst Jenni and Claus Westermann. Translated by Mark E. Biddle. 3 vols. Peabody, MA: Hendrickson, 1997.

Jidejian, Nina. *Tyre through the Ages.* Beirut: Dar El-Mashreq, 1969.

Jipp, Joshua. "Luke's Scriptural Suffering Messiah: A Search for Precedent, a Search for Identity." *Catholic Biblical Quarterly* 72, no. 2 (2010): 255–74.

Kaminsky, Joel S. "Did Election Imply the Mistreatment of Non-Israelites?" *Harvard Theological Review* 96, no. 4 (2003): 397–425.

———. *Yet I Loved Jacob: Reclaiming the Biblical Concept of Election.* Nashville: Abingdon Press, 2007.

Kamuf, Peggy. "Author of a Crime." Pages 187–207 in *A Feminist Companion to Judges.* Edited by Athalya Brenner. Feminist Companion to the Bible 4. Sheffield: Sheffield Academic Press, 1993.

Keel, Othmar. *The Symbolism of the Biblical World: Ancient Near Eastern Iconography and the Book of Psalms.* Translated by Timothy J. Hallett. 1978. Reprint, Winona Lake, IN: Eisenbrauns, 1997.

King, Martin Luther, Jr. *Strength to Love.* Philadelphia: Fortress Press, 1981.

Kirk-Duggan, Cheryl. "Violence." Pages 1357–58 in *Eerdmans Dictionary of the Bible.* Edited by David Noel Freedman. Grand Rapids: Eerdmans, 2000.

———. *Violence and Theology.* Horizons in Theology. Nashville: Abingdon Press, 2006.

Klein, Lillian R. *The Triumph of Irony in the Book of Judges.* Bible and Literature Series 14. Journal for the Study of the Old Testament Supplement Series 68. Sheffield: Almond Press, 1988.

Kriegshauser, Laurence. *Praying the Psalms in Christ*. Notre Dame, IN: University of Notre Dame Press, 2009.

Lapsley, Jacqueline E. *Whispering the Word: Hearing Women's Stories in the Old Testament*. Louisville: Westminster John Knox Press, 2005.

Levenson, Jon D. *Creation and the Persistence of Evil: The Jewish Drama of Divine Omnipotence*. San Francisco: Harper & Row, 1988.

———. *The Death and Resurrection of the Beloved Son: The Transformation of Child Sacrifice in Judaism and Christianity*. New Haven, CT: Yale University Press, 1995.

———. *Esther: A Commentary*. Old Testament Library. Louisville: Westminster John Knox Press, 1997.

———. *Sinai and Zion: An Entry into the Jewish Bible*. Minneapolis: Winston Press, 1985.

Levine, Étan, "The Syriac Version of Genesis IV 1–16." *Vetus Testamentum* 26, no. 1 (1976): 70–78.

Lind, Millard C. "The Concept of Political Power in Ancient Israel." *Annual of the Swedish Theological Institute* 7 (1970): 4–24.

———. *Yahweh Is a Warrior: The Theology of Warfare in Ancient Israel*. Scottdale, PA: Herald Press, 1980.

Lohfink, Norbert. "חָרַם *ḥāram*." Pages 180–99 in vol. 5 of *Theological Dictionary of the Old Testament*. Edited by G. Johannes Botterweck and Helmer Ringgren. Translated by David E. Green. Grand Rapids: Eerdmans, 1986.

Long, Burke O. *1 Kings; with an Introduction to Historical Literature*. Forms of the Old Testament Literature 9. Grand Rapids: Eerdmans, 1984.

Luckenbill, Daniel David. *Ancient Records of Assyria and Babylonia*. 2 vols. 1926–1927. Reprint, New York: Greenwood Press, 1968.

MacGregor, G. H. C. *The New Testament Basis of Pacifism*. London: Fellowship of Reconciliation, 1953.

Mays, James L. *Amos: A Commentary*. Old Testament Library. Philadelphia: Westminster Press, 1969.

———. "Justice: Perspectives from the Prophetic Tradition." *Interpretation* 37, no. 1 (1983): 1–17.

———. *The Lord Reigns: A Theological Handbook to the Psalms*. Louisville: Westminster John Knox Press, 1994.

————. *Psalms*. Interpretation: A Bible Commentary for Teaching and Preaching. Louisville: Westminster John Knox Press, 1994.

Mazar, Amihai. *Archaeology of the Land of the Bible: 10,000–586 BCE*. 2nd ed. New York: Doubleday, 1992.

McBride, S. Dean, Jr. "Divine Protocol: Genesis 1:1–2:3 as Prologue to the Pentateuch." Pages 3–41 in *God Who Creates: Essays in Honor of W. Sibley Towner*. Edited by William P. Brown and S. Dean McBride Jr. Grand Rapids: Eerdmans, 2000.

McCann, J. Clinton, Jr. "The Book of Psalms." Pages 641–1280 in vol. 4 of *The New Interpreter's Bible*. Edited by Leander E. Keck. Nashville: Abingdon Press, 1996.

————. *Judges*. Interpretation: A Bible Commentary for Teaching and Preaching. Louisville: Westminster John Knox Press, 2002.

————. "The Single Most Important Text in the Entire Bible: Toward a Theology of the Psalms." Pages 63–76 in *Soundings in the Theology of the Psalms: Perspectives and Methods in Contemporary Scholarship*. Edited by Rolf A. Jacobson. Minneapolis: Fortress Press, 2010.

McCarter, P. Kyle. *I Samuel: A New Translation with Introduction, Notes, and Commentary*. Anchor Bible 8. New York: Doubleday, 1980.

————. "The River Ordeal in Israelite Literature." *Harvard Theological Review* 66, no. 4 (1973): 403–12.

McGinnis, Claire Mathews. "Swimming with the Divine Tide: An Ignatian Reading of 1 Samuel." Pages 240–70 in *Theological Exegesis: Essays in Honor of Brevard S. Childs*. Edited by Christopher Seitz and Kathryn Greene-McCreight. Grand Rapids: Eerdmans, 1999.

Meyers, Carol. *Discovering Eve: Ancient Israelite Women in Context*. New York: Oxford University Press, 1988.

————. "The Family in Early Israel." Pages 1–47 in *Families in Ancient Israel*, by Leo G. Perdue, Joseph Blenkinsopp, John J. Collins, and Carol Meyers. Family, Religion, and Culture. Louisville: Westminster John Knox Press, 1997.

Middleton, J. Richard. "Created in the Image of a Violent God? The Ethical Problem of the Conquest of Chaos in the Biblical Creation Texts." *Interpretation* 58, no. 4 (2004): 341–55.

————. *The Liberating Image: The Imago Dei in Genesis 1*. Grand Rapids: Brazos Press, 2005.

Miller, Patrick D. "Animal Names as Designations in Ugaritic and Hebrew," *Ugarit-Forschungen* 2 (1970): 177–86.

———. "Divine Council and the Prophetic Call to War." *Vetus Testamentum* 18, no. 1 (1968): 100–107.

———. *The Divine Warrior in Early Israel*. Cambridge, MA: Harvard University Press, 1973.

———. *The God You Have: Politics and the First Commandment*. Facets. Minneapolis: Fortress Press, 2004.

———. *The Ten Commandments*. Interpretation: Resources for the Use of Scripture in the Church. Louisville: Westminster John Knox Press, 2009.

———. *They Cried to the Lord: The Form and Theology of Biblical Prayer*. Minneapolis: Fortress Press, 1994.

———. *The Way of the Lord: Essays in Old Testament Theology*. Grand Rapids: Eerdmans, 2007.

Moberly, R. W. L. *The Old Testament of the Old Testament: Patriarchal Narratives and Mosaic Yahwism*. Overtures to Biblical Theology. Minneapolis: Fortress Press, 1992.

———. "Toward an Interpretation of the Shema." Pages 124–44 in *Theological Exegesis: Essays in Honor of Brevard S. Childs*. Edited by Christopher Seitz and Kathryn Greene-McCreight. Grand Rapids: Eerdmans, 1999.

Moessner, David P. "Two Lords 'at the Right Hand'? The Psalms and an Intertextual Reading of Peter's Pentecost Speech (Acts 2:14–36)." Pages 215–32 in *Literary Studies in Luke-Acts: Essays in Honor of Joseph B. Tyson*. Edited by Richard P. Thompson and Thomas E. Phillips. Macon, GA: Mercer University Press, 1998.

Moltmann, Jürgen. *The Crucified God: The Cross of Christ as the Foundation and Criticism of Christian Theology*. Translated by R. A. Wilson and John Bowden. Philadelphia: Fortress Press, 1974.

———. *The Way of Jesus Christ: Christology in Messianic Dimensions*. Translated by Margaret Kohl. 1990. Reprint, Minneapolis: Fortress Press, 1993.

Monroe, Lauren A. S. "Israelite, Moabite and Sabaean War-Ḥērem Traditions and the Forging of National Identity: Reconsidering the Sabaean Text RES 3945 in Light of Biblical and Moabite Evidence." *Vetus Testamentum* 57, no. 3 (2007): 318–341.

Moran, "Ancient Near Eastern Background of the Love of God in Deuteronomy." *Catholic Biblical Quarterly* 25, no. 1 (1963): 77–87.

Moye, Richard H. "In the Beginning: Myth and History in Genesis and Exodus." *Journal of Biblical Literature* 109, no. 4 (1990): 577–98.

Murphy, Frederick J. *Fallen Is Babylon: The Revelation to John.* Harrisburg: Trinity Press International, 1998.

Nelson, Richard D. *Deuteronomy: A Commentary.* Old Testament Library. Louisville: Westminster John Knox Press, 2002.

———. *First and Second Kings.* Interpretation: A Bible Commentary for Teaching and Preaching. Atlanta: John Knox Press, 1987.

———. "Josiah in the Book of Joshua." *Journal of Biblical Literature* 100, no. 4 (1981): 531–40.

Niditch, Susan. *Judges: A Commentary.* Old Testament Library. Louisville: Westminster John Knox Press, 2008.

Niskanen, Paul. "The Poetics of Adam: The Creation of אדם in the Image of אלהים." *Journal of Biblical Literature* 128, no. 3 (2009): 417–36.

Noth, Martin. *The Deuteronomistic History.* Journal for the Study of the Old Testament Supplement Series 15. Sheffield: Sheffield Academic Press, 1981.

Olson, Dennis T. "The Book of Judges." Pages 721–888 in vol. 2 of *The New Interpreter's Bible.* Edited by Leander E. Keck. Nashville: Abingdon Press, 1998.

Origen. *De Principiis.* Translated by Frederick Crombie. Pages 239–384 in vol. 4 of *Ante-Nicene Fathers.* Edited by Alexander Roberts and James Donaldson. Reprint, Grand Rapids: Eerdmans, 1956.

———. *Homilies on Joshua.* Translated by Barbara J. Bruce. Edited by Cynthia White. Fathers of the Church 105. Washington, DC: Catholic University of America Press, 2002.

Pagels, Elaine H. "Exegesis of Genesis 1 in the Gospels of Thomas and John." *Journal of Biblical Literature* 118, no. 3 (1999): 477–96.

Paine, Thomas. *The Age of Reason.* Reprint, New York: Citadel Press, 2000.

Patrides, C. A. "The Salvation of Satan." *Journal of the History of Ideas* 28, no. 4 (1967): 467–78.

Petersen, David. *The Prophetic Literature: An Introduction*. Louisville: Westminster John Knox Press, 2002.

The Presbyterian Hymnal. Philadelphia: Presbyterian Board of Publishers, 1874.

Pritchard, James B., ed. *Ancient Near Eastern Texts Relating to the Old Testament*. 3rd ed. Princeton: Princeton University Press, 1969.

Pope, Marvin. *El in the Ugaritic Texts*. Supplement to Vetus Testamentum 2. Leiden: Brill, 1955.

Rad, Gerhard von. *Genesis: A Commentary*. Translated by John H. Marks. Rev. ed. Old Testament Library. Philadelphia: Westminster Press, 1972.

———. *Holy War in Ancient Israel*. Translated by Marva J. Dawn. Grand Rapids: Eerdmans, 1991.

Ramelli, Ilaria, and David Konstan. *Terms for Eternity: Aionios and Aidios in Classical and Christian Texts*. Piscataway, NJ: Gorgias Press, 2007.

Rediger, G. Lloyd. *Clergy Killers: Guidance for Pastors and Congregations under Attack*. Louisville: Westminster John Knox Press, 1997.

Rhoads, David. "Zealots." Pages 1043–54 in vol. 6 of *Anchor Bible Dictionary*. Edited by David Noel Freedman. Garden City, NY: Doubleday, 1992.

Ricoeur, Paul. *The Confllict of Interpretations: Essays in Hermeneutics*. Edited by Don Ihde. Evanston: Northwestern University Press, 1974.

———. *The Symbolism of Evil*. Translated by Emerson Buchanan. New York: Harper & Row, 1967.

———. "The Narrative Function." *Semeia* 13 (1978): 177–202.

Roberts, J. J. M. *Nahum, Habakkuk, and Zephaniah: A Commentary*. Old Testament Library. Louisville: Westminster John Knox Press, 1991.

———. "The Davidic Origin of the Zion Tradition." Pages 313–30 in *The Bible and the Ancient Near East: Collected Essays*. Winona Lake, IN: Eisenbrauns, 2002.

Sagi, Avi. "The Punishment of Amalek in Jewish Tradition: Coping with the Moral Problem." *Harvard Theological Review* 87, no. 3 (1994): 323–46.

Schechter, Solomon. *Aspects of Rabbinic Theology*. 1909. Reprint, Woodstock, VT: Jewish Lights, 1993.

Schmid, Hans Heinrich. "Creation, Righteousness, and Salvation: 'Creation Theology' as the Broad Horizon of Biblical Theology." Translated by Bernard W. Anderson and Dan G. Johnson. Pages 102–17 in *Creation in the Old Testament*. Edited by Bernard W. Anderson. Issues in Religion and Theology 6. Philadelphia: Fortress Press, 1984.

———. *Gerechtigkeit als Weltordung: Hintergrund und Geschichte des alttestamentlichen Gerechtigkeitsbefriffes*. Beiträge zur historischen Theologie 40. Tübingen: Mohr, 1968.

Schneemelcher, Wilhelm, ed. *New Testament Apocrypha*. Vol. 2, *Writings Relating to the Apostles; Apocalypses and Related Subjects*. Philadelphia: Westminster Press, 1964.

Schneidau, Herbert N. *Sacred Discontent: The Bible and Western Tradition*. Berkeley: University of California Press, 1977.

Schwartz, Regina. *The Curse of Cain: The Violent Legacy of Monotheism*. Chicago: University of Chicago Press, 1997.

Seibert, Eric A. *Disturbing Divine Behavior: Troubling Old Testament Images of God*. Minneapolis: Fortress Press, 2009.

Seitz, Christopher. *Word without End: The Old Testament as Abiding Theological Witness*. Grand Rapids: Eerdmans, 1998.

———. *Zion's Final Destiny: The Development of the Book of Isaiah: A Reassessment of Isaiah 36–39*. Minneapolis: Fortress Press, 1991.

Simon, Uriel. *Jonah*. Philadelphia: Jewish Publication Society, 1999.

Simpson, Gary M. *War, Peace, and God: Rethinking the Just-War Tradition*. Minneapolis: Augsburg Fortress, 2007.

Sizgorich, Thomas. *Violence and Belief in Late Antiquity: Militant Devotion in Christianity and Islam*. Philadelphia: University of Pennsylvania Press, 2009.

Steinmetz, David C. "The Superiority of Pre-Critical Exegesis." *Theology Today* 37, no. 1 (1980): 27–38.

Stern, Philip D. *The Biblical Ḥerem: A Window on Israel's Religious Experience*. Brown Judaic Studies 211. Atlanta: Scholars Press, 1991.

Stoebe, H. J. "חָמָס ḥāmās violence." Pages 437–39 in vol. 1 of *Theological Lexicon of the Old Testament*. Edited by Ernst Jenni and Claus Westermann. Translated by Mark E. Biddle. 3 vols. Peabody, MA: Hendrickson, 1997.

———. "רעע r' to be bad." Pages 1249–54 in vol. 3 of *Theological Lexicon of the Old Testament*. Edited by Ernst Jenni and Claus

Westermann. Translated by Mark E. Biddle. 3 vols. Peabody, MA: Hendrickson, 1997.

Stone, Lawson. "Ethical and Apologetic Tendencies in the Redaction of the Book of Joshua." *Catholic Biblical Quarterly* 53, no. 1 (1991): 25–35.

Strong, John T. "Israel as a Testimony to YHWH's Power: The Priests' Definition of Israel." Pages 89–106 in *Constituting the Community: Studies on the Polity of Ancient Israel in Honor of S. Dean McBride, Jr.* Edited by John T. Strong and Steven S. Tuell. Winona Lake, IN: Eisenbrauns, 2005.

———. "Shattering the Image of God: A Response to Theodore Hiebert's Interpretation of the Story of the Tower of Babel." *Journal of Biblical Literature* 127, no. 4 (2008): 625–34.

Tanner, Hans Andreas. *Amalek: Der Feind Israels und der Feind Jahwes: Eine Studie zu den Amalektexten im Alten Testament.* Zurich: Theologischer Verlag, 2005.

Tate, Marvin E. *Psalms 51–100.* Word Biblical Commentary 20. Waco, TX: Word Books, 1990.

Tertullian. *The Five Books Against Marcion.* Translated by Peter Holmes. Pages 271–475 in vol. 3 of *Ante-Nicene Fathers.* Edited by Alexander Roberts and James Donaldson. Reprint, Grand Rapids: Eerdmans, 1976.

———. *The Shows.* Translated by S. Thelwall. Pages 79–91 in vol. 3 of *Ante-Nicene Fathers.* Edited by Alexander Roberts and James Donaldson. Reprint, Grand Rapids: Eerdmans, 1976.

Thrane, James R. "Joyce's Sermon on Hell: Its Source and Its Background." *Modern Philology* 57, no. 3 (1960): 172–98.

Tillich, Paul. *The Shaking of the Foundations.* New York: Scribner, 1953.

Trible, Phyllis. "Exegesis for Storytellers and Other Strangers." *Journal of Biblical Literature* 114, no. 1 (1995): 3–19.

———. *Texts of Terror: Literary-Feminist Readings of Biblical Narratives.* Overtures to Biblical Theology. Philadelphia: Fortress Press, 1984.

Tucker, W. Dennis Jr. "Revisiting the Plagues in Psalm CV." *Vetus Testamentum* 55, no. 3 (2005): 401–11.

Tuell, Steven Shawn. *Ezekiel.* New International Biblical Commentary. Peabody, MA: Hendrickson, 2009.

VanderKam, James C. "Genesis 1 in Jubilees 2." *Dead Sea Discoveries* 1, no. 3 (1994): 300–321.

Wapnish, Paula, and Brian Hesse. "Pampered Pooches or Plain Pariahs? The Ashkelon Dog Burials." *Biblical Archaeologist* 56, no. 2 (1993): 55–80.

Weippert, Manfred. "'Heiliger Krieg' in Israel und Assyrien: Kritische Anmerkungen zu Gerhard von Rads Konzept des 'Heiligen Krieges im alten Israel.'" *Zeitschrift für die alttestamentliche Wissenschaft* 84, no. 4 (1972): 460–93.

Welker, Michael. *Creation and Reality.* Minneapolis: Fortress Press, 1999.

Wellhausen, Julius. *Israelitische und jüdische Geschichte.* 7th ed. Berlin: Reimer, 1914.

Westermann, Claus. *Genesis 1–11: A Commentary.* Translated by John J. Scullion. Continental Commentary. Minneapolis: Augsburg Publishing House, 1984.

White, Marsha C. *The Elijah Legends and Jehu's Coup.* Brown Judaic Studies 311. Atlanta: Scholars Press, 1997.

Whybray, Roger N. *Isaiah 40–66.* New Century Bible Commentary. Grand Rapids: Eerdmans, 1981.

Wildberger, Hans. *Isaiah 13–27: A Commentary.* Translated by Thomas H. Trapp. Continental Commentary. Minneapolis: Fortress Press, 1997.

Williams, James G. *The Bible, Violence, and the Sacred: Liberation from the Myth of Sanctioned Violence.* San Francisco: HarperSanFrancisco, 1991.

Wilson Robert R. "The Death of the King of Tyre: The Editorial History of Ezekiel 28." Pages 211–18 in *Love and Death in the Ancient Near East: Essays in Honor of Marvin H. Pope.* Edited by John H. Marks and Robert M. Good. Guilford, CT: Four Quarters, 1987.

Wink, Walter. *Jesus and Non-Violence: A Third Way.* Facets. Minneapolis: Fortress Press, 2003.

Wolff, Hans Walter. *Hosea: A Commentary on the Book of the Prophet Hosea.* Translated by Gary Stansell. Hermeneia—A Critical and Historical Commentary on the Bible. Philadelphia: Fortress Press, 1974.

Yoder, John Howard. *The Politics of Jesus: Behold the Man! Our Victorius Lamb.* Grand Rapids: Eerdmans, 1994.

———. *The War of the Lamb: The Ethics of Nonviolence and Peacemaking.* Edited by Glenn Stassen, Mark Thiessen Nation, and Matt Hamsher. Grand Rapids: Brazos Press, 2009.

Zenger, Erich. *A God of Vengeance? Understanding the Psalms of Divine Wrath*. Translated by Linda M. Maloney. Louisville: Westminster John Knox Press, 1994.

Zevit, Ziony. "The Priestly Redaction and Interpretation of the Plague Narrative in Exodus." *Jewish Quarterly Review* 66, no. 4 (1976): 193–211.

SCRIPTURE INDEX

263

269

SUBJECT INDEX

Abbadon, "the grave," 176
Abel. *See also* Cain
  blood of, cries from ground, 30
  murder of and first reference to sin
    in Bible, 32
  offering of, accepted as compared
    with Cain's, 32
  story of, in Genesis 4 linked to
    Genesis 3, 32
Abraham
  called to maintain justice and righ-
    teousness, 11, 45, 75
  conduit of blessing for humankind,
    11, 43–45, 74
  election of, understood as catalyst of
    violence, 45 (*see also* election)
  as focus of creation, 43–44, 74
  responsible for staving off violence,
    43, 75–78
  role related to humans in image of
    God, 11, 43–44 (*see also* human
    being).
Achsah
  Caleb's daughter, 129
  possessor of watered land as sign of
    high status, 129, 152
Adoni-zedek, 117, 131–32
Agag, Amalekite king, 12, 93. *See also*
    Amalek; Esther
Ahaz (King), as unfaithful ruler in
    Isaiah 1–39, 233
Ai, 116
alien, resident
  Abraham as, 76–77
  Lot as, 76
  protection prescribed for, 76–77,
    229
  as vulnerable, 77
"all flesh," 39, 74
allegorical interpretation
  application to Pharaoh and Egyp-
    tians in Exodus, 9, 80–1
  of ban, 8, 99, 101–5, 107–8, 112 (*see
    also* ban; Origen)

characteristic of early church, 8
  (*see also* early church; Origen;
  Augustine).
fallen out of favor with modern
  readers, 8, 103–4
philosophical foundation of, laid
  by Paul Ricoeur in modern
  period, 9.
supported by predominance of chaos
  and evil in creation accounts,
  9, 88–9
supported by plain sense of text,
  105–8, 208
supported by study of historical
  context of writing, 9
Allison, Dale, 175, 227, 238
Amalek
  battle in wilderness against, charac-
    terized by prayer, 94
  compared to native Americans by
    Cotton Mather, 112
  in Deuteronomy, presented like ter-
    rorist, 88
  as enemy of God, 12
  in Esther, 93–94, 96
  fighting against as dividing line
    between Saul and David, 90–93
  historical identity of, 90
  memory of to be wiped out by non-
    violent word, 96
  messenger from, reported death of
    Saul to David, 93
  represented by Haman in Esther,
    12, 93–94
  Saul ordered to put under the ban, 2,
    89–93, 226 (*see also* ban; Saul)
  as symbol of evil, 12, 74
Amalekites. *See* Amalek.
Ammonites, 57
Amos (prophet)
  call for righteousness and justice,
    168
  declared mistreatment of poor equal
    to war crimes, 167–69

273

symbolic importance of dismembered body, 151
Levites, lamented loss of Zion in Psalm 137, 208
liberation
exodus story concerned with, 47
violence sometimes approved for, 9, 126, 130–32, 135–38
Lind, Millard, 53
Lohfink, Norbert, 109
Lord's Prayer, and Old Testament concern for justice, 195, 214, 233
love, as covenant language, David and Jonathan as example of, 211 (*see also* hate)
Luther, Martin, 232

ma'at, Egyptian concept of, 75 (*see also* righteousness)
man–woman relationship. *See also* woman; image of God; patriarchy
disrupted by human rebellion, 30
hierarchy in against God's intention, 31
intended for mutual sharing, 30
intentions of God for recovered in Jesus Christ, 31
as model of and basis for community, 31
Marcion, 14
declared heretic, 2–3
rejected Old Testament and portions of New Testament, 2, 48–49
thought God of Old Testament violent, 2
views of, many remain sympathetic with, 3
Marduk
created world by conquering chaotic forces, 20, 22
invoked by power-grabbing Babylonian kings, 24
marketplace, violence in
message of eighth-century prophets concerning, 200
practices characteristic of, 200
vulnerability of widows, strangers, orphans, 200

Mather, Cotton, Puritan preacher, proclaimed native Americans as Amalek, 90, 96, 112. *See also* Amalek; ban
Mays, James L., 61, 64, 168, 228
McCann, J. Clinton, 130, 142, 202, 210
McCarter, Kyle, 55, 90
Mesha, King of Moab, placed Israelites under ban, 100 (*see also* Moabite Stone).
Meyers, Carol, 128
Middleton, J. Richard, 25
midrash on Exodus 15, 59
military, on not trusting in, 233–34
Miller, Patrick, 15, 48, 110–111, 198
Moabite Stone, concerning evidence of ban outside Bible, 100
Moberly, R. W. L., 105–7
modern period
characterized by rejection of figurative interpretation of Scripture, 8, 99
human reason as guide to morality in, 3
rise of criticism of Bible within, 3
Moltmann, Jürgen, 218
monotheism, violence blamed on, 111
Mordecai, 93–94
Moses
absence of as actor in God's battle with Pharaoh, 53
declared God fights for Israel, 53
time of, 98

Nabal, name meaning "vile," 151
Naboth, as victim of Ahaz and Jezebel, 156
Nahum (prophet)
concern for those who take refuge in God, 172
focus on God's jealousy, 171
oracles against Nineveh, capital of Assyria, for its brutality, 171–73
and vengeance as expression of justice, 171–72
name
men of, as self-promoting heroes in Genesis 6:1–4, 37
nations
bring desolation through war, 64

281

response to rescue from Egyptian
 slavery, 106
Sheol, 176
 God's presence in, 210
sin
 as desire for what belongs to another
  in Genesis 4, 33
 presented as predator in Genesis
  4, 33
 related to desire in Genesis 3:16
  and lack of mutuality between
  sexes, 33
 of residents of Sodom, 78
Sisera, Canaanite general, defeated by
 Deborah, killed by Jael, 135–37
Sisera's mother
 compared to Deborah, 137
 representative of female deity, 137
 symbol of aristocracy, 137
 viewed women as spoils of war,
  137–38 (*see also* women,
  violence against)
Sodom and Gomorrah
 crime of, 74
 residents of as enemies of God, 12
 sin of, cosmic implications, 78–79
  (*see also* creation)
 as symbol of evil, 74
sojourner. *See* alien, resident
soldiers, included in kingdom, 230
Solomon (king), reign of anticipates
 Messiah, 234
spiritual interpretation. *See* allegorical
 interpretation
stranger. *See* alien, resident
Stone, Lawson, 117
Strong, John, 26

Tanner, Hans Andreas, 94
temple (Jerusalem)
 conceived as paradise, 50–51
 place God's reign is celebrated, 51,
  57
 worship of, anticipated in Song of
  the Sea, 50
Testament of Abraham, as parallel to
 Luke 9:51–56, 159
Tiamat. See also Babylonian creation
 epic.
 representative of unruly waters, 20

sound of, similar to word for "deep"
 in Genesis 1:2, 20
Tiglath-pileser. *See* Assyrians, kings of
Tiglath-pileser III. *See* Assyrians,
 kings of
till
 in Genesis 2:15 with nuance of
  "serve," 29 (*see also* keep).
Tillich, Paul, 224
travel, danger of, 77 (*see also* alien,
 resident)
Trible, Phyllis, 140, 156
Tyre
 birthplace of Jezebel, 156
 prince of, imagined himself divine,
  165

unrighteousness. *See* righteousness.

vengeance
 expressed in prophetic speech and
  action, 13
 and God's concern for justice, 213
 as God's exclusive prerogative, 195,
  212, 234
 in imprecatory psalms, 195
 negative associations of term, 66, 213
 not seeking revenge, understanding
  of, 66
 relation to final judgment, 13
 relation to judicial action, 66, 195

war
 as context of God's judgment, 56
 as God's exclusive prerogative, 14,
  123
 difficult to justify according to
  biblical values, 58
 end of, portrayed in context of God's
  reign in Psalm 46, 63 (*see also*
  Zion, God, as king)
war crimes, conquest and ban often
 considered examples of, 97 (*see
  also* ban; conquest of Canaan)
warrior, God as
 actions of, related to wrath, 66
 covered in blood of enemies, 65
 and destructive actions, 64
 fought directly against Pharaoh and
  Egyptians, 47

285